A Short Account of the Land Revenue and its Administration in British India; with a Sketch of the Land Tenures

A Short Account of the Land Revenue and its Administration in British India; with a Sketch of the Land Tenures

B. H. BADEN - POWELL, C.I.E.
F.R.S.E., M.R.A.S.

GYAN

Published by

GYAN

Gyan Publishing House
5, Ansari Road
Daryaganj, New Delhi-110002
Phone: 011-47034999, 9811692060
E-mail: books@gyanbooks.com

Distribution Network
gyanbooks.com
India, USA, Canada, UK, Australia, France

ISBN: 978-81-212-8730-2 (PB)
First Published, 1907

2nd Impression 2023

Printed at: Gyan Press, Delhi.

A Short Account of the Land Revenue and its Administration in British India; with a Sketch of the Land Tenures
Author: B. H. Baden -Powell

LAND REVENUE AND TENURE IN BRITISH INDIA

B. H. BADEN-POWELL

A Short Account of the Land Revenue and its Administration in British India; with a Sketch of the Land Tenures

BY

B. H. BADEN-POWELL, C.I.E.

F.R.S.E., M.R.A.S.

LATE OF THE BENGAL CIVIL SERVICE; AND ONE OF THE JUDGES OF THE CHIEF COURT OF THE PUNJAB

WITH MAP

Oxford

AT THE CLARENDON PRESS

1894

CONTENTS

PART I.

GENERAL CONCEPTION OF THE LAND REVENUE.

PART II.

THE LAND TENURES AND THE LAND REVENUE SYSTEMS.

NOTE

ON THE PRONUNCIATION OF INDIAN WORDS.

In pronouncing the vernacular words which occur in this book, it is only necessary for the general student to remember, that the words are *not* to be read with the peculiarly English sound of vowels: that is sure to be wrong. Adopt generally the Italian or 'continental' vowel list. The most prominent feature is the unaccented *a*, a short vowel pronounced as in 'org*a*n' or as the *u* in j*u*g; *never* like the *a* in fat. The accented *á* is the broad *a* of the French or Italian *gâteau*, *lago*; *i* and *í* are respectively, as in the English words *pit* and *peat*; *u* and *ú* are—'oo'—the former shorter, the latter more prolonged. In this book, the *u* in any Indian word is *never* to be sounded like the *u* in 'j*u*g', for that would be short *a*. The letter *e* is a diphthong, and sounded like *é* in French; *au* is like 'how,' *not* like 'awe'; *y* is always a consonant.

Of consonants, it is only necessary to mention that *th* is never a sibilant (either as in *th*is or *th*in) but only *t* with a slight aspirate[1]. The *kh* and *gh* (with a line under) are the gutturals of the Perso-Arabic (like 'loch' and 'lough' in Scotch or Irish). As there are two kinds of *k*, we use for the one *k*, and the other *q* without the conventional *u* added.

ABBREVIATIONS.

To save space, the letters L. R. are occasionally used instead of printing 'Land Revenue' at full length; so S. for 'Settlement;' and P. S. for 'Permanent Settlement.'

As 'Settlement' is a word which has other meanings (e.g. it may refer to a location or place of settlement of a colony, a tribe or a family), it is written with a capital S whenever the term is used in its technical or Revenue sense.

'*L. S. B. I.*' refers to my *Land Systems of British India*, 3 vols. (Oxford: Clarendon Press, 1892.)

[1] In Burmese the sibilant *th* occurs, not in any Indian dialect.

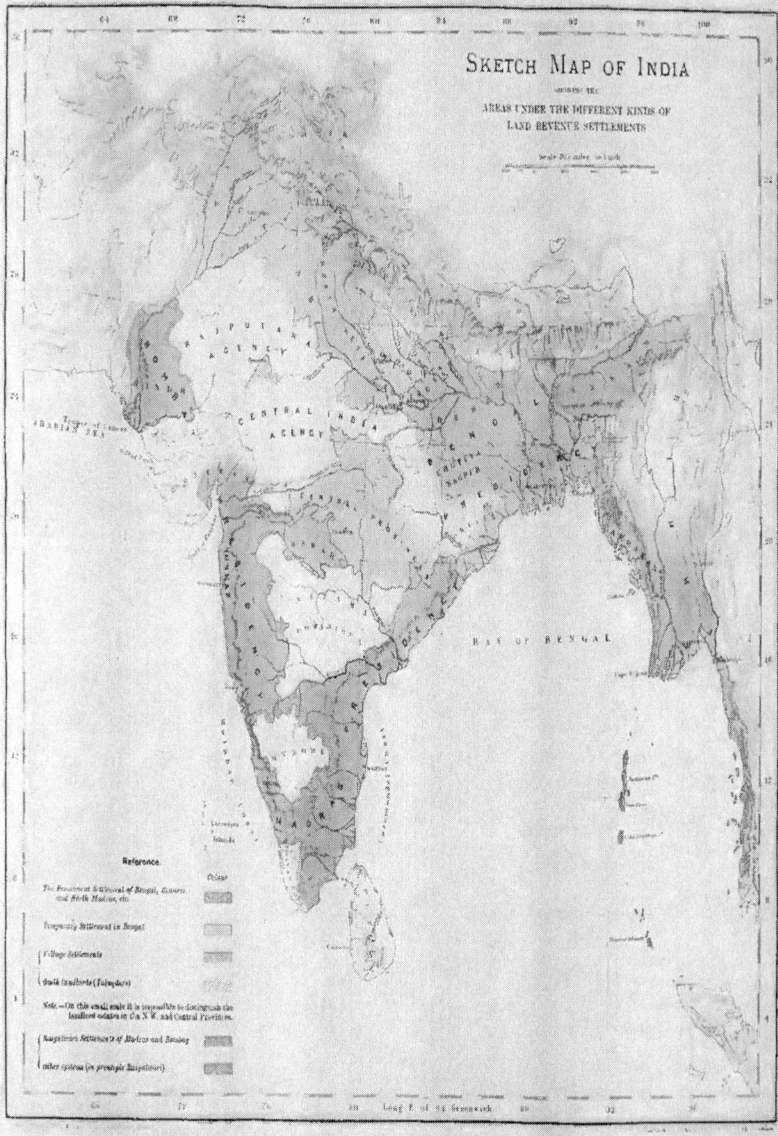
SKETCH MAP OF INDIA
AREAS UNDER THE DIFFERENT KINDS OF
LAND REVENUE SETTLEMENTS
RAJPUTANA AGENCY
CENTRAL INDIA AGENCY
ARABIAN SEA
BAY OF BENGAL
Reference

THE LAND REVENUE

AND

ITS ADMINISTRATION IN INDIA

PART I.

GENERAL CONCEPTION OF THE LAND REVENUE.

CHAPTER I.

INTRODUCTORY.

THE LAND REVENUE is of such importance to our Indian Empire that many persons desire to have some general knowledge of what it is and how it is levied and managed.

Intimately connected on the one hand with the past history and later development of Land-Tenures, it appeals to the jurist and the student of the growth of institutions and customs; not less connected on the other hand with questions of taxation, land-valuation, rent and agricultural conditions in general, its administration invites the notice of the economist. To assess and to collect the Land Revenue has been the chief care of all past governments for many centuries; and for this purpose territorial divisions and official agencies have been devised; and these, however modified, still form the basis of modern arrangements, and naturally have affected all other departmental jurisdictions and official forms. To understand the Land Revenue system, is to gain a greater knowledge of Indian government than could be acquired in any other way. For the agricultural class, which pays this Revenue, represents about five-sixths of the entire population; and the assessment and collection of such a widely levied impost demand an intimate knowledge of land-customs and the social features of country life. And so it is that the Government of India itself requires from various departmental officials, e. g. those of the Forest Department, an elementary knowledge of the Land systems, as essential to the discharge of their general duty.

But the difficulty is to find the desired information in a suitable form and within convenient limits.

My *Land Systems of British India* is too detailed for the purpose. It was designed as a kind of 'Gazetteer' of Land Revenue-Systems and tenures; and to form a series of Provincial monographs (preceded by a general summary) which I would willingly have divided into separate volumes instead of joining them in three large ones. Its object is to furnish a compendious outline of systems, giving references from which all further details can be obtained. It might be supposed that such a task was not worth attempting, because students of detail would wish to go to original sources at once. But these sources are much easier to speak of than to produce or even catalogue. In any case they are so voluminous, so scattered over reports and books now scarce and inaccessible, that a compendium of their contents had become desirable. But whatever may be the justification of the larger book, it contains too much for the many readers who do not care for full details, and too much for the official student who wants only the leading principles indicated, or needs only to be enlightened as to those portions of Revenue work which bear directly on his own duty.

The necessity then arises to provide such a book as shall answer the purposes of the ordinary student of Indian affairs, and shall yet give sufficient practical information to serve as a text-book for Forest Officers and others outside the Land Revenue Department.

The fact is that it is much easier to write a detailed account of any given Provincial system, than it is to select the precise features, and the proper amount of illustrative detail, which will give a correct view of the system in a short form and in comparatively untechnical language. If we try to be too brief and general, we simply reproduce a semblance of those loose generalized sketches of the 'village community' and the 'Land-tax of India' with which readers of Indian histories and text-books are only too familiar, and which, from the conditions under which they were written, *must be* inadequate for any practical purpose, and *are*, in some cases, positively misleading.

The following chapters represent an attempt to describe the Land Revenue Administration of British India, and the forms of land-holding on which that administration is based, in the compass of one small volume. The attempt has been made with some misgiving; but it has been made with care, and with the endeavour to direct attention to what is important from a general reader's point of view. I have, however, given references whence some detail on special points may be obtained.

To those who are going to use the book as a text for examination or otherwise, may I add, that it is expected that *they* will arm themselves further with (1) the Land Revenue Act and Rent or Tenancy Act, and (2) the Revenue Circular Orders, of the particular Province with which they are concerned.

CHAPTER II.

General Features of the Country affecting the Land Revenue Administration.

There are certain general features of Provinces and districts, and certain facts regarding the soil, climate, and institutions of the country, which are often alluded to in describing the Land Revenue systems, and which, though familiar enough to residents in India, will need explanation to the reader in England. It is convenient, therefore, to open proceedings by briefly describing the facts and features alluded to.

'British India.'—In the first place it is often convenient to allude to 'British India' as a whole; meaning the territories subject to British Government, and to the law as enacted by the Central and Provincial Legislatures of India, and in some matters by the Imperial Parliament in England. The rest of India is governed by native princes.

These rarely or never represent the indigenous rulers of the people, but are descendants of Rájput and Maráthá conquerors, or of the Deputies whom the Mughal Emperor established locally, and who, in the decline of the Empire, assumed independence. These States vary in size and importance and in the degree of independent authority they possess. All of them are aided by a British 'Resident' (or by Political officers with other titles). All of them are bound by treaty to enter into no dealings with foreign powers without the approval of the Suzerain. If internal affairs should be grossly mismanaged, the Governor-General would interfere; otherwise, the administration of the Land Revenue, local taxes, police, and public justice are not meddled with. In the smaller States the powers of life and death are not unrestricted; a reference for approval may be needed before a prisoner can be put to death.

'**India.**'—The name 'India,' however, has a purely geographical use; the different parts or provinces included in it have populations widely different in customs, language, and physical appearance. Even where there is a common Muhammadan faith, it does but little to obliterate natural and caste characteristics[1]. The aggregation of races under the general name of 'Hindu' has even less meaning as indicating anything like unity; for the Hindu sects, as well as their deities and customs of worship, are local and multiform; hardly anything is common to all, except certain general religious ideas and various caste rules and social principles[2]. Vast numbers not only of low-caste or outcaste people, but of fine races (like the Panjáb *Jat*) are 'Hindus' in hardly any other sense than that they are neither Muhammadan, Christian, nor Parsí. These always follow their own land tenure and inheritance customs, in total ignorance of the Hindu Law Schools and their text-books. They have, however, a general respect for Brahmans, and a certain tincture of Hindu religious ideas.

'**Bengal.**'—The term 'Bengal' is sometimes vaguely used as if it meant all India that is not Madras or Bombay. It is used in these pages only for the territories under the Lieutenant-Governor of Bengal, whose capital is at Calcutta; and it does not include Assam, which has been separated since 1874, under a Chief Commissioner.

'**North India.**'—The term 'North India' is generally used to mean very much the same as 'Hindustán'—the country north of the group of hills, locally known by various names, but conveniently described in the aggregate as the Vindhyan Range. These hill-ranges form a barrier across the 'peninsula' nearly from east to west.

[1] Especially when such numbers are perfectly ignorant converts, and retain a great many Hindu caste ideas and superstitions generally. In many parts local custom governs inheritance and other matters, and the law of the text-books is hardly known.

[2] 'The people of the great kingdoms known to history are an immense mixed multitude broken up into tribal or religious groups and united under one rulership by force or accident.' (Sir A. Lyall, *Rise of the British Dominion in India*. Murray, 1893.)

'The Dakhan' (Deccan).—Southern India is often referred to as 'the Deccan' (Dakhan), though the terms are not quite identical, for the Dakhan includes the west and upper part of the south country, between the *Ghát* or line of hills on either side. As this country is generally undulating high land (descending very gradually from the Western Ghát), it has distinctive features. On the whole, we may say that 'Dakhan' does not include Southern Madras, but may be taken to extend from the Narbada Valley (amid the Vindhyan hills) as far south as the Kistná river.

Variety of districts as to climate and staple produce.—The districts of India represent, in the aggregate, almost every conceivable variety of climate, from the Alpine districts of the North Panjáb and the North-West Provinces to the nearly tropical districts of Southern Madras and the West Coast. Their agricultural products are equally varied; the only general distinction that can be drawn is that part of the country is a large producer of wheat and barley, and in part the staple is rice. Millets and pulses are everywhere raised in some variety, as well as the sugar-cane, tobacco, oil-seeds, cotton, and vegetables, including a large variety of gourds, cucumbers, and melons. Some staples, like 'jute' and indigo, are confined to districts where the climate is suitable.

Character of the surface. Alpine hill-districts. Submontane districts. Tarái.—As might be expected, the surface is extremely diversified, but usually preserves the same character over extensive areas. In the extreme north the valleys and cultivable slopes within the system of the Himalayan mountains are largely in the hands of Native States—Kashmir, Naipál, Sikkim, &c. But there are a few British districts. There is also a series of submontane districts among the valleys and lower hills which intervene between the higher mountains and the level plain. Some of these districts (of which the Dehra Dún may be taken as an example) are enclosed valleys with much forest land. Others receive the drainage from the outer hills, and thus have certain peculiarities of soil and an unhealthy climate; districts of this character are known as 'Tarái.'

Alluvial plains.—Throughout the great Ganges plain, and the Panjáb plain traversed by its five rivers, the deep alluvial soil is often a dead level for miles together, and a stone or pebble is never seen. The Panjáb rivers, coming down from the hills on to a soil of this character, are constantly changing their course, as the water rises or falls with the melting of the Himáláyán snows or the floods of the 'monsoon' season or both [1].

There is a vast tract of arid sandy country south of the Panjáb. Indeed all the country from Hisár across to the 'Run of Cutch' and including Sindh, is more or less arid, and cultivation is entirely dependent on the moisture from the rivers which percolates a certain distance inland.

Districts south of the Vindhyan range.—When we leave Northern India and come to the Narbada valley and the districts beyond the Vindhyan hills, we find great diversities of level; and generally a country quite distinct in character from that of the Northern alluvial plains.

'Black cotton' and red soil country.—We come to the 'black cotton' soil (which produces the well-known cotton of Northern Central India and Bombay) and the 'red soil.' A number of the districts occupy plateau-land—a succession of wooded hills, with fertile valleys between; others are uniformly at a lower level. The upper districts are often distinguished as '*bálá-ghát* (above the *ghát* or passes of the hills) and the lower ones as *talá-ghát* or *páyín-ghát* (at the foot or below the *ghát*).

Seasons and harvests.—The climate of the provinces is very various. There is generally a part of the year cooler than the rest; but only in the North is this season (November to February) really cold. In Madras there is a 'N. E. monsoon' or late

[1] In these countries the tract between two rivers is called a Doáb (*Do* = two, *áb* = water). 'The Doáb' *par excellence* is the great plain between the Ganges and Jumna (Jamuná) river in the North-West Provinces. The tracts so called in the Panjáb are distinguished by some addition, e. g. the 'Bári Doáb' (between the Beás and Rávi rivers). In these tracts it often happens that the level of the central part of the Doáb is higher than the rest, and as wells cannot here be sunk, the country is covered with 'jungle.' It is here in fact that the *rakhs* or fuel forests, afterwards mentioned, are chiefly found.

autumn rainfall; elsewhere the short period of winter rainfall that often occurs about December or January, is due to other causes. The general S.W. monsoon or rainy season ('the rains') begins with June and goes on till September; but the dates vary, and so does the amount of fall. In some places there is a steady wet season, in others only occasional downpours, and in others hardly any rain at all, only the air becomes somewhat moister.

Rabí and Kharíf harvests.—This results generally in there being two chief harvests; one is the *rabí* (*rabí'*) or spring harvest (in the northern and central districts this is the harvest for wheat and barley) and the other the *Kharíf* or autumn harvest [1] (e.g. the rice harvest of Bengal). The season of sowing and reaping varies with the locality: speaking generally, in the *rabí* or spring harvest, the ground is prepared after the summer rains, the wheat is sown in October, and reaped at dates varying from early April to as late as May 15. The *Kharíf* crops are rapidly growing plants; they are put in as soon as the soil is moistened by the first rain, and reaped in the autumn. Sugar-cane is cut gradually and frequently stands till the end of winter [2].

[1] These are the terms used in Revenue books. In the Hindí districts they call them *Hárí* and *Sáwaní* respectively, and by other local names. The relative importance of these harvests varies; e.g. in the Panjáb the *Kharíf* is the less important, except as far as sugar-cane is concerned. Fodder plants and millets are the chief produce. In other parts the importance is reversed. All land is not, however, cultivated twice. Land that bears two crops is said to be *do fasli*, (*fasl* = harvest or crop); that which only bears one, is *ek-fasli*.

[2] **Agricultural Year. 'Faslí era.' Official Year.**—Land Revenue instalments and other arrangements often depend on this harvest division. Tenant ejectments and rent-enhancements are managed with reference to certain periods prescribed by law, called the 'agricultural year'; these are so arranged that changes are made when it is convenient; a tenant is not ejected, e.g., after his ploughing and sowing is all done, and before his crop is ready for the sickle. The Mughal emperors invented a date or era for the financial and revenue accounts which they called the *Fasli* year; it was more convenient than the Hindu, or Muhammadan calendar year, which varies owing to the use of *lunar* months. The *Fasli* era is now generally disused.

For all official purposes the year begins April 1 and ends March 31 following. These official years always contain two numbers; thus 1890–1, means the year which began on April 1, 1890, and closed March 31, 1891.

Irrigation.—Whether the rains fall in due time, or not, the operations of the two harvests begin at the usual dates whenever there is irrigation. Land that is dependent solely on rainfall is generally called *báráni*; that watered by wells is *cháhí*: land irrigated by canal is *nahrí*: land moistened by river percolation is *sailába*.

The Canal Acts.—Canals are mostly the property of the State and are managed by a special staff. Each province that has canals, has its own Irrigation or Canal Act. And the Land Revenue Collectors often have duties in connexion with them; hearing appeals from the orders of canal-officers, and settling questions about water-rates, about the arrangements for taking channels across the land of another person, and so forth. In South India there are also canals, but the State Irrigation Department is more concerned with great tanks, and the channels that lead from them; and with irrigation systems which depend upon weirs thrown across rivers, as in the delta of the Kistná and Godávarí rivers.

Value of land increased by Canal irrigation being provided.—It may here be mentioned, that as land rises greatly in value by its being more or less completely protected by a canal, this difference in value may greatly affect the Land Revenue. But it is the usual practice to let the assessments regard the land in itself, apart from the fact that it is canal watered; and the extra advantage owing to the canal (which was provided at the expense of the State) is arranged for in Upper India, by charging what is called an 'owner's rate' levied per acre on the area affected. The charge for the use of the water itself is called the 'occupier's rate,' because that is paid by the person who actually reaps the crop, and he may or may not be the owner of the land. The water always belongs to Government; and it is important to remember the distinction (in whatever form it is practically made or may hereafter be made in amended Acts) between the price of the water as a commodity and the increased acreage value of the land itself, consequent on its general improvement resulting from the possibility of permanent irrigation.

In Southern and Western India the matter is somewhat

differently managed. There, lands that grow rice crops which always require tank or river irrigation are separately assessed at special rates; and, for Revenue purposes, all cultivation is broadly classified as 'wet' and 'dry.'

Irrigation by Wells. Means of raising water.—Wells give rise to many customs of land-holding in Northern India [1]. As each well can only be worked a certain number of hours, and the flow during that time will water a certain number of acres (more or less according to situation, nature of soil, requirement of crop, &c.) the sharers in a well arrange 'turns'—each working it so many hours each day, or on certain days in the week. In the Central Panjáb water is raised from the well by the 'Persian wheel,' which is an apparatus of earthern pots fastened on an endless band of grass rope which passes over a great wheel turned by cattle. This is local. Elsewhere a large leather bag furnished with an iron rim and hung by a stout rope over a pulley-wheel, is drawn up and down by cattle moving on a roadway sloping up from the well's mouth (*láo-charsa*). Or a lever-pole weighted at one end and furnished at the other with a bucket or earthern pot, is used (*dheṅklí*). Small wheels (*ráoti, jhalár*) are often erected on the edges of rivers and creeks and on low level canals where the water requires raising.

Tank irrigation.—Tank irrigation is common in Central and Southern India. The word *tank* is said to be a Central Indian term and not the English word [2]. It refers to some natural soil depression, which, being dammed up at one end, catches and retains the rain-water as it flows off the high land or hills in the vicinity. Some tanks in Ájmer and elsewhere are great lakes, sometimes they contain water perennially; often, however, when the water has run off, the level bottom (enriched with the water-deposit) is allowed to dry for a time and is then ploughed up and sown [3]. In South India the term *ayacut* refers to the area com-

[1] So that the term 'well' in Land Revenue Papers often means not merely the water source itself, but an area of land watered (or protected) by the well.

[2] Hence the 'irrigation taṇk' is not a reservoir or a masonry enclosure; the latter is found commonly, but only at temples, &c., for religious ablutions.

[3] This is the *ábi* cultivation of Ájmer.

manded by the tank and its distributary channels. Where irrigation is effected by a dam or weir for confining the waters of a river and distributing the aggregate by suitable channels, the arrangement is called an 'anicut' (*annekattu*).

'Villages.' 'Mauza.'—We shall speak hereafter about 'Villages,' but it is here convenient to notice that by that term we mean *a group of cultivation* of a permanent character[1] in one place, having a known area and a name in the map. In Revenue language, the village is the *mauza*. A survey, a record, &c., is said to be *máuzawár* when it proceeds by villages —i.e. takes the village as the unit. Other common terms for village are *dih* (Persian), *gáñw*, *gám* (Hindí dialects), *grámam* (Sanskrit).

Boundary marks in use.—The fields and holdings within the village, as well as the outer boundaries, are everywhere demarcated. In North India, important points (as e.g. a point of junction of two or more village boundary lines) are indicated by stout masonry pillars, lesser boundaries usually by clay pillars or small mounds.

In Bombay and Madras, where what is called the *Raiyatwárí* system prevails, the boundaries of fields or holdings are invariable[2]. Each field is therefore elaborately demarcated by a system of corner stones or earthen banks; each of the stones enclosing the angle, is set so as to point in the direction of the boundary line, and strips of land between the marks are left unploughed, and soon become covered with bushes. In Bombay it is an express rule that such a strip must be left unploughed. I may add that in countries where irrigation is much used, there will often be plots surrounded with low earthen ridges to keep in the water: these do not necessarily indicate any boundary line or limit of property or landed interest.

Measures of weight; area measures. 'Maund' and 'seer.'

[1] I say 'permanent' because there are many soils where crops are only taken for two or three years in succession, and the place is then abandoned. And in hill countries where there is bamboo and other forest, as in Burma, East Bengal, Assam, South India, and in the Western Ghát, local tribes still carry on a process of shifting cultivation which is described later on.

[2] This will be explained in the sequel.

As we frequently refer to measures of weight and still oftener to land measures, it will be convenient to add in conclusion, that while measures of grain, &c., are locally very various, the *man* (anglicized into 'maund') is perhaps most commonly referred to. If *pakká* (that is, of standard weight) it is 40 *seers* (*sír*) or 80 lbs. Where the local weight of the *man* is different from the standard it is said to be *kachchá* (i.e. raw or imperfect).

English Acre. Bighá.—In some places the public records adopt the English Statute acre as the land-measure: in others the vernacular records are made only in local measures; and for imperial returns and published statistics these are 'translated' into acres. The commonest native measure is the '*bíghá*,' first adopted under Akbar's Land-Settlement (of which we shall presently speak). But the standard of the succeeding reign is that now in general use. The *Sháh Jahání-bíghá* is the square of a linear unit, which is 60 *gaz*—each *gaz* being 33 English inches in length. The *bíghá* is thus 3,025 sq. yds. $= \frac{5}{8}$ of an acre. In Bengal, however, the *bíghá* is 1,600 sq. yds. $= \frac{1}{3}$ of an acre.

Its divisions.—The *bíghá* is divided into 20 *biswa*, and that into 20 *biswáńsí*. In Bengal the corresponding divisions are 'cotta' (*katthá*) and *gandá*.

The Ghumáo.—In the Panjáb the *bíghá* (as above) is only locally used: more generally a measure called *ghumáo* (from *ghumáná* = to turn the plough) is used; it is divided into 8 *kanál*, and the *kanál* into 20 *marla*. The *ghumáo* is unfortunately rather various: rarely it is = 1 acre; more commonly it varies to a little above or a little below $\frac{8}{10}$ of an acre[1].

Forms of cultivation. Shifting cultivation in hill ranges.—A very interesting account might be given of the forms of agricultural cultivation in the different provinces, but it would lead us too far away from our direct object; it is necessary, however, to call attention to the fact that all cultivation is not permanent. Apart from the fact that in Assam (and other places also) large areas are only cultivated for a year or two and then abandoned for a long time, there is a still extensively practised

[1] A full detail, with *formula* for reduction to acres, will be found in the Panjáb Revenue Circulars.

mode of cultivation, which is characteristic of places where there are large tracts of forest and jungle-clad hills, inhabited by more or less primitive (often non-Aryan) castes or tribes. In these cases a temporary location of bamboo huts forms the village residence; and the families, having selected a suitable hill slope, where the angle is not too steep[1], proceed to cut down all the bamboos and smaller vegetation, killing the larger trees by ringing or girdling. The stuff is collected in heaps during the early hot season and allowed to dry thoroughly. Just before the rains set in, the whole is fired, and the ashes are raked up, mixed with suitable kinds of seed, and dibbled into the soft forest-soil with a hoe. The only further care—which, however, involves heavy labour—is weeding the crop, and sometimes fencing it strongly against the depredations of deer, &c. One, or perhaps two, crops are taken off, and then the site is abandoned. It is not returned to till a period of years has elapsed sufficient for the re-growth of the forest. This period depends largely on the numbers of the tribes, the area available, and other circumstances; it may be as long as twenty to forty years, or it may be as short as five to seven years. This form of cultivation is called *júm* in Bengal, *kumrí* in South India, *taungyá* in Burma, *dahyá* in the Central Provinces[2].

There are other forms of permanent cultivation which require ashes for manure, and for this purpose tracts of jungle land are often *attached* to cultivated holdings as part of the necessary area (e.g. in Coorg, Bombay, &c.).

These methods are interesting, because in ancient times all village cultivation must have begun, even in the plains, by similar forest clearings; only that in level land, when once the jungle was removed, and the *plough* came into use, there would be no necessity for shifting the site; and thus from a small clearing, a large permanent village would grow up[3].

[1] Otherwise the soil (and the seed with it) would be washed away by the heavy rainfall.

[2] Some interesting particulars as to how the system may gradually develop into something resembling a fixed tenure, may be seen in *L. S. B. I.* vol. iii. pp. 504–508.

[3] The process is illustrated in an extract given in *L. S. B. I.* vol. ii. p. 451.

CHAPTER III.

How the Provinces and Districts are Organized with Reference to Land Revenue Administration.

I. The Governments.

General Government, in India and in England.—The whole of British India is divided into *Provinces*, each under its own local Government or local Administration. These Governments are in general subordinate to the Supreme Government, i. e. the Government of India, whose head-quarters are at Calcutta and Simla. In England the Secretary of State for India, assisted by a Council of ten members, exercises a general control and supervision on behalf of the Crown [1].

'Presidencies.'—Three of the Provinces—Bengal, Bombay, and Madras—have the designation of 'Presidency.' This is owing to the fact that, in the early days of the trading Charters, the 'Factories [2],' which formed the centres of establishment,

[1] The 'East India Company' ceased to exist as a governing body—holding delegated authority from the Crown—when the 'Act for the better Government of India' (21 & 22 Vict. cap. 106) became law, and the Queen's proclamation was issued in November 1858. (The Act has been several times amended.) Before this the management of Indian affairs at home was conducted by the 'Court of Directors' of the Honourable E. I. Company, with a certain supervision exercised on the part of the State, by a 'Board of Control.' The authority was given by means of Royal charters. The earlier of these were concerned chiefly with trade and commercial matters. In 1773 the 'Regulating Act' was passed, and is noticeable as the first statute which directly dealt with the local government of provinces: this was supplemented by further statutes in 1780, 1784, and 1786. After this as each charter was renewed (after twenty years), further Acts of Parliament were passed (concurrently with the charter) to provide for matters which it had become necessary to regulate. Thus it is that the principal statutes date 1792–3, 1812, 1833, 1853. There is a convenient collection of 'Statutes relating to India' published by the Legislative Department (Government Press, Calcutta).

[2] The capitals were called Fort William (Calcutta), Fort St. David

were under the management of a 'President' and a Council of senior merchants. When, in after-times, territories were conquered or ceded to the Company, they were attached to the Presidency town which was nearest, or whose forces had been concerned in the acquisition; and so the whole territory became the 'Presidency.' When the Company came to be a governing power rather than a trading company, the organization of President and Council gave way to that of 'Governor' and Council, but the term 'Presidency' was retained.

The 'Governors' of Madras and Bombay have the aid of Executive and Legislative Councils; and they retain some privileges of direct correspondence with the Secretary of State, survivals from the old times when the capitals of the three Presidencies were really distinct and widely separated places. The Bengal Presidency (p. 5 ante) is larger and more populous than either of the others, and its Governor became the 'Governor-General' of India[1]; and then a separate Governor was not appointed for the local Government, but a 'Lieutenant-Governor' who has a Legislative, but no Executive, Council.

The North-Western Provinces (so called because the districts lay N.W. of the capital, and formed what was then the N.W. frontier of our Indian Empire) were at first part of the Bengal Presidency; but they were separated in 1834–5, and a Lieutenant-Governor was appointed. A Legislative Council has existed since 1886.

The Province of Oudh was annexed in 1856 and placed under a 'Chief Commissioner.' In 1877, this office was combined with that of the Lieutenant-Governor of the North-West Provinces, and various arrangements have been made for

(Madras), Bombay Castle (Bombay). It was in 1687 that the Company first undertook to administer the internal affairs of the fortified stations at which the traders were established. The local native Government was not able, even if it had wished, to interfere. It was not till nearly a century later that territorial government began.

[1] At first the 'Governor of Bengal' was both local governor and also general superintendent of the other Governments; but as time went on, a separation was inevitable. Authority was given to appoint a Governor for Bengal, or a Lieutenant-Governor; and the latter was adopted.

assimilating the powers; so that for all practical purposes the whole forms one Government—the full style of the Executive head being 'Lieutenant-Governor and Chief Commissioner.'

The Panjáb (annexed March 31, 1849) was at first placed under a 'Board of Administration'; then (1853) under a single Chief Commissioner; and finally (1859) under a Lieutenant-Governor. There is no Legislative Council[1].

The other territories which never could (owing to geographical and other considerations) have been attached to the 'Presidencies' were organized in a somewhat different manner. Ájmer, the Central Provinces[2], Assam, Coorg, and Burma, (and at the date of annexation, Oudh also as above mentioned) were placed under 'Chief Commissioners.'

Local Government and Local Administration.—This is a convenient point at which to explain the difference between a Local Government under a Governor or Lieutenant-Governor, and a Local Administration under a Chief Commissioner. In the former case the territories were either part of the old historical Presidencies, or could be separately aggregated into Provinces under a responsible executive head. But other territories were provided by law to be taken under the direct management of the Government of India itself; and the Governor-General appointed a chief officer locally to 'administer' his orders. Hence the Presidencies and Provinces under Governors and Lieutenant-Governors (who though subordinate in general to the Central Government, are yet primarily responsible and have many direct and independent powers) are called 'Local Governments' and the others 'Local Administrations.'

As it would be inconvenient in practice for the Government of India to exercise directly all the functions of a local Government in so many places, it was provided by certain Acts of the Legislature that various powers were to be delegated to Chief Commissioners *ex officio*; and the matter was further simplified by the 'General Clauses Act 1868[3], which provided that the term 'Local Government' when used in Acts of subsequent date, should include 'Local Administration' unless there was something in the context or some

[1] The Panjáb could not be attached to either of the distant Presidencies; nor could it conveniently have been added to the North-West Provinces, for the whole territory would have been unmanageable in size.

[2] The reader will perhaps need to be reminded that the 'Central Provinces' (capital Nágpur) and the Military Station at Kamthí (Kamptee) is a distinct province from 'Central India'; the latter is a group of native States under the 'Agency' of a Political officer.

[3] An Act passed to define once for all certain terms that are in constant use in Legislative enactments.

express provision otherwise. Practically, therefore, Chief Commissioners have much the same powers as Lieutenant-Governors, and the details of such differences as exist (locally and otherwise) need not occupy us.

The Government of India.—The Government of India is presided over by 'the Governor-General in Council[1].'

This phrase is used in all official proceedings and orders, because all acts—except some special ones on emergent occasions—are considered to be the acts of the Government as a whole. For this reason also formal letters or 'despatches' to the Secretary of State are signed by the Governor-General and all the members of his Executive Council; and so in Madras and Bombay when they write to the Secretary of State.

The Governor-General is aided by an Executive Council, which usually includes the Commander-in-Chief as an extra member. Each 'Honourable Member' takes charge of some department of public business; and the secretaries in that department look to him for necessary orders. Thus there is a Legislative member, a Finance member, a Military member (besides the Commander-in-Chief), a member who has charge of the Home Department, &c. The portfolio of Foreign business is usually held by the Viceroy himself, directly, with the aid of the secretaries and attachés of the Foreign Office.

Legislature. I do not propose to give details about the *Legislature*; but it will be well to indicate that when the Governor-General and his Council sit for legislative business they are reinforced by a number of extra members to constitute the Legislative Council, which makes laws for the country, and to some extent (since the amending Act of 1892) controls the financial and general administration, as it can discuss the budget and interpellate the Government on public questions. As regards the provision of laws, the Imperial Parliament has power to legislate for any part of India; but in practice it does not do so except in matters of imperial or constitutional import. When local legislative powers were first given, the Councils of Bengal, Madras, and Bombay respectively, passed 'Regulations' some of which are still in force. This plan was pursued up to 1834, when a single General Legislative Council for all India was substituted, and its enactments were then called 'Acts,' which besides having certain titles, also

[1] In other State functions this high official has also the title of 'Viceroy and Governor-General.' This latter title was first used in 1858 in the Queen's Proclamation on assuming the Government under the Act (p. 14 note).

bore a serial number for the Calendar year. (Thus we have the 'Indian Penal Code' as Act XLV of 1860, and so on.) This practice has been continued ever since. After some improvements of the Council as regards its constitution, in 1853, the present law of 1861[1] re-established provincial Councils as well as the Central Legislative Council of India. Provincial Councils pass Acts relating to their own province only, and their enactments must be approved by the Governor-General; there are certain restrictions regarding the nature of the provisions enacted, so as to prevent any clashing with the 'general Acts' of the Central Council which legislates on matters common to the whole of British India.

Scheduled Districts.—It is also convenient to mention that there are parts of the older territories, and also some newly annexed, and otherwise specially situated, provinces (or parts of provinces) for which the ordinary law of the Regulations and Acts, as a whole, would be unsuited. In 1874, a list of such places called 'Scheduled districts' was enacted (Act XIV of 1874); and in any place on the list, the Government is empowered to notify what laws are to be, and what are not to be, in force[2]. Further there is an Act of Parliament (33 Vict. ch. 3) of 1870, by which the Governor-General is empowered to make special 'Regulations' (not passed by the Legislative Council) for territories in a backward state which may be *notified* as places for which such provision is desirable. This notification not only enables such special Regulations to be put in force, but has the further effect of practically making the places 'Scheduled districts,' i. e. the ordinary laws do not apply except so far as they may expressly be extended. These modern Regulations are distinguished from the old Bengal (and other) Regulations before 1834, by their date—which is after 1870[3].

[1] Indian Councils Act, 24 & 25 Vict. ch. 67 (with subsequent amending Acts, including that extending the council and its sphere of action in 1892).

[2] In the same year Act XV set at rest doubts which had arisen as to the local application of various Acts and Regulations to certain territories which had never been annexed formally to the Presidencies, and about which certain doubts had arisen.

[3] These Regulations are simple practical codes of rules adapted to the special purpose; though not subject to all the formalities and discussions of the Legislature, they are really just as carefully drafted, and worked up by the Legislative Department as if they were Acts. The 'Regulations' for Upper Burma are an instance of this class.

Special Inspecting and advising Agency of the Government of India. Imperial Department of Agriculture and Revenue.—This will suffice to give a general idea of the scope of the work of the Government of India ; but it should be added that besides the Secretaries in each department, the Central Government has the aid and advice of Special Officers who are also deputed on tours of general inspection in the Provinces. Such are the Inspector-General of Forests, the Consulting Engineers, Sanitary Commissioners and others. The Department of Revenue and Agriculture which especially directs the Department of Land Records (of which presently) in the provinces, has not a Director called by that name, but the head of it is a Secretary to the Government of India.

The Local Governments.—In each province the Local Government divides its work of correspondence into Departments, with Secretaries and Under Secretaries in each. If the province is small there may be one Secretary only, or perhaps no more than two, who divide the work between them. It may be also that the heads of Executive Departments (as the Chief Engineer, the Inspector-General of Police, and the Director of Public Instruction) are also Secretaries or Under Secretaries to Government for those departments.

Chief Controlling Revenue authority.—In smaller Governments the Chief Commissioner is himself the head or Chief Controlling authority in Land Revenue matters; but in the larger provinces there is a separate Chief Controlling authority in direct communication with the Government. In Bengal, Madras, and the North-West Provinces (including Oudh) the control is centred in a 'Board of Revenue' which has its own Secretaries. The members divide the work; and there is legal authority for the orders of one member being deemed to be the orders of the Board, except in certain specified matters of importance. Usually one member takes control of the Land Revenue Settlements and other connected subjects, while another deals with Excise, Customs, Stamps, Pensions and other branches. In Madras, where there are more than two members, the work is otherwise distributed. In the Panjáb there are two Financial

Commissioners (first and second) who in fact, but not in name, constitute a Board. In Bombay the system is exceptional; there is no Board, but the whole Presidency is divided into large divisions (Northern, Southern, and Central, and the Province of Sindh), and the Commissioners of these are the controlling Revenue authorities in direct communication with the Government and its Revenue Secretary.

Course of Correspondence.—Correspondence with Government on all official matters is addressed to the Secretary in such and such a department, not to the Governor or Lieutenant-Governor or Chief Commissioner direct. The Government of India is officially addressed by the Secretaries to the Local Governments, &c., and addresses them in reply.

The Governor-General, Lieutenant-Governors and Chief Commissioners have 'military' or 'private' Secretaries (or both), but these are not addressed on public official questions, only on personal and semi-official matters.

The heads of Departments (Directors, Conservators of Forests, &c., &c.) address their Local Government direct (unless it is a matter for the Chief Controlling Revenue authority). Subordinate officers communicate through their Departmental Superior.

Provincial Departments of Land Records and Agriculture.—Before passing on to the District Organization, special notice should be taken of an important Provincial agency which works in direct communication with the Chief Revenue Authority. In each province there is a '*Department of Land Records and Agriculture*,' under a Director (or he may have some other title) with or without an assistant. The general work and the plan of operations of these departments are systematized and directed by means of the Imperial Department (of the Government of India) to which allusion has already been made.

The Directors are able to give important aid at Land Revenue Settlements, and also in times of famine, according to the official code of Instructions known as the 'Famine Code.' They also pay attention to agricultural experiments and improvements, to public gardens, experimental and stud farms, and the prevention and treatment of cattle disease. But their uniform and perhaps most important duty is to supervise the agency in districts for keeping up the land records and statistical returns (of which we shall speak presently). For the District Officers or Collectors have, under various Acts and orders, such a variety of duties that, if not assisted in this matter, they could hardly see to it sufficiently.

The essential object aimed at by the correct keeping of village maps, records and returns, is not only the facility of collection (of the Land Revenue) and the security of all classes of rights and interests in the land, but also the more perfect knowledge of the agricultural condition and prospects of the estates, so that on the first warnings of famine, the requisite action may be taken in time, and indications of distress may not be thrown away for want of definite information. Moreover, a hardly less important object is that, when a *revision* of Settlement becomes due, the records may be found so to correspond with actual facts, that the necessity of costly and harassing operations of re-survey, re-valuation of land, and revision of records of rights, may be as far as possible obviated.

The attention of these departments is also specially directed to the official organization, personal improvement, training and instruction (in surveying, &c.), of the local subordinate staff.

II. Local Land Revenue Jurisdiction.

The important point, for our purpose, is to be familiar with the internal arrangements of the Provinces—the Divisions, Districts, Revenue local subdivisions, and village offices. It may be stated at once, that the Land Revenue has, under every form of Government, and at all times, been so essentially the mainstay of the State income, and its administration has so necessarily involved a network of local jurisdictions and a graded staff of local officers, that the Land Revenue local jurisdiction is the basis of all other administrative divisions of territory. The Criminal, Police, and Civil jurisdictions do not indeed always, or wholly, follow the Land Revenue divisions; but even they coincide to some extent.

The Division.—The provinces are always divided into 'DISTRICTS' (the old term 'Zilla' is now completely disused[1]). In all provinces except Madras, a number of these districts —three, four, or even more, are aggregated into DIVISIONS, under the superintendence of a COMMISSIONER[2]. This officer is in general the medium of communication between the District officer and the Chief Revenue authority or the Government (as the case may be). He is the *appellate* authority in Land Revenue matters, from orders of the District Officer, and the first grade of his Assistants; he is charged with duties of inspection and general control, and with the sanctioning or refusing certain expenditure, and with various matters of appointment or discipline in respect of certain grades of public servants. He is called on to advise the Government, and to report on a great variety of matters. Land Revenue Settlements in the Division are conducted under his supervision.

The District.—The DISTRICT is really the fundamental administrative unit. It varies in size and population, its limits being formed partly on considerations of administrative convenience, and partly as the result of physical features or of historical developments. The law gives power to the Local Government (usually in the Land Revenue Acts) to alter the boundaries of existing districts, and to erect new ones[3].

Where the districts are very large they may be primarily sub-

[1] Except of course in vernacular documents. The district is sometimes referred to as a 'Collectorate.'

[2] In some places the full title is 'Commissioner and Superintendent.' Even in Madras the exception is more in form than in reality. The Officers styled 'Commissioners' in that Presidency are the members of the Board of Revenue. Instead, that is, of having separate *territorial* charges of groups of districts, they are Commissioners for certain *subjects* or branches of *duty* (Settlements, Land Revenue, Excise, &c.), and sit together as a Board: in Bombay the Commissioners act territorially, and this dispenses with a Revenue Board; in the other Provinces, there is both the agency of Commissioners and the Supervision of a Board or Financial Commissioners.

[3] Alteration may be necessary because a district is too large for convenience, or because it is desirable to aggregate, under one head, groups of lands affected in common by certain local features; as e.g. where it is convenient to have the Permanent Settled estates separate from those under Temporary Settlement in the North-West Provinces; or where, as in the Kistná and Godávari districts of Madras, it is desired to have the delta irrigation (and special Revenue arrangements) of each river under the same officer, and not divided between two.

divided, as in the case of the Madras districts; and in that case the subdivisional Assistant Collector is practically a district officer for his own locality, though in general subordination to *the* District officer.

The Collector. Deputy and Assistant Collectors. The District Officer regarded in his Land Revenue Capacity is the COLLECTOR, and is always so spoken of in the Land Revenue and Rent Laws[1]. The Collector has the help of Assistant Collectors, and of native 'Deputy Collectors[2].' The Assistants are usually classed in two grades (first and second).

They may be employed either in definite local charges or subdivisions (in which case there is a regular Gazette appointment), or when there are no such local subdistricts, they give general assistance, and dispose of such cases as are sent them by the Collector; or perhaps they take up all work (within their legal competence) arising in certain local areas (without being otherwise in charge of those areas); or they may be instructed to take up certain classes of cases. This is a matter of general control and disposal of business arranged by the Collector with reference to the important object of training and giving experience to the younger officers.

The powers of first grade Assistants are wider, and more nearly approach those of the Collector; and appeals from their orders will, in most cases, lie to the Commissioner. Second grade Assistants have lesser powers; they can perform a number of acts that do not involve any decision of disputed points; and they can inquire and report on various matters on which the

[1] His ordinary or general official title is 'Magistrate and Collector,' in the older provinces that were subject to the Regulations from the first. In districts and provinces annexed after the era of the (old) Regulations or expressly exempted from their operation (and called 'Non-Regulation Provinces' accordingly) the title usually is 'Deputy Commissioner.'

[2] And where the District Officer is called 'Deputy Commissioner' the corresponding titles will be Assistant Commissioner and Extra Assistant Commissioner: but in the Land Revenue Laws they are always 'Assistant Collectors.' The origin of this distinction of title was that in the older districts, the officers are always, by Statute, selected from the Covenanted Civil Service. In the others the rule did not apply; so that the staff might be drawn partly from the Covenanted Service, but partly also from the Uncovenanted; and military officers might also be employed. Collectors and Assistant Collectors may be natives of India if they are Covenanted Civil Servants or if they are what are called 'Statutory civilians' in India. This is a detail I cannot enter on.

Collector will pass orders. In cases where they are empowered to decide, the appeal from their decision will be to the Collector. We shall have something more to say about the work of District Officers and the law relating to them in Chapter VII.

Local Revenue subdivisions in North India; in Madras; in Bombay; in Bengal.—An essential feature of the District organization and one on which the working of the whole system largely depends is, that *independently* of there being any major division such as the above-mentioned, every district is divided up into a number of convenient local Revenue charges. The Officers in charge of these are a special grade of Native officers, appointed locally, under certain rules as to qualification, pay and promotion. In North India and in the Central Provinces, this charge is called the *Tahsíl* (which means 'place of collecting') and the officer is the *Tahsíldár*; and he usually has a '*Náib*,' i.e. assistant or deputy [1]. In Madras the officer is also called *Tahsíldár*, but his local charge is a *táluk*. In Bombay, the local division is the *táluka*, and the officer is the *mámlatdár*; he is assisted in official work by one or more subordinates (*kárkun*). There may sometimes be a division of a large *táluká*, and then a *mahálkarí* is the assistant in charge, answering very much to the *Náibtahsíldár* of other parts. In Bengal, owing to the history of the Native Administration, the local Revenue subdivisions of Mughal times had only faintly (and in certain places) survived, and were not restored as local charges in the first years of British rule; the Collectors managed all estates from their head-quarters' office. But in some places (as Sylhet, Chittagong, &c.), where a number of small estates always existed, *tahsíls* were recognized. And now in Bengal generally, 'Sub-Deputy Collectors' are appointed at local centres; and for practical purposes may be regarded as taking the place of the *tahsíl* or *táluka* organization of other provinces.

Organization of the Tahsíl, &c.—The *Tahsíldár* (under

[1] The *Tahsíldár* has himself inspection duties, so that it would be inconvenient to leave the *Tahsíl* office without any one in charge; there is usually a Deputy of some kind, and matters are so arranged that one or other is always there.

which name I include similar Local Officers of all denominations) has under him

(1) A staff of accountants and treasury clerks for the purpose of receiving the local Land Revenue, and sending it on (with the proper accounts, statements of balances outstanding, and the like) to the District Treasury (the '*Sadr*' or '*Huzúr*' as it is sometimes called).

(2) He has a staff called 'Revenue Inspectors' (or *Kánúngo* in some places). One of these remains at the *Tahsíl* headquarters, to have charge of the returns and statements submitted, and to issue the necessary blank forms for use. He has also to compile the village returns into total returns for the entire *Tahsíl*. The others are allotted, one to so many village accountants (of these we shall speak directly), in order to be always on tour and see that the village accounts and returns are properly kept up, and village inspections of crops duly made. *Local* and repeated *inspection* is the mainstay of Land Revenue administration.

Retrospect of the origin of the local jurisdiction. The Pargana.—At this point, the mention of the officials called Revenue Inspectors (and also *Kánúngo*) reminds me that before passing on to the ultimate administrative unit—the village, it should be explained that our modern system of district, *tahsíl* (or *táluka*) and village, officers, is a direct descendant of the Mughal Imperial System, and that again was derived from the old Hindu (Aryan) State organization—as it still exists in Native States, and as it is traceable in the 'Laws of Manu' and other Sanskrit writings.

The Mughal rulers treated the several geographical divisions of the empire as great provinces (*Súbá*) under Governors or Deputies (*Nawáb*, &c.) in direct subordination to the Court at Delhi[1].

Each province was divided into a number of '*Sirkárs*,' something like our 'districts,' only larger—each under its *Díwán* and *Názim*, for Civil and Revenue and for criminal work, respectively. (In some cases, and at a later time, a division into *chaklá* was preferred.) The important local unit was however the *pargana* (*pergunnah* of books); and this was in general the older '*des*' of the Hindu kingdoms. In Hindu States (and so under the Maráthás) the

[1] In later times the heads of these Súbás—Bengal, Oudh, Hyderabad, &c., threw off allegiance and set up as independent Sovereign princes.

executive and Revenue officer was the *desái*, and the accountant the *despándyá*[1].

Under the Mughals the *pargana* officer was the *Kánúngo* (properly *Qánúngo*, and meaning *go*=speaker, *qánún*=the 'canon' or rule;—one who declares the standard or rule in Revenue matters[2]. The executive officer of Land Revenue—the *'ámil*, had a jurisdiction which might or might not coincide with the *pargana*, because it depended on the amount of Revenue which he was responsible to levy[3].

It is important to remember about the *pargana*, because these divisions are still locally remembered and are often referred to or made use of[4]. But for administrative purposes in general, they were too small; and the modern *Tahsíl* usually contains three or more *parganas*. In Bombay, I believe, the *táluka* is still (generally) conterminous with the old native jurisdiction, though the former official titles have given place to that of the *mámlatdár* and his assistants.

Village Officers.—Immediately below the *tahsíl* or *táluka* with its *tahsíldár*, &c. and the Revenue Inspectors, come the 'Villages' (p. 11).

The headman, pátel, lambardár.—Each village has, at any rate, an official headman. In one class of villages (as we shall understand more fully in the Chapter on Land Tenures) the headman is a natural part of the constitution; in the other he is not; but as, in the latter case, some one must act as representative of the village with the Collector, one of the leading co-sharers is selected (and to some extent elected) as official headman or *lambardár*[5].

[1] These titles still survive as hereditary titles in certain families. The reader may perhaps remember to have heard of Bombay gentlemen with the name (or rather appended title) of 'Desai.'

[2] The *Kánúngo's* office was the depository of the Revenue Accounts, lists of Rates, and the Survey and Estate records; hence he was the general official referee in all such matters.

[3] Hence he was afterwards called *karorí*—the officer who collected a *karor* (ten millions) of the 'dám' or copper coins used (said to be 40 to the rupee) or about 2½ *lákhs* of rupees (1 *lákh* = 100,000).

[4] The *pargana* was sometimes subdivided into '*tappa*,' each being in fact a group of two or three or more villages, also still locally remembered. In fact it sometimes happens that local landholders of influence in *parganas* or *tappas* may be recognized as *zaildárs* or otherwise as local petty magistrates. *Zaildár* is an honorary office intended to secure the goodwill and service in suppressing crime, &c. of certain influential persons.

[5] '*Lambardár*' means the holder of a 'number' in the Collector's list of persons primarily responsible to bring in the Land Revenue of the village or a section of a village. *Muqaddam* (or in the Hindí form *mukádam*) was the

In *Raiyatwárí* countries, the village heads retain their natural title (of *pátel, mandal, maniyakáran.*, &c, according to the dialect). They have no direct responsibility for any revenue but that of their own holdings, but they have their general duties, and are often petty magistrates, and act as official arbitrators or Civil Courts in petty cases. In these countries, also, the headship is not only hereditary but sometimes still has a *watan* or official landholding attached to it; all the family are sharers in the *patelgí* (i.e. headship) and its land and emoluments, but only one man is selected to perform the actual duties of office [1].

In the provinces where the Settlement regards the whole village as the unit of assessment, there may be as many *lambardárs* as the village has *pattí* or sections; and *each has a direct responsibility* (differently defined, however, in the several Land Revenue Acts) for the revenue. Where there is a custom to that effect, or otherwise, where allowed because of a real responsibility, the *lambardárs* receive a *pachotra* (or *haq-lambardárí*) which is a fee of five per cent. on the Revenue, and which they collect as one of the legal Cesses or rates [2].

Patwárí. Karnam.—Even more important than the headman is the *patwárí* (called *Karnam* in the South and *Kulkarní* in Bombay [3]), sometimes referred to as 'village accountant' or 'village Registrar.' The office originated in remote times

older term in use under Native rule. In the Central Provinces *both* terms are still used, because the functions of headman are sometimes divided; '*lambardár*' then refers to the revenue paying aspect of the office; *muqaddam* or *mukádam* to the Executive, i.e. to the responsibility to give aid to public officers in general, and specially in suppressing and informing about crime; a duty which has always been laid by law on village heads (cf. Criminal Procedure Code, sec. 45; Ind. Penal Code, secs. 154, 156, &c.).

[1] It is highly probable that, originally, the headman and the accountant were always renumerated in this way: but succeeding governments having refused to leave the official lands revenue free, the privilege was lost. Speaking generally, it is in Central India and the Dakhan that the *watan* is best preserved. Besides the *land*, the *watan* also included certain dignities and privileges, some of which are very curious. *L. S. B. I.* vol. i. p. 180.

[2] In the Panjáb, the number of sectional headmen is sometimes so considerable that it is convenient to have a single representative of the several representatives; and an *'ala-lambardár* or chief-headman is recognized by the Land Revenue Rules.

[3] In Bombay, where a village accountant of the hereditary class exists, he is the *kulkarní*, where a stipendiary official is appointed he is called *talátí*. The latter term is chiefly used in Gujarát.

when writing and cyphering were rare accomplishments, and the headman or leader of the village could not be expected to possess them, so that a separate writer became a necessity. And as the Revenue system grew, this officer became more and more important as being indispensable to the due realization of the State Revenue. At the present day he is, or may be, equally valued as the means of preserving village rights and keeping the co-sharers from getting into difficulties, while his duties as a Revenue servant and recorder of statistics are still more important.

Provincial details of organization vary, but in the North-West Provinces, Panjáb, and Central Provinces, *patwárís* are appointed not to single villages but to circles which are smaller or larger according to value, density of population, &c.; they may vary from a charge of 1,200 to even 5,000 acres of land. Appointments to the office are now carefully protected by rules to secure proper qualification and intelligence. The office is fairly well paid by fixed salary and by certain fees [1].

Duties of the village patwárí in general.—The different Land Revenue Rules and Circular Orders must be referred to for all details as regards each province, but a very general account may be given which applies primarily to the North of India, but also fairly enough describes the sort of work done in Madras and Bombay.

The *patwárí* has—

I. To keep the village accounts.

(*a*) Of revenue payments, and outstanding balances by the proprietor or co-sharers.

(*b*) Of rent payments by tenants.

(*c*) Of *malba* or items chargeable to the common expenditure of the village [2].

[1] It is allowed to be to a certain extent hereditary, that is to say that a son of a *patwárí* will have a prospect of succeeding before other applicants, provided he is capable and has been sent to a *patwárí* school and learnt the special subjects (surveying, &c.) which a *patwárí* requires. A boy who turns out well in this respect is pretty sure of his place in the course of time.

[2] In joint villages (owned by a body of co-sharers) there are various charges, such as entertaining strangers, keeping a festival, repairing the

This involves giving receipts in due form or in making entries for landholders and tenants (who usually cannot write) in certain books of receipts with which they are furnished.

II. To have official charge of the village maps, field registers and other records of landed rights, shares and interests, as prepared at survey or Settlement. *Patwárís* are bound to allow inspection, and to furnish, on payment of fixed fees, extracts from these records, when such are required for the purpose of being filed in suits and proceedings or otherwise.

III. They are charged with periodically preparing returns in the same forms as those last spoken of, and keeping copies of the village-map, all corrected up to date, so that the information in the Land Records may never get obsolete, but be kept in correspondence with the actual facts for the time being.

IV. They also make certain inspections and fill up various statistical returns, which show the crops sown and harvested, the number and kind of wells, of cattle, of groves and orchards, and give details of other matters on which a complete knowledge of the state of the village depends.

V. They also have to take note of all *changes* that occur in the ownership of land, and have a special register for noting transactions of sale, mortgage, or under the law of inheritance [1].

VI. The *patwárí* is bound to report at once to the *Tahsíl* any unusual occurrence—destruction of boundary marks,

village meeting-place, or the well or tank, or some charity or payment to the village mosque or temple, which are chargeable to the village in common. These charges the headman will himself disburse and, after the harvest, recover the amount from all the co-proprietors rateably; there may be local rules limiting the amount that may be so spent. In Raiyatwárí villages the headman himself bears such costs, but in the old days he used to make it an excuse for levying dues and cesses on the villages; and the *táluka* officers did the same for the '*pargana* expenses' as they called them. I have not heard of any charge on the village landholders allowed on this account at the present day.

[1] We shall speak of this again under the head of Revenue business and Procedure, Chap. VII.

encroachment on public land, occurrence of cattle disease, approach of locusts, &c.; and he keeps a *Diary* which he has to fill in regularly, noting practically everything that goes on, and that in any way concerns public business.

Patwárí's duty in Raiyatwárí Provinces.—In Madras and Bombay, and other provinces where the Land Revenue officer deals with individual fields and land-holdings, not with estates or groups taken together, the village accountant's duties are in many respects the same; for the maintenance of maps, and statistics of crops and cattle, are equally important under all systems. So is the report of all important occurrences, the keeping account of revenue payments, and seeing that every ignorant landholder gets a receipt or an entry in his receipt-book for every payment he actually makes whether against current dues or for arrears. 'Mutations'—or changes in the occupancy of land—have to be noted in *Raiyatwárí* countries no less than in others, not because the system is directly concerned with rights in land, but because all such changes affect the Collector's procedure in recovering revenue from the right person.

Annual Jamabandí or occupant's revenue account.—In Madras the *Settlement Manual*, and in Bombay *Hope's Manual*, give rather formidable lists of the village accounts and records. But the documents that are necessary have here a special reference to a proceeding characteristic of the *Raiyatwárí* system, namely, the making out an annual account for each occupant, giving a list of the lands actually held by him in the year, and the revenue due for each. This will be further noticed in Chap. VII.

Settlement Officers.—It will be observed that the gradation of Officers just described refers to the permanent staff of Land Revenue officials. For the express purpose of assessing the Land Revenue, and making the initial inquiry into rights, rents, and land customs, a special staff has hitherto been appointed: this consisted of a *Settlement Officer* with, perhaps, one or more

Assistant Settlement Officers, and various subordinates called Superintendents of Settlement (or by other titles locally), Inspectors, Surveyors, &c. Some of the Land Revenue Acts still mention separately the appointment and powers of Settlement Officers. In a modern Revenue Act, like that of the Panjáb (XVII of 1887), no such distinction is drawn. Officers engaged in revising a Settlement are regarded as ordinary Land Revenue Officers empowered to do certain things which are required in connexion with a Land Revenue Settlement—either the whole work, or revising the assessment only, or making or correcting the Record of Rights only. And this is indeed all that is necessary. For in future Settlements, the work will become simpler and simpler—all re-survey, and re-valuation, and fresh record of rights becoming unnecessary—and the work of revising the revenue and rent-rates will be carried out entirely by Land Revenue Officers of the ordinary grades. At present, however, a certain number of Settlement *Tahsíldárs* and subordinates as well as European Settlement Officers are usually maintained in parties, ready to attack the work in four or five districts simultaneously. In order that such establishments (as long as they are required) may be fully employed, the periods of Settlement have to be adjusted so that they may fall in successively, and thus enable the Staff to find continuous employment, and not have a number of Settlements falling in all at once, which would oblige them to keep districts waiting for re-settlement, and occasion loss to the Treasury.

Résumé.—Let us now briefly collect in one paragraph a summary of administrative agencies. Immediately below the Local Government is the Chief Revenue authority—be it a Board of Revenue, or one or more Financial Commissioners. In small Provinces there is no such control separate from the Chief Commissioner himself.

Then comes the *Division*, a superintending charge over three, four or more districts, under a *Commissioner*. (In Madras this gradation is omitted.)

Then the *District* under the *Collector* with his 'Deputy' and 'Assistant Collectors'—European and Native. If the district is not primarily subdivided owing to its size, the next stage is its complete allotment into small local charges called *táluka* and *tahsíl.* In Bengal, the 'Sub-Deputy Collector's' charge virtually answers to this arrangement. The experienced (native) officer who has charge is provided with a *Náib* or *Deputy*, and also a staff of Revenue Inspectors (or *Kánúngo*), who are trained and rendered capable of minutely and constantly supervising the *village* agency below them.

In the village, or rather in a *circle*, the *patwárí* is the really important functionary of the administration. Village headmen and watchmen have their duties and their responsibility, but on the *patwárí's* efficiency and on his records and statistics being really correct (and in accord with existing facts) depends almost the whole of the Revenue management present and future.

CHAPTER IV.

What is the Land Revenue?

On commencing a study of the Land Revenue Administration, we naturally first ask, what is the nature of the contribution to the State income, known as the Land Revenue?

Originally a share of the grain heap on the threshing-floor.—Briefly, it is a historical fact that from very ancient times, long before the Mughal Empire, the kings or *Rájás* and other lesser chiefs were accustomed to take from the cultivators of the soil in their dominions or chiefships, a certain share of the produce of every cultivated acre, unless, as a special favour, that share was remitted.

Associated with the early Hindu Rulers.—As our earliest literary mention of the State share is in the Sanskrit books[1] we naturally associate this plan of raising a revenue with the early kingdoms resulting from the Aryan immigration. When an important section of these tribes had crossed the Panjáb, and settled down in the regions of the Jumna and the Ganges plain, they developed not only the literature, law, and philosophy which have become famous, but also a distinct State-craft and a territorial organization, in which the influence of tribal divisions and groups is plainly discernible. The leading military caste furnished the ruling prince and a number of subordinate (quasi-feudal) chiefs managing portions of the

[1] The compiler of the 'Laws of Manu,' a well-known Hindu text-book, speaks also of traders, cattle-owners, and artificers contributing a share of their gains to the king; here, however, we confine our attention to the land.

territory. The Brahman caste furnished the ministers and advisers of the Court. The share in the produce of all cultivated land was the principal source of the Rájá's Revenue.

State Revenue of Non-Aryan kingdoms. But we are acquainted with other tribal groups in India—before the Aryan advent, who also had organized territorial settlements, though some of them showed no sign of a 'State' more developed than the patriarchal rule of the clan or tribe. Among these we do not find any direct evidence of a Land Revenue or share of the produce appropriated by the ruler. But there are evident traces—especially in Eastern, Central and Southern India—of tribes (whom we associate with the name 'Dravidian') who had a curious method of giving the ruling chief an income in a somewhat different way; at first they allotted a portion of the land in each village group, for the chief: and this was cultivated by slaves, or by some special arrangement. Traces of these 'chief's farms' or 'royal lands' are still to be found in more than one locality. But from whatever cause, whether by the influence of contact with the Aryans or otherwise[1], the time came when a share in the produce was levied (additionally) from all land except certain privileged holdings of the priests and of the old founders and heads of the village[2].

Extent of the State share.—Whatever its real origin, there can be no doubt about the fact that the levy of a produce-share became general at a remote period. It is mentioned, as a thing long known and established, in the 'Laws of MANU.' The share was one-sixth of the gross produce, i. e. of the grain heap

[1] Though the Aryan advance only affected, directly or primarily, the countries north of the Vindhyan hills and the upper part of Western India, there can be no doubt that smaller parties of Aryans travelled further. The Brahmans with their ideas of pilgrimage and ascetic life, wandered everywhere, and found in the south a fertile soil for the propagation of their social and religious ideals; they doubtless found a welcome in many of the rude courts of non-Aryan chiefs or princes, and gradually leavened the country with Aryan ideas; and the State organization became modified accordingly. Military adventurers, too, appear to have been welcomed at courts, and to have been employed in organizing and leading the local armies. Whatever the precise truth may have been, it is quite certain that the 'Rájás' of Central and Southern India became in time quite 'Hinduized,' though no general Aryan advance or conquest can be historically traced—indeed on various grounds, can be distinctly denied.

[2] It can be only conjectured that the princes had been induced to grant away to dependants and relations, their 'royal lands,' so that they found themselves unable to support their State without a more extended source of Revenue. The grain share in time became universal throughout the originally non-Aryan States just as much as in the Aryan. Whether they learnt the system from the Aryans or vice versâ, I cannot pretend to discuss.

made up at the threshing-floor; and Manu notices that the sixth might be raised to one-fourth in time of war or other emergency[1].

Was soon raised to a higher proportion.—Though *the sixth* became a traditional share, the growing requirements of States in a perpetual condition of warfare, and the frequent demands of conquerors, often caused it to be raised. At first various devices would be resorted to—e. g. of demanding husked rice instead of unhusked—without apparently increasing the share. But at a later time, we find *one-half* was a common rate of sharing. The Mughal Emperors fixed *one-third* as a fair rate.

Advantages of the plan.—There was a primeval simplicity about this plan, that offered many advantages, in an early stage of society. Being a share of the gross produce, there was no question of any complicated calculations of the cultivator's profit, or the costs of production, nor about the relative value of land, or the productiveness of the season. Whatever the land produced, little or much, was heaped on the threshing-floor, and the king's officer superintended its division in kind. In a famine year there might be nothing to divide and so revenue relief followed automatically.

It is still made use of locally, in Native States.—The collection in kind is still largely practised in India. In many Native States (especially in the Hill country and in the more primitive districts) the State share is still paid in grain; and in some British districts (very commonly, e. g. in the Panjáb) where the land has passed into the hands of a landlord class, what was once the State share, and is now the landlord's rent, is taken in kind.

But has also disadvantages.—But there are also many disadvantages attending the system, which gradually cause it to be modified, and ultimately given up, in favour of a cash equivalent.

[1] Long after the days of Manu, 'the sixth' remained a customary share; thus in *Kálidásá's* time (beginning of the Christian era) we find allusion to the revenue sixth (*Sakuntalá*, Act ii):—

Máthavyá. You are the king are you not?
The King. What then?
Máthavyá. Say you have come for the sixth part of their grain which they owe you. . . .

Modification of the grain payment system. Gradually changes into a cash payment.—As population grows and cultivation extends, the task of collecting in kind becomes a difficult one; for unless actively supervised, the peasantry conceal or make away with the grain, and local collectors, on their part, cheat both the peasant and the treasury. At first, modified plans of collecting are adopted. The crop is no longer divided at the threshing floor (the process being called *batái* or *bháolí*). An estimate of the standing crop (*kankút*) is made, and appraisers become extremely skilful in the art of judging. The appraiser announced his opinion that such and such a field would yield so many '*maunds*' (p. 12) of grain, of which the State share would be so much. When the grain was reaped this quantity had to be paid over to the State collector, whatever the actual outturn might prove, more or less. Other devices also were adopted. But in time as farms got more and more subdivided, the old theoretical shares became impracticable; and at the same time coined money came more into use, and thus it was easier, as well as more profitable, to fix a roughly calculated money payment.

Effect of the Mughal Imperial system.—This general change was largely brought about by the action of the astute Emperor Akbar. It will be sufficient to state briefly, that on the establishment of the Mughal Empire, it was found impossible to apply the strict theory of the Moslem law as to the taxation of conquered countries. There was indeed a tax in kind known to that law as '*khiráj*[1],' but in any case it was necessary to manage the Hindu population according to their long-established usages.

The Mughal Revenue administration, in fact, merely reduced the customary and unwritten usages of the Hindu Administration to a system. It introduced regular records and revenue accounts, and provided a whole set of revenue terms and

[1] In fact a plan of taxation in kind is a very natural one. The Arabs knew it; and hence the Muhammadan theory could, without much difficulty, be adapted to the practice found in India at the conquest. We remember also the mention of a fifth share of the produce for the king, levied by Joseph, as mentioned in the book of Genesis.

phrases: it fixed the official charges and gave new names to them; but in all essentials the Mughal Revenue Administration was simply the older plan in a new form. One change was, however, made. A great empire like Akbar's required some definite knowledge of the financial resources of the provinces; and the Land Revenue was the chief item. Hence it became necessary to measure the land and to have some regular assessment of an average quantity of grain (of each principal kind) that would be received from each class of land. Akbar made such a measurement and estimate; in fact establishing—in a rough and simple manner—the process (of which we shall speak hereafter) of a Land Revenue Settlement.

Akbar's Land Revenue Settlement.—His first essay was made with the help of his Hindu minister, *Rájá Todarmal* (A. D. 1571, and in Bengal 1582); it was a settlement of the Revenue in kind. But after a few years this was revised in favour of a cash assessment. The rates were fixed by calculating the price of grain on an average of the previous nineteen years of the reign [1], and applying it to a share which was one-third of the average gross produce.

An average amount of produce per *bíghá* (p. 12) was ascertained for certain established kinds or classes of land, and for each of the crops commonly cultivated. (Where there were exceptional crops or such as could not be divided in kind, an arbitrary cash rate was charged, and indeed had long been customary [2]. The average produce was ascertained by experimental reapings and weighments; it was intended to be a fairly low average rate, so as to allow for changing rates of production in good and bad years: it was fixed higher in the best and regularly yielding lands, and lower in the poorer and more precarious soils. The Revenue Officers, who were closely supervised, had always an elastic power of reduction in bad years.

Akbar at first softened the novelty of his system by leaving it optional with the cultivators to give grain or cash as they preferred [3].

[1] Nineteen years was believed to be a cycle during which all the ordinary varieties of good and bad years would come round; so that an average of the cycle gave an average of all possible degrees of good or bad.

[2] Almost always, certain exceptionally valuable crops, or those which are not easily divisible in kind, paid cash rates known as *Zabtí*.

[3] As a matter of fact, when the soil and climate render the crop precarious,

Attempt to value the grain share in cash given up in favour of independent land rates. Plough rates and soil rates.—It will be observed that Akbar's Settlement deliberately proceeded on the basis of an attempt to convert a share (fixed at one-third) in kind, into a direct average equivalent in money. But in many places to which the Akbarian Settlement did not extend, and in many later Native States, the process of change from kind to cash did not follow this order. I cannot here go into the causes, but recourse was had to a feature of agricultural life which has in most countries been found to affect the size and form of holdings as well as the apportionment of rent or other charges. There are always a certain number of ploughs, each of which represents the tilling of a certain area of land; and it is easy to levy a rough rate *per plough*. In other cases a rough classification of the chief kinds of soil (markedly different in productive power [1]) was made, and an area rate was imposed—arbitrarily or by bargain. When once such rates find their level (being lowered if not practically payable, or if too light being raised) they become customary rates and are left unaltered for several years. Other subsequent rulers accept these rates as a basis, and proceed to add so much more, to represent *their* Settlement; of this we shall see examples presently.

Ideas of assessment under Native rule.—Money rates when once they became general, always adjusted themselves to practical conditions. The oriental financiers soon came to hold (virtually) that the limit of land assessment was what could be extracted from the cultivator without reducing him or his cattle to semi-starvation, and without causing him to

when the country is backward, and export difficult, grain payments will often be preferred. But when there is a ready sale for produce, and the means of getting it to market, and where there are competition prices, the cultivator is the loser, in the long run, by having to give grain. The landlord, on the other hand, likes to take grain, because even though the quantity is less in a bad year, prices are sure to be higher. Those who wish to see more details about grain collection, and the varieties of method adopted, and the oppression that can be exercised on the one side and the petty cheating that is usual on the other, may be referred to *L. S. B. I.* vol. i. p. 269; ii. p. 716; iii. p. 341.

[1] As might be expected, the Native agriculturist recognizes (and has endless local names for) varieties of soil, the relative value of which and their capacity for growing certain staples he is well aware.

lower the standard of cultivation or throw up his holding and decamp. Their officers became skilful at alternately squeezing and letting go. It was only a few rapacious tyrants and short-lived Revenue-farmers who habitually transgressed the rule of not killing (or even overtasking) the 'goose that laid the golden eggs.'

Example of the Maráthá States.—The Maráthá rulers afford a good example. Keen financiers they always were, and in some provinces were mere plunderers, extorting Revenue with savage cruelty, and everywhere leaving depopulated villages and lands abandoned. But in their more firmly established provinces, they accepted the original rates fixed by the Muhammadan kingdoms in Central India, as a basis, spoke of them as the *aín* or 'essential' rates, and then levelled them up to what they called the *kamál* or 'perfect' assessment. In each village they employed some energetic headman (or a farmer, if the natural headman was inefficient or non-compliant), and his business was to exact all that could be got up to the limit of not destroying the village. The village heads and contractors were backed by the keen efforts of the *desáí* or *kamísdár* or other district officer, who wanted the *táluka* total as full as possible for the treasury—with a good extra slice for himself.

Ideas of the Native State as to permanence of the assessment.—This leads me to remark that no native ruler ever intended that when an assessment was once made there should be no future rise or alteration. The best rulers would have only gradually, and at long intervals, raised their rates. Akbar's Settlement was in fact made for ten years. It was doubtless intended that only additional measurements should be taken as cultivation extended; and that ordinarily the existing '*pargana* rates' (as they were called) should be applied. But we have everywhere proof that from time to time additional rates were levied; indeed as the government declined in character and ability, *annual* Settlements became almost everywhere the rule: the standard rates of the last formal provincial assessment being used only as a basis for the calculation of the year's demand.

Expedient of levying cesses or extras.—Unfortunately as the Empire grew older the Land Revenue methods instead of improving and ripening, got laxer and laxer. We might have expected to find some practical, if rather arbitrary, method of re-adjusting rates, as prices rose and the value of money, or its purchasing power, altered; but it was not so; the local Governors hit on no better expedient than that of raising the total amount by demanding arbitrary percentage or other additions or 'cesses' (called *abwáb*, and locally *bábti* and *hubúb*). These they called by various names according to the name of the Governor who ordered them or the pretence on which they were levied[1]. When the head of the province thus levied extra charges, the local officials and Revenue farmers began to levy such rates also, on their own account. The old Settlement rates thus disappeared. Then the state of things would become intolerable; a compromise would be effected, the revenue and extras would be consolidated into one sum, and a new start would be made.

Revenue farming.—But the increasing difficulties of Revenue management and the impossibility of a weak government giving efficient local control to its subordinates, suggested that it would be easier to divide the districts into large blocks or estates, to calculate (from the Treasury Accounts) a rough total sum which the tract ought to yield, and then to get some capitalist or local landholder of wealth and influence to undertake the entire management and be responsible that the required total should be paid into the Treasury every year.

The Revenue farmer so appointed was armed with large powers (often very arbitrarily used) to make the collections from villages, holders of small estates, and the like. This saved the Governor all trouble of controlling local Revenue officials of all grades and checking their accounts. The Treasury officer in future only looked to the totals due from the different estates, and cared for nothing else so long as these total sums were duly realized without further deduction than what was authorized for the remuneration of the farmer.

It is suggested also by the necessity of employing and conciliating the Hindu princes and chiefs.—There was another circumstance which, in several provinces, recommended if it did not necessitate this plan. There had been

[1] Thus in Bengal one was called the *chauth Maráthá* or *Maráthá fourth*, being levied to enable the Governor to satisfy the Maráthá chiefs who had got as far as levying a tribute, though they had not assumed the Government of Bengal.

a number of local Hindu kingdoms, usually comparatively small, and these had succumbed to the Mughal arms, leaving the Rájás in many cases unable to resist openly, but still capable of giving a great deal of trouble directly a chance of revolt appeared. These Rájás and their chiefs or 'barons' had a strong territorial influence, and could to some extent be conciliated by being left in enjoyment of their local rule and dignities, provided they would consent to accept a 'patent' of tenure from the Governor, and agree to hand over part of their Land Revenue as a fixed annual tribute or assessment to the Treasury. The Rájá in fact became the Revenue farmer under Imperial warrant, and in time as ex-officials, capitalists, and Court favourites acquired a similar connexion with tracts of land or estates, the position became assimilated, and the difference of origin forgotten.

All kinds of farmers called Zamíndár and Taluqdár.— The persons, whether territorial Rájás or others, thus employed, were generally called '*Zamíndár*,' and sometimes *Taluqdár*[1]. Neither term implied any definite right of ownership in the soil; it simply implied in the one case that the Rájá or other person was managing the State right in the land; and in the other that he was a 'dependant' (Arabic *ta'alluq*=dependency) of the ruling power.

First position of great Revenue farmers.—When the system of Revenue farming began, the Empire had not yet reached its final stages of disorganization and collapse. The

[1] **Origin of the term.**—*Zamíndár* means holder (*dár*) of land (*zamín*). The later rulers of the countries that once were provinces of the Mughal Empire, it will be remembered, had come to claim to be owners (by conquest) of all land: at any rate they reckoned among the State rights, not only the administration of justice, the command of the military force, &c., but (most chiefly) the right to the land, including its revenue and other perquisites, which they spoke of as the *Zámíndári* right; and when the management of this was made over to the Rájá or a capitalist farmer, they called him the *Zamíndár*. In Oudh, the Government was too tenacious of its own *Zamíndári* rights to allow the turbulent local Rájás to call themselves *Zamíndár*, lest they should assume that they had really recovered their old territorial claims—they called them therefore *Taluqdár*. These Oudh landholders never were pleased with this distinction; and to this day none of them calls himself *Taluqdár*, but always *Rájá*. In Bengal, the term *taluqdár* was generally employed to indicate a smaller class of estate sometimes subordinate to the *Zamíndár*.

Revenue farmer, or Zamíndár as we may now call him, was at first appointed regularly and with much form and care, giving in a written bond of acceptance, and receiving a warrant (*sanad*) which declared his duties and gave a schedule of the local subdivisions, estates and villages, for the Revenue of which he was responsible, and the amount due from each; it also indicated what deductions for remuneration, collection charges, police, charities, and the like, he was entitled to make. Usually he had to pay in about nine-tenths of the whole collections, but he was allowed also some lands free of revenue for himself and for police charges. The Government pargana officer (or *Kánúngo*) was still responsible to check accounts and see to the due execution of the Revenue responsibility. The Office of Revenue farmer was not hereditary. In the case of the territorial chiefs, as the son would succeed to the estate of his father, it was almost a matter of course that he succeeded also to the Zamíndárí; but in other cases the son only succeeded on sufferance, and on taking out a new warrant, probably paying a handsome succession fee.

As control was released the Revenue farmer's responsibility is fixed by bargain.—As the authority of the Emperor grew less and less, so the local Governors of Bengal, Oudh, &c., became more and more independent of the Court at Delhi; but they also became more careless of the details of administration; and, as usual, when bad government is rife, the treasuries became empty; and then the Revenue farmers were the only persons who could be looked to for money. They naturally felt that they were indispensable, and enlarged their pretensions accordingly. They were left more and more unchecked, and the sums they had to pay became more and more a matter of bargain. The official organization for Land Revenue control disappeared, or was only retained in name and quite under the Zamíndár's influence. The Zamíndárs, in fact, did just as they pleased, and made the villagers pay whatever they demanded or whatever they could extract from them.

Condition of the Revenues at the commencement of British Rule.—In Bengal (and the same is true of other parts when the districts came under British rule), the land Revenue had for generations past been levied in cash payments; its assessment (often by contract for the year) was determined on no known principle. All traces of a share in the produce, and a valuation of that share in money, had long disappeared. The sum actually paid into the Treasury was just as much of the total collections as the Zamíndár could not avoid paying. The sums received through the petty estate-holders or through the village headmen from the cultivators were levied at certain rates spoken of as 'pargana rates.' They were supposed to be rates fixed at the last formal assessment but modified by those subsequent compromises of which I have spoken. But these rates varied from place to place, and were levied with various additions and impositions as the Zamíndár chose or was able to levy [1].

This then is a summary of what the Land Revenue was, and what it had come to be, at the end of the last century. The retrospect has been entirely historical; and as our limits will prevent us indulging in much more reference to times long passed away, it will be desirable here to review each province, briefly, and see in what condition its Land Revenue Administration was found at annexation.

Review of the provinces as to the prevalence of Revenue farming.—BENGAL (where our first attempt at Land Revenue management was made) had been assessed under the Akbarian system, and there had been more than one later formal re-assessment. By 1765–1772 (when British rule began) the greater part of the districts—the central and more populous ones in fact—were entirely managed (and had been for a century past) by Zamíndárs. Here and there smaller estates paying lump sums were found independent of the Zamíndárs. There were also some State grantees of other descriptions.

The NORTH-WEST PROVINCES, began with the 'Benares Province' districts (1775). This territory was all under a Rájá,

[1] Even in Warren Hastings' time, the old Revenue Rolls showing the rates formally assessed for the *pargana*, were described as 'mere objects of curiosity' which had long since ceased to have any relation to actual payments.

who, however, did not become the 'Zamíndár' of the whole. Consequently there were no great revenue farmers, but only smaller landlords who were answerable for the revenue.

In 1801, the districts of the Ganges plain were 'ceded' by the Oudh Wazír to pay for the expenses of British protection; and in 1803, others were conquered from the Maráthás. A certain territory was acquired in the Himáláyán region at a later date (1815), but substantially the districts first named make up the Province. It may be said generally that the bulk of the districts had been farmed, but had not become a regular network of Zamíndárís as Bengal was. In some cases the Revenue management had been left with local territorial Rájás and other notables who farmed large areas; in some cases the State officers (*'ámils* and others) had held the districts directly for the Government; but in fact they managed very much on the terms of Revenue farmers. But in many cases, owing to the stronger constitution of the village bodies which we shall afterwards describe, farming, village by village, was resorted to.

Oudh, annexed in 1856, was in the last stage of Revenue disorganization; its districts were mostly held by Rájás, but in some cases by *Názims* or State officers, and in others by bankers, Court favourites and others. All of these practically farmed the revenues, and virtually acted as landlords.

The Panjáb was a country where the villages also had a strong constitution, and no extensive system of 'Zamíndárs' ever prevailed. Farming was, however, common enough in Sikh days[1], and revenue collection in kind was still practised locally.

In the Central Provinces the country had been mostly under the Maráthá rule. A part of it was held by local chiefs who had been left alone on condition of paying a tribute to the ruling State; otherwise the villages were farmed one by one

[1] When British rule began, in 1849, it was found that the country had been divided into *taluqa* charges: of these there were fifty-nine in all: forty-three were managed by State officers (*kárdár*); eight were farmed village by village to the headman; and in eight the *kárdár* was treated as farmer of the whole, taking as much, and paying in as little, as he could. *L. S. B. I.* vol. ii. p. 541.

to the old headman, or to a more efficient revenue agent (afterwards called *málguzár*) who undertook to be responsible for a certain sum.

In BOMBAY farming had been very general, but it was by means of local land-officers, who for the most part did not succeed in getting a permanent hold territorially. The whole system was worked by the *desái* (or *desmukh*) and *despándyá* or other officers of districts and *tálukas* through the village headmen or *pátels*[1].

In MADRAS, the Northern districts had been under Mughal rule, and Zamíndárs were established; but they were frequently old territorial chiefs, and do not seem to have destroyed rights and reduced the tenantry as other Zamíndárs did. The Carnatic districts, under a Nawáb (tributary to the Nizám), had been mercilessly farmed; but with the result, not of creating landed estates, but of destroying all rights in land. In other parts there were local chiefs who also may be called Revenue farmers in a sense, but their influence was not lasting, Other districts, held either by Nawábs (or Deputy-Governors) tributary to the Hyderabad State, or temporarily by the Mysore Sultans, or by Hindu Princes, or by the Maráthás, were all more or less farmed and cruelly mismanaged; but revenue-farming produced no lasting effect on the tenures (as a rule) except in breaking down old privileges and making landholding a burden rather than a valuable right.

Reasons for giving these details. They influence the land tenures.—This brief review of the progress of the farming system in past days was introduced (as I have said) primarily to explain the condition of the Land Revenue Administration at the close of the eighteenth century, and to account for the *absence of any practical plan of administering the Land Revenue* which could be adopted by the new British rulers. But it was also desirable to notice the subject for another reason. The growth of the Revenue farmer is one of the important factors in the development of the local land-tenures in more

[1] It will be remembered that the Mughal Empire was only established in the Gujarát districts. Beyond that, a Muhammadan kingdom—the relic of the earlier Mussalman invasions, had flourished in spite of its having broken up into five smaller kingdoms. These were overthrown by the last of the Mughal Emperors and by the Maráthás, who at the beginning of the century had established their dominion everywhere throughout the Bombay territory.

than one province. In some cases, as we shall see, revenue farmers developed into great landlords, and were so recognized by law. In others they founded smaller village estates: in others, again, they retained nothing but some overlord dues; in other places, again, they passed away altogether, leaving no mark. Bengal seemed to have been the home of the regular revenue-farmer who grew into a landlord; the other provinces, speaking generally, never exhibited this growth to anything like the same uniform extent. It is important to recollect that though Revenue farming (as a method of land management) very generally prevailed, in one shape or another, it did not equally result in the growth of permanent estates in land. And where landlord rights have been recognized, their growth was often due to the fact that the landlords were old territorial chiefs, Imperial grantee families of rank, or local land-officers of exceptional strength and ability, all of whom had various ties and connexions with the land from the first.

Difficulty of devising a principle for fixing the land Revenue.—But we must return to our consideration of what the Land Revenue is at the present day. When, in Bengal, the British Government undertook the direct government of the districts, the first and most formidable task that confronted it was the re-organization of the Land Revenue Administration.

It is hard, at this distance of time, to realize the enormous difficulties of the position. The country had just been decimated by a famine of unprecedented dimensions; there was, as I have said, no principle or rule of assessment; there were only fragmentary, and often unreliable, official lists of estates with their (nominal) assessment, and tolerable accounts of past collections; there was no survey, no staff of experienced native subordinates on the spot, for the old Revenue Agency had fallen into complete decay, and there was only a small and wholly inadequate staff of English district officials, and those at first ignorant of Indian land-tenures, and skilled only in questions of commercial investment.

Nor did the experience gained in Bengal materially profit when the Settlement of the newer provinces had to be undertaken. For the conditions of the 'ceded' and 'conquered' districts that made up the bulk of the North-West Provinces were widely different; and for them, a separate system had to be worked out. The same was the case with Madras, and afterwards with Bombay. Each province had laboriously to work out a Revenue system adapted to its own special requirements, with many failures by the way and many disappointments.

The other provinces, the Panjáb, Sindh, Oudh, and the Central Provinces, were not acquired, or at all events were not ready for a formal Settlement, till principles had been fairly well established; but even so, some difficulties had to be encountered, though mostly of our own making—in the not unnatural desire to apply to them, wholesale, systems which were really only suited to the Provinces for which they had originally been devised.

These considerations will explain why it is that Land Revenue Administration in India has been a plant of slow growth, which has only of late years come to maturity. They will also explain why there have been stages of progress and periodical modifications in the methods of work, so that the working of the Land Revenue system in each province got to be looked on as a sort of mysterious craft which no outsider could presume to understand.

Remarks on the principle of assessing the Revenue.—As a matter of fact, the Governments, while justly proclaiming that the basis of their Land Revenue is the old grain share, and that a money assessment is only its modern representative, have been driven to devise actual methods of assessing the amount, which have departed more and more from the idea of valuing in money a certain share in the produce. At one time, indeed, they tried to make such a valuation (as we shall see presently), but they had to give it up. And in some provinces, e. g. in Burma and in Madras, there is still a certain reference made, in assessment reports, to the average produce of land, to its value, to the costs of production and profits of stock which have to be deducted, and to a fraction of the balance, as representing the Land Revenue.

Two principles emerge.—Assessment methods have of course to vary according to the kind of estate and its mode of working. But practically underlying all methods, there are only two principles which emerge as ultimately distinct. One is to fix empirical rates, which are first ascertained only as maximum rates, on the basis of those actually paid in the past, but with such increase as can now be taken with reference to the rise in prices and progress in prosperity indicated by statistics, and then to apply those rates, in full or in part, according to a sliding scale, the land being accurately valued according to the relative excellence of one kind of soil as compared with another. The other principle is applied to all varieties of landlord estate (including village estates) where there are tenants; and it consists in finding out the rents which the tenants actually pay, and thence devising average rent-rates at which each acre of the different classes of soil in the estate may be valued. The Land Revenue is then a fixed fraction of the total rental 'assets.' To put it more shortly, modern Land Revenue is either an empirical but nicely graduated rate per acre of each kind of soil, or it is a fraction of the actual rental assets of an estate treated as a whole.

The merits of the Land Revenue as a source of State income.—It is impossible to enter on any discussion as to the merits of the Land Revenue as a source of State income; it must suffice to say briefly, that no Government could, in the past, have for a moment contemplated giving it up; and it is in the ast degree improbable that any future Government will be able to find a substitute. It is acquiesced in throughout the country, as part of the natural order of society: and that, in India, is a consideration of first-rate importance. The first requirement of a good taxation is that the people should be accustomed to it, and that it should be collected with the minimum chance for oppression on the one hand and for evasion on the other[1]. These considerations far outweigh any theoretical arguments of political economy.

[1] It might perhaps be objected that the brief account above given, shows the Land Revenue to be a form of impost that, in the past, has been attended with the greatest oppression. That is true; but it is due, not to the system as such, but to bad government and want of control. As a matter of fact these defects can be, and for many years past have been, completely obviated.

Nature of the Land Revenue, whether a 'tax' or what.— It is also fruitless to discuss exactly what the oriental institution of a Land Revenue is, whether a 'land tax' a 'rent' or what. Certainly it bears very little resemblance to the land tax in England. At one time the tendency was to regard the ruler as the ultimate landlord or owner of the soil; the revenue was then called a 'rent.' We shall have something to say about this hereafter; at present it will only be necessary to note that the British Government has everywhere conferred or recognized a private right in land, and in large areas of country (Bengal, Oudh and the whole of Northern India for example) it has expressly declared the proprietary right of the landlords and the village owners; it is then impossible any longer to say broadly that the State takes a rent from the landholders regarded as its tenants. There are no doubt cases where Government is the immediate owner of particular lands, as it is of all waste and unoccupied land in general; but we are speaking of cultivated land in villages and estates. The Government is certainly not owner of this: the utmost it does is to regard the land as hypothecated to itself as security (in the last resort) for the Land Revenue assessed on it. The Government also fulfils some of the functions of a landlord, inasmuch as it watches over the welfare of the agricultural population, it advances funds to landholders to help them in making improvements—well-sinking, embanking, draining and the like. It is these vestiges of the landlord character claimed by the former rulers, and perhaps the sort of residuary right which the Government still has in provinces where the landholders are called 'occupants' and not 'owners' (*eo nomine*), that keep alive the question whether the Land Revenue is in any sense a 'rent.' Practically, the discussion is a profitless war of words, and we may be content to speak of the 'Land Revenue' as a thing *per se*. It *operates* as a tax on agricultural incomes—a contribution to the State out of the profits of land-cultivation, just as the 'income tax' is a contribution out of the proceeds of other industries and occupations.

Question of a Permanent Settlement for all Provinces.— A few words may be added, about the question which, up till 1882, was more or less under discussion ; namely whether, when a suitable assessment had been once arrived at, for estates that had received a fairly full development, it would not be better to declare that assessment permanent, i. e. not liable to any further revision. This proposal derived such strength as it had, from the fact that, owing to the difficulties of the case, the task of making a Settlement had hitherto been both serious and costly. The work lasted for several (sometimes five to ten) years ; it subjected the districts to a prolonged period of agricultural disorganization ; and it was anticipated that the whole process would have to be gone over again every thirty years—or whatever the period of Settlement was. Such a prospect was more or less alarming both for the State and the landholders. But the first check which the proposal received was the consideration that it proved next to impossible to determine the essential preliminary question, what is the criterion by which to judge whether an estate is sufficiently developed to be fit for a permanent Settlement[1]? No sooner is one test proposed than another appears ; and the practical result of all inquiries has been that a Permanent Settlement must be deferred, so long as the land continues to improve in value by any causes which are not the direct result of the holder's own efforts and expenditure.

And two other objections are also obvious; one is the fact that a century's experience has failed to show that permanently settled districts are in any way more prosperous or better to do than those in which a fairly long term of Settlement is allowed[2]: the other is the impolicy of an existing Government assuming to bind its successors to all time, regardless of what the future may bring forth and of changes in value of money or of land and its produce.

It may seem strange that in face of these grave objections, it was not earlier seen that the better way to attack the problem was to inquire whether the only real advantage of a Permanent Settlement—namely that it would avoid all the cost and prolonged trouble of future Settlement operations—could not be attained in another way? At last it became recognized that it was quite possible to obviate almost wholly any necessity for lengthened re-settlement operations.

The establishment of the 'Land Record Departments' and their new duty (p. 20) was the first practical step. We are now, it may be fairly said, well on the way to the conclusion that in future re-settlements, a simple revision of rates on certain general and intelligible principles—whether on the ground of rise in prices or any other grounds that may be most satisfactory—will become practicable ; and then the work of revision will be carried out without any perceptible ruffle in the smooth course of agricultural work. The Secretary of State was then amply justified, in 1882, in declaring the policy of a Permanent Settlement finally discarded.

[1] Obviously an estate cannot be permanently valued when as yet a third of it, perhaps, is not cultivated, or when canal and railway construction, which so affect the value of land and its produce, are in an elementary stage.

[2] And it is a fact, that land is not more valuable and does not sell for a higher price in Permanently Settled estates, than in those settled for a term of years.

CHAPTER V.

WHAT LANDS ARE LIABLE TO PAY LAND REVENUE.

Section I. Lands not liable.

In general theory all land is liable. Certain lands not included in the area assessed to Land Revenue.—The various Land Revenue Acts (in force in the different provinces), following the old Regulations[1], have declared that the Government 'is entitled to a share in the produce of every *bíghá* of land.' This would seem to render any remarks under such a heading as the above, unnecessary. But, as a matter of fact, there are some practical distinctions. Land is, e.g., occupied by the houses and streets of towns and cities, cantonments and 'stations' (as we call the places where the European population, official and non-official, resides): there is also land devoted to special purposes, such as public forests or plantations; camping grounds used when troops march from place to place; public parks and gardens; grazing farms for the cavalry or for stud-breeding, &c. Then within the area of villages (p. 11) there is often, I may say usually, a certain extent of land occupied by the groups of village houses and the open space around them, where the cattle stand, and where the weavers stretch their webs; here also is the village grove, and the place of public meeting, and probably the village pond or tank. Speaking generally, Land Revenue is not levied on such areas; at all events not in the same way as it is on agricultural land.

[1] See for example the preamble to Regulations XIX and XXXVII of 1793 (Bengal Code); and for a modern example see the Bombay Land Revenue Code (Bombay Act V of 1879), sec. 45.

When gardens and other cultivated lands are found within the area of cities or stations, they do pay Land Revenue, but often under special rules. In villages, when the Settlement survey takes place, the area distinguished as that appropriated to the residence-sites and their suburbs is marked off by a line: and the Settlement does not record or assess the land within [1].

Assessment of waste-land allowed to be included in estates.—In all Settlements where an entire estate (large or small), waste and cultivated together, is settled for, the waste is often spoken of as 'unassessed waste [2]': but that only means that the waste area given over to the village was not assessed in detail like the cultivated acres; it was a matter for the discretion of the Settlement officer whether he would make some general addition to the total assessment, to discount (so to speak) the advantage of this area available for future cultivation.

But we shall speak of the general subject of waste lands in a separate section, and now pass on to another important matter.

Section II. Revenue free lands and Revenue assignments.

Revenue free lands. 'Lákhiráj.'—Besides lands that are not assessed to Land Revenue, there are others on which the payment ordinarily leviable is either remitted or made payable to some grantee. At all times the rulers of Indian States have been accustomed to *remit* the Land Revenue on certain lands, or to make such *grants* or *assignments*. Lands that were expressly granted in this way, were in Revenue language said to be *lákhiráj* [3] (Arabic *lá*=not, and *khiráj*=the land tax under the Moslem law).

'Alienated Lands.'—In Bombay and Madras, such lands are now generally called 'alienated lands'; and this term may be

[1] Nor does the Revenue officer exercise exclusive jurisdiction (in those provinces where otherwise he has it). A dispute about a house site, about the right of a tenant, on leaving a village, to sell his cottage, or to remove the roof-timbers, or his liability to pay certain ground rents or other dues to anybody in the village, would all be matters for the Civil Court, not for any Land Revenue Court.

[2] Waste is classified in estate-records as 'culturable' or 'not-culturable' (*mumkin* and *ghair-mumkin*.) The former will gradually be brought under the plough—unless permanently reserved for grazing and other purposes. The 'not-culturable' consists of the house-sites, the graveyard, &c., &c.

[3] This is the only instance in which the Muhammadan law term *khiráj* is generally made use of. In Assam a term *nisf-khiráj*, for certain lands allowed to pay half-revenue, is in use, but this is a term invented within the last thirty years, by British officials.

found in use in other places also, but not generally. It really pointed back to a time when the Government claimed to be (and was to some extent) owner or landlord of all land, as well as of the Land Revenue. When, therefore, the Government gave up its right to take anything from the land, in favour of a grantee, it was said to *alienate* the land, as it had no further concern with the soil or its revenue; and it came to pass that such grantees were always held to have a perfect title to the land itself as well as to the revenue [1].

How far such grants affect the title to the land itself.—The Mughal rulers formally distinguished such grants into two classes—those which gave a title to the land (*milk*), and those which only assigned the revenue. A very common class of *milk* grants was made in favour of pious and learned persons or reputed saints, or for the support of a school, a mosque, a temple, or some tomb or shrine; here either a bit of land was granted revenue-free, or the land was already owned by the grantee and the revenue was remitted: the term *mu'áfí* (Arabic = pardoned) or *in'ám* (reward or benefaction) was used for such grants. In this way also the official holdings of land enjoyed by village officers in some districts (as remuneration for their services) were allowed to be held free, and village-servants had their petty grants in payment for their service (sweeping, water-carrying, shaving, &c.).

In some States provision was made by petty grants of this kind for the support of the families of soldiers who had fallen in the Rájá's service. But in fact, there are very many varieties, and quite a host of local names for such free holdings; the names having reference to the origin or purpose for which the grant was made.

Mughal system of Revenue assignments or Jágír.—But besides these smaller and special grants (which were hereditary as long as the family survived or the purpose of the grant continued) the native Governments always and everywhere had been in the habit of making over tracts of land, and assigning the revenue of them (as shown in the public accounts) to some

[1] Even under modern conditions, in the Bombay Presidency and some other provinces, the law only recognizes the *raiyats* as 'landholders' or 'occupants,' not as owners *eo nomine*; therefore when the Government makes or confirms a grant, it may be said to 'alienate' not only the revenue but also its own ultimate right (whatever that may be).

person on condition of military or political *service* of some kind. This was regularly done in the case of Mughal Officers of State, each of whom held a *mansab*, i.e. a title with an assignment of revenue (so many rupees per annum) to support his dignity and also to maintain a certain number of troops, which he had to call out when he was required to join the Imperial Standard in war or on ceremonial occasions, or for duty at Court.

Very often frontier tracts, or those which were troublesome to manage, were made over in this way to military chiefs or others capable of developing the district, and then the amount of revenue assigned was probably merely nominal; the holder was expected to make what he could, by extending cultivation, and founding new villages. He had the right to apply to his own purposes the proceeds of the Land Revenue which he realized, on condition that he maintained the necessary military or police force for keeping the peace, and that he made due provision for the administration generally.

This class of assignment was called *jágír*[1]. At first the grant was only for life (unlike the grants first named) but in later times it was allowed to become hereditary. We are here only concerned to note that, owing to these institutions, large areas of land, to this day, pay no revenue to the State.

Confusion caused by irregular and invalid grants.— When our Revenue Settlements began, the number of claims to revenue-free holdings, in one form or another, was enormous; and it was found a very difficult matter to deal with them. For in the days of disorder, such grants had been greatly abused; they were issued by impecunious Governors who had no other way of meeting claims on their empty treasuries; they were issued by subordinate officials who had no right to make them; and worst of all, they were often fraudulent, intended only to keep money out of the Treasury; in short they threatened to eat up a large portion of the provincial Land Revenue. As far as the *liability to Revenue* was concerned, it was entirely a matter

[1] Variously represented in books as *jagheer*, *jaguire*, &c. The word is a contraction from the Persian *jái* = place, and *gír* = holding or taking possession.

of option to the new Government, whether it would recognize any such grants at all, and whether it would remit (or assign) the Revenue in future or not[1]. But all the Provincial Governments desired to act liberally and equitably; they all, in fact, recognized such grantees as had a real claim to consideration. As for any *right in land* which the grants conveyed, or which they had given rise to, that was a question for private litigation in case there were rival claimants. (The right in land acquired by such grants is considered later on when we come to the Land Tenures.)

As an example of the labour involved in these inquiries I may mention that in Madras and Bombay the matter was dealt with by official 'Inám Commissions,' and they sat for several years and issued many thousands of title-deeds to the persons whose right was admitted; but even so, a great economy was effected[2].

Every other province had to make a more or less extensive adjustment of such claims; and each had its own rules on the subject. All questions of this kind have long ago been settled; but some of the old grants still occasion a certain amount of official reference, because, as the lives for which they were

[1] See (for example) the declaration of the Government at the head of the Rules for determining the validity of grants, issued on the annexation of the Panjáb (reprinted in the Financial Commissioner's Circulars). No native Government ever doubted that it had full right to resume any *jágír* as far (at any rate) as the Revenue-right was concerned: but it was thought beneath the dignity of the State to resume such grants as were made for pious or charitable purposes. Purely political grants were resumed at pleasure, at any rate after the life of the original grantee. The Maráthá rulers very generally avoided the odium of resumption, by imposing a 'quit-rent' called *jodí*, *salámi*, &c. (often as heavy as the Land Revenue itself). When the British Government in Bombay and Madras began to deal with claims, it found many grants already liable to such a quit-rent; and this no doubt led to the practice which obtained in these Presidencies, of settling the question in the rough and allowing the claimant to have a certificate or title-deed, on his consenting to a general definition of the area of his estate, and to paying a moderate lump assessment for the whole.

[2] Thus in Bombay, the Inám Commission found that the various grants, (political, religious, personal, or for village-service) affected about *Rs.* 132,50,000 of the Land Revenue. The Commission reduced this to *Rs.* 80,38,000, of which part represents land-grants managed by the grantees, and part cash allowances paid through the Treasury, the holders not being direct owners of the land, or their claims having been commuted for a cash payment.

continued terminate, or otherwise the grants lapse, there is often an application to Government for some consideration; either to prolong a grant or to allow some part of it for the maintenance of a widow or other relative who may not be strictly entitled to succeed.

Modern Jágírs.—Jágírs are occasionally granted at the present day (apart from the maintenance of such grants of former rulers as have been allowed to continue); that is to say the Land Revenue of a village (or of a certain territory) is assigned to some retired native (military) officer of distinction, or to some local magnate, as a reward for political service, or to recognize and secure valuable local influence. Sometimes grants of waste-land are made Revenue free, and these then convey the Revenue remission as well as the proprietary title to the land. 'Service' in the sense of the old condition attached to such grants is not now required: but in another sense, it is often rendered. Many *jágírdárs* are most useful as honorary magistrates in their estates.

Section III. The waste lands.

One other class of land remains to be considered, land that does not yet pay any revenue, because it is still waste and unoccupied.

Enormous area of waste in India.—When British rule began in Bengal, it was estimated that from one-third to one-half of the total area of the province was waste and uncultivated. And in all provinces there was much waste[1].

[1] I allude to the (generally) culturable waste which was found in the districts without taking account of the great *desert* tracts about Rájputána and the South Panjáb; and apart also from the hilly regions, where it is natural to find great stretches of timber-forest, or smaller 'jungle.' It must be recollected that the districts had gone through many vicissitudes, wars, and invasions; and that many of them had been laid waste owing to the rapacity of particular rulers and Governors. There was not only therefore the large area of waste due to the population being naturally undeveloped or insufficient, but the fact that whole tracts had been abandoned (*khánd-khâli* or *ghair-ábád*) and entire groups of villages left untilled and deserted. See for example an old account of Rohilkhand, in *L. S. B. I.* vol. ii. p. 12 ff.

Disposal of it in Bengal.—At first no notice was taken of this. In Bengal, the estates were settled (as we shall see) without any survey; most of them included—and were freely allowed to include as their own—as much of the waste (often forest land) as naturally adjoined the estate. It was always contemplated, that, as the Land Revenue was fixed in the lump for the whole estate, the extension of cultivation into the parts at present waste should be wholly for the benefit of the estate, making the Revenue burden lighter and lighter as more and more success in this direction was attained. But as time went on and as estates became better known and their limits practically fixed, attention was called (in 1819) to the fact that lands were being taken up that really did not belong to any estate; the first thought, however, was only to make them pay the proper Land Revenue;—the title by mere occupation was allowed, or at least passed over in silence. But in 1828 Regulation III asserted the right of Government (which had always existed in theory), and then various efforts were made to separate the waste tracts and deal with them. This especially affected districts like Chittagong and others in Eastern Bengal (now in the Assam Province), but also the vast tract of forest land towards the mouths and delta of the *Húghlí* and other rivers, known as the 'Sundarban.' There were also great tracts of waste in the districts of Jalpaigúrí and Darjfling; and some forest land in the Chutiyá Nágpur districts and in Orissa. These lands were henceforward taken in hand, and afterwards leased to cultivators, or made into public forests, as I shall presently explain.

In the North-West Provinces and Oudh.—In the North-West Provinces, in the ordinary districts, the whole of the waste was divided up and given over to the village-estates to which it was adjacent; this is true of all the populous Ganges plain districts. But where there were large tracts of jungle land, in the hill districts, and in Dehra Dún, Jhánsí, Mirzapur, &c., these tracts remained as Government waste. In Oudh very much the same procedure was followed; only the excess waste lands (exceeding 500 acres in any one plot) were reserved to Government and have since become State forests.

The Central Provinces and the Panjáb. Panjáb colonization of waste supplied with canal irrigation.—In the Central Provinces and the Panjáb, the waste area between the cultivated villages was much too large to be entirely given over. A rule was adopted in both, that a certain area of waste (usually about 200 per cent. on the cultivated area) should be included as village property, the surplus being marked off as Government land.

In the Panjáb, the areas so cut off became the '*rakh*' or 'Fuel reserves,' so called because they mostly contain a peculiar stunted growth of wood admirably adapted for fuel. These lands are partly kept as forest and grazing lands, partly for the extension of cultivation.

In the Central Provinces, the area so left was enormous: it was declared originally as 'Government forest,' under the Forest Act of 1865; but the arrangements were not always well carried out, and of late it has been found desirable to give up some of the area to cultivation, or for village purposes generally.

In the Panjáb, I should mention, that area of Government '*rakh*' or waste is very far in excess of the needs of Forest conservancy; and in some parts there are large stretches of poor woodland where no market at all for the wood exists. Moreover cultivation would be economically much more valuable than forest (of such a class as could be raised in such land), and nothing is wanted but the means of irrigation in order to ensure large areas being profitably cultivated. Of late years the Goverment has arranged for the extension of canals, and on the land so provided with means of irrigation, it has marked blocks out of a convenient size and fitted with the requisite water channels, so that each block may be occupied by colonists and become a village. Rules exist for the colonizing of these tracts, and provide for the Land Revenue assessment in such a manner as to make things easy during the first years, when there is much outlay and little return [1].

[1] It will be observed that this is a new (and interesting) departure from ordinary practice of leasing waste lands. Under the ordinary rules, the Government surveys and marks out the limits of the block in its native wilderness, and hands it over to the lessee, who finds the entire plant and capital and the means to bring about cultivation. In these Panjáb tracts, the Government itself supplies the principal requirements of cultivation (viz. an irrigation system), and then seeks for colonists (from over-peopled districts), and locates them on sites already prepared in all respects, save that of clearing the land.

Waste land in the Raiyatwárí Provinces.—In the *Raiyatwárí* countries (Madras, Bombay, &c.) the Settlement system does not deal with 'estates,' and there is therefore no question of allowing surplus waste to provide for expansion or for lightening the Revenue burden. Each field or holding is separately assessed on its own merits. Consequently all the waste land (except that allowed for use to the village for grazing ground, &c.) remains Government property and is made into 'survey numbers' and assessed (lightly) according to its class; any one therefore who wants one of these plots has only to make application at a certain time to the local Revenue Officer, and agree to pay the assessment: in this way the expansion of villages and family holdings is amply provided for.

This remark applies to the villages in the plains: but in parts of Bombay, in Coorg, and on the West Coast, there are local forms of landholding, and local methods of cultivation, which always involve a certain patch of wood and grass-bearing land being attached to each cultivated landholding: in such cases, a certain 'waste' area is allowed to form part of the holding, and cannot be used for public forest or other State purposes. The waste is however in this case held on definite conditions; it cannot be permanently cultivated or separately alienated.

In these Provinces, it is consequently only in hill ranges, and more remote places, that considerable tracts of waste exist, which were not brought within the Settlement survey, nor made available in the manner alluded to. It is only in the hilly country and large jungle-tracts therefore that the 'Waste Land Rules' (next to be spoken of) apply, or that State or District Forests have been constituted.

The Waste Land Rules.—Though various rules had from time to time been issued in different districts, for the disposal of Government Waste Lands, the state of the country and its general development had not allowed of many areas being taken up. In 1861, under the Viceroyalty of Lord Canning, the subject was first seriously considered. The value of State Forests—to be made out of the best and most usefully situated wooded and grass lands—was not even then recognized, and the occupation of the waste by capitalists and settlers was alone discussed.

The first ideas on the subject were developed in a Minute on the Waste Lands, sent home in 1861:—

It was pointed out that the waste in its present state was only a burden to the Government, and it was recommended that it should be sold outright without any conditions as to its being utilized or cultivated in a certain time, and that the liability to Land Revenue should be discounted by allowing the purchaser to redeem it by certain payments.

Subsequent developments have left no doubt that this policy was based on erroneous but very natural assumptions. Had it been extensively acted on the result would have been disastrous. The loss to the State would have been very great, both owing to the rise in the value of land, which was entirely overlooked, and to the heavy sacrifice of future Land Revenue. The rules would also directly encourage the taking up of land by mere speculators, who had no intention of using it, but desired simply to hold it till it rose in value, so that they could re-sell it in blocks at a profit. It was fortunate that the state of affairs did not invite capitalists, and that the area parted with under the first rules was not, on the whole, large.

The policy changed. Modern Rules.—Since the first rules (promulgated for the various Provinces in 1865) the policy has entirely changed. The great rise in the value of land, and the consequent demand for it, has led to a better system, which prevents the speculative purchase of lands by persons not intending to make use of them; and prevents the loss of Revenue in the future. The main features of the Rules at present in force are:—

1. That lands covered with trees, or otherwise useful for State Forest purposes, are not disposed of. Of course there are many areas densely wooded where, nevertheless, the establishment of cultivation, tea-planting, &c., is desirable; but lands are first inspected and their Forest capabilities judged of before giving them up under the 'Waste Land Rules.'
2. The land is only leased for a term of years (under a moderate scale of payments), which allows ample time to develop the cultivation.
3. The areas given are all surveyed and mapped, and necessary rights of the State in roads and sidings, in rivers, fisheries, mines, quarries, &c., are reserved.
4. The lease-right can be ultimately converted into ownership-right on prescribed terms, when the lease-holder has shown that he has really put the land to the intended use—by bringing a specified proportion of it under cultivation in a certain time.

5. The land remains liable, like any other proprietary-estate, to a Settlement of the Land Revenue under the ordinary law. At first, however, favourable terms are allowed to facilitate the establishment of cultivation.

For all details, the Rules of each Province must be consulted; but it may be here further observed that some of the rules draw a distinction between—

(*a*) Large areas suitable for capitalists intending to undertake tea-planting, coffee, cinchona or other staples on the large scale, where capital will have to be largely expended, and so special terms are desirable.

(*b*) Small areas (from 10 to 200 acres as the extreme limit) suitable for the ordinary agricultural occupation of villagers, and others in the same position.

In some cases it will be found that the applicant for land will be dealt with direct (without competition) on his accepting the terms of the rules: in others, when a block is applied for, the lease of it is put up to auction: there is usually an 'upset price' or entrance fee, payable in certain instalments, to be deposited; also the expenses of survey and demarcation; and then only light annual payments (until the time comes for the regular assessment of the Land Revenue).

PART II.

THE LAND TENURES AND THE LAND REVENUE SYSTEMS.

CHAPTER VI.

INTRODUCTORY.

WE have now completed the first stage of our inquiry.

In that stage it has been our object to form a general conception of the Indian Land Revenue as 'an institution'—if I may be allowed the phrase. For this purpose we have taken a rapid survey of the Indian Provinces and their Government, and more especially of the District organization; we have considered the origin of the Land Revenue, and its history up to the commencement of British rule: we have taken notice of certain questions commonly asked about the subject in modern times; we have seen what lands pay revenue and what do not, and in so doing we have taken the opportunity of describing the rules under which the area of waste-land, still large in some of the provinces, has been, and is being, colonized and cultivated.

Our second stage is to inquire how our modern Land Revenue is assessed, and how it is collected, and how the general business connected with its management is conducted.

But when we speak of assessment, we are reminded of the peculiarity of the conditions under which the Indian Land Revenue is levied. It is not a mere question of obtaining, by survey, a detailed account of the area of each different kind of soil, and of finding a suitable rate thereon—to be levied per acre, or other unit of measure. In many Indian provinces that is only one part of the work. In all cases, the revenue is assessed with more or less reference to the tenure of land, to the sort of estate or holding which may be regarded as a unit paying a certain sum, and with reference to some definite person (or a body of persons) who is to be held responsible.

Without going into details which would at present be unintelligible, it may be usefully stated in general terms, that land is held in one of these ways:—

(1) In various forms of landlord-tenure; the estates varying in size from half a district to a few acres, but generally being of at least considerable extent: in these there is one person (or at most a few joint owners) distinctly vested with a proprietary or landlord character; and the system accordingly lays one sum of revenue on the whole estate, and makes the landlord (or the co-sharers together) liable for it[1].

(2) In smaller estates, really of the same character as the first, but with certain features which render it convenient to distinguish them,—these being in general, *village estates* where the village (or part of two or more villages together) is held by a co-sharing body or community; here the community is treated as jointly and severally liable; the body regarded as a whole is, in fact, the (ideal) landlord.

(3) In single independent holdings; though aggregated locally in

[1] In some estates of this class the law of primogeniture applies, and so the estate remains undivided in the hands of the eldest heir; in others the estate may be divided or again united under one head, by the effect of the ordinary law of inheritance.

villages, the group of holdings does not form one estate: the circumstances of past history have either caused the disappearance of any landlord (person or class), or such an interest has never existed; and the direct occupant is dealt with individually.

It might be supposed that under these conditions, it would still be a simple thing to determine the *person* who is to be liable for the revenue *and to have the remaining profits of the estate*, after the revenue has been paid; but here the complications of Indian tenure begin to appear. Only in the third case above noted, it is a simple matter to determine that the 'occupant' is to pay the Land Revenue and to take the remainder. Even in his case it may be that he has to settle with some other party above or below him, who has a claim, which essentially is (whatever the form) a title to some part of the profits of the land. And in other cases it usually happens (owing to causes which we shall discuss in the sequel) that there is not only the middleman landlord or landlord body, but that this middleman is often in a position much more doubtful or complicated than that of an English landlord with tenants under him paying a contract rent.

These considerations will not only point to the study of the Land tenures, as necessary in order to understand how the Land Revenue Settlements are made, but also remind us that Government has never been content merely to tax the land and leave the different parties interested in it to their own devices in order to get practical recognition of their several rights.

Absence of all legal security for titles in old days.—From the very first, our administrators saw that, while securing the State Revenue, they must also secure private landed rights, if wealth and prosperity were ever to return to the agricultural population. Under native rule, there had been no such thing as *legal* security for titles to land; especially not for interests that had been partially submerged or reduced to a secondary grade. There was nothing but the autocratic government of a conquering chief or Emperor, whose will was law,—will tinctured indeed by a respect for the texts of a semi-sacred, but not very definite, law, and largely influenced by the great regulator of Indian affairs—CUSTOM. The 'law and constitution' of India spoken of by some writers, had no existence except in a purely metaphorical sense. Even if it were otherwise the changes in landed property, the growth of one class of rights and the extinction or diminution of others, could not be systematic or legalized, because such changes were not the consequence of law or State policy, but of the gradual usurpation of Revenue farmers, of the rise and fall of families, of forcible seizure, or of compact extorted by the necessities of self-preservation; they were the result of those never-ceasing tribal and personal conquests and adventures that make the past history of India what it is—an almost unbroken record of invasion, war, and intrigue. Hence the British Government, while determining to limit and render moderate its own demands on the land, and to give up for ever the inordinate pretensions of the rulers it superseded, found itself face to face with the task of giving legal security and definition to various degrees and kinds of right or interest in the land; from that of the great landlord who received a 'title-deed of perpetual ownership[1]' to the humbler 'subproprietor' or 'tenure holder' or 'occupancy tenant.' This recognition and definition, it will be observed, was not only necessary to give a secure position to the person directly responsible for the Revenue, it was equally necessary for the due apportionment of the remaining profit (after the Revenue was paid) arising from the land.

Before then we can attend to the formal operations of a Settlement, we had best gain some general idea of the Land Tenures.

[1] This phrase is actually used in Madras, where each great landlord or Zamíndár received from the British Government a title-deed officially called *sanad-i-milkíyat-i-istimrárí*—a Persian phrase of which the English equivalent is that given in the text.

CHAPTER VII.

THE LAND TENURES.

Section I. The Village.

Use of the term village.—At the outset of any inquiry into the way in which land is generally held in India, we are struck by the fact that almost everywhere cultivation is aggregated into local groups which we call 'villages.' The term 'township' has occasionally been made use of; but general usage has established the term 'village.' It is needless to say that this word is used in a special sense different from that which it bears with reference to modern English agricultural life [1].

Usual features of a village.—The 'village' is an aggregate of cultivated holdings with or without some waste area, belonging to, or attached to it: and usually it has a central site for the dwelling-houses congregated together. In some cases, small homesteads and farm buildings are found separately located on the holdings [2]. The village, moreover, often boasts a grove, or at least a single tree under which local assemblies will take place; there is also some kind of public office where the village *patwárí* (p. 27) keeps his books, and where he sits for the disposal of his business.

[1] Though not altogether dissimilar to what it meant in mediaeval times.

[2] In the Himáláyan districts the narrow extent of valley land or terraced hill slope suggests separate holdings with their own buildings; and so in Kánara and the West coast; in the latter country the people have no word for 'village.' The only term in use is supposed to be equivalent to 'street';—because the families would build their houses in a line, at the further end of which, the menials and village artisans have their cottages. The whole group is merely the homestead of a single family whose members keep together.

Whatever changes may be undergone the village as a local feature remains.—The village area once established, it soon acquires a local name and becomes a permanent feature in the map. Its constitution may change; it may be bought and sold; it may begin as a village of one kind and gradually turn into another kind; it may be absorbed in the estate of a great landlord, or remain as a small separate property under a body of joint-owners. If once owned by a family proud of its hereditary right, it may again return to be only an aggregate of separate landholders. But under all such changes, the village itself remains; its fields are tilled and irrigated, the money-lender sits at his shop, the menials and artisans do their work, no matter who is managing the land or its rents and revenues, or how the landed rights change their character or pass from one hand to another.

Its value for administrative purposes.—The village as a unit may be of great importance for administrative purposes; and is hardly ignored even in Bengal where the Revenue administration deals not with villages, but with entire landlord estates. In places (such as those mentioned in a previous note) where villages do not naturally exist, the Government has always found it desirable to aggregate several holdings, hamlets or farms, into some kind of circle, for administrative purposes.

What is the bond which aggregates the village landholders.—If we next inquire what bond unites the landholders or cultivators in a village together, or determines their aggregation into separate groups, we shall easily perceive that there are certain natural and social causes which from the first invited the formation of villages in general; and further, that the actual bond of union depends on certain peculiarities of land custom—certain features of tenure.

Natural causes of village aggregation.—In the first place it is to be remembered that originally, at any rate, throughout entire regions, villages must have been established in a country then covered with forest or jungle; and the labour of clearing this, as well as of maintaining an unceasing struggle against the re-growth of semi-tropical vegetation, required co-operation;

and union would also be necessary for defence against the depredations of deer, pigs and other animals which are dangerous not only to the cultivation but to human life. And any group of cultivators would have to be prepared to present a common front against neighbours with whom they were probably at feud. Often too defence would be needed against marauding chiefs or some regularly invading force on the march, to say nothing of the ruthless freebooters and Revenue-farmers of later days[1].

Cause of the groups being limited.—And then there are other reasons, why not only should there be aggregation, but also why the groups should be limited in size. All popular settlements in India—those which resulted in permanent cultivation, and were not mere occupations of territory in a nomadic form—were first effected by *tribes*, that is by groups with a natural organization into clans, septs and family groups. These divisions naturally suggested a certain limit to the number of families that would wish to settle together in one spot. And when in later times new villages were established one by one, it was by individual leaders with associated followers, or by limited groups of grantees, settlers and colonists. Indeed in all cases where there was a natural organization of tribes, not only village groups but other territorial divisions also resulted. It was doubtless tribal divisions, and the limits of the authority of greater and lesser chiefs that gave the first idea of *parganas* and *districts*. Indeed several interesting cases are on record in which a whole clan was established on one considerable area, each family having its own share, without any *village* grouping at all. But in the course of time quarrels, rivalries and differences of habit would be sure to end in division into smaller groups.

[1] It is owing to this that villages were so often surrounded with stout mud walls and defended by gates, within which the cattle could be driven against an apprehended raid. In Central India it was quite common for the headman's residence to be called *garhí*, i. e. fort or castle; and in the Karnál district (S. E. Panjáb) I find an account of walled and gated villages with the houses so built as to prepare for street-fighting. In Oudh, in the later days of misrule, the readers of *Sleeman's Journey* may remember the author's account of how the revenue was collected by a regular siege, and with the aid of field guns!

Nature of the bond uniting the groups internally.—So much for the natural and social causes of village aggregation; we have next to inquire what is the bond which internally unites, or holds together, the village groups when formed.

Two forms of village observable.—On taking a general survey of the villages in the different Provinces, we are struck by the fact that there are two main forms of village constitution, which are practically quite distinct. In the one, the village contains a number of individual cultivating holders (who usually work the land themselves with the aid of their families, but often employ tenants). These holdings are separate units; the cultivators do not claim to be joint-holders of a whole area, nor do their holdings represent, in any sense, *shares* of what is in itself a whole which belongs to them all. They are, however, held together by their submission to a somewhat powerful village headman[1] and other village officers, and by use in common of the services of a resident staff of village artisans and menials, who receive a fixed remuneration on an established scale, and sometimes have hereditary holdings of service-lands[2].

[1] **Village headman and artisan staff.**—The headman's title is very various. In Bombay, Berár and Central India generally, he is the *pátel* (or *pátil*). In Bengal (where this type of village also is commonly found) he is called *mandal* (but there are other tribal and local names). In Madras the titles are still more numerous, *maniyakáran*, *nátamkar*, *reddi*, &c. These are quite distinct from the official representative headman or *lambardár* of the North Indian village system.

[2] The staff varied with the locality and the size and wealth of the village. In Western and Central India the ideal staff was supposed to consist of twelve (the *bára* (twelve) *baluté* village servants in Maráthí—sometimes contrasted with *alute*, the official headman, *kulkarnl*, &c.). The artisans usually included a carpenter, potter, blacksmith, cobbler, barber-surgeon, washerman (sometimes also a dancing girl; even a 'witch finder' may be locally discovered). Such servants are usually hereditary and are never paid by the job; they are given houses in the village, and perform all services for the residents (who only provide, or pay for, the *materials* employed). Their labour is rewarded by regular annual remuneration (of service land or an allowance in cash, grain, clothes, tobacco, &c.) paid at the harvest. Only strangers getting something made or done, would pay for the job. This system is common to all villages, and was necessitated by the circumstances of their position. No one could venture to set up a business on speculation in a village, unless it was a very large one. Nor could the village people go for all their simple but indispensable requirements to a distant town: so they attracted the necessary staff by giving them homes and a regular remuneration.

Importance of the headman and village officers. Official holding of land.—The headman and his aid, the writer or village accountant, have always a considerable importance, and were early taken, so to speak, into the State system, and were remunerated by the State (or turned out if inefficient). In Madras and Bombay, for example, it will be found that the village *pátels* have often petty magisterial powers, and can decide civil cases under certain rules. They were *formerly* also entrusted (practically) with the farm of the village revenue, and in such a position had authority to dispose of the waste, and settle the annual revenue-payment with each landholder. In some districts we can still read how, in past days, the headman stood up as the protector of the village, fortified his house and resisted the marauder or other enemy. Very often it would be the case that the headman was the person[1] who had led the party who first established cultivation and founded the village; and he may have planted the village tree or grove, and have furnished the means for making the tank, and so forth. But though the headman owned the central site where his house stood (and the site accommodated his whole family and their dependants), he made no claim to be owner of the entire village. He was quite content with his hereditary position, and above all with the holding of land (probably the best in the place) that was allotted to him as headman. This *ex officio* holding (accompanied as it was by *mánpán* or various rights of precedence on ceremonial occasions, and other dignities) was dearly cherished. In early times it was allowed to be free of Revenue, and was called by the Muhammadan rulers, *watan*. It was hereditary in the pátel's family and shared among all his descendants, even though only one of them was performing the official duty of headman[2]. The waste land that was left round the residences for general use, did not belong to the headman; and the culturable waste adjoining the village belonged to the

[1] Or the direct descendant of such a person.

[2] The *watan* disappeared in later times in many villages and even in whole districts, but this was the result of revenue oppression. There can be little doubt that the institution was once universal through the Dravidian countries. It is apparently alluded to in Manu.

Rájá; the headman only took official charge of it and located cultivators or gave it out to applicants.

Besides the headman and the accountant or writer, there was also a village watchman and messenger, and perhaps a guardian of the boundaries. The accountant and the other officers also had their (smaller) *watan* lands.

Prevalence of the first form of village.—This form of village is universal in Madras, Bombay, Berár, and Central India: it was the original form in the Central Provinces until a certain artificial proprietary right was created; it was also the characteristic form in the greater part of Bengal, although there, the importance of villages had been thrown into the shade, and the influence of the village officers much broken down, by the growth of the Zamíndárs.

The second form of village.—The second form of village may be briefly described as similar in many respects to the first, but with one essential feature superadded, and others modified in consequence. The important feature is that there is an individual, or a family (or a group of ancestrally connected families) which has the claim to be superior to other cultivating landholders, and in fact to be the owner or landlord of the entire area within the ring fence of the village boundary, as already existing, or as established by their own foundation[1].

The proprietary body may now consist of twenty or fifty or more co-sharers, usually of common descent: the founder may be perfectly well known; or in the case of older foundations, the original ancestor may be rather a shadowy being, and the existing body can trace descent more definitely from a few persons more or less reasonably supposed to be—say—great-great-grandsons of the patriarch[2].

[1] I take the case of a single village forming the estate, because it is very common and is simpler to understand. As a matter of fact there may be two distinct groups, each holding (in the same way) a part or *tarf* of a village; or it may be that the family has not obtained its lands all in one village, but some in one village and some in another; for which reason the actual estate is spoken of in Revenue language as the *mahál*—because it does not always coincide with the *mauza* though it very often does, and quite usually so in the Panjáb, for example.

[2] The descent may be real or have got so mixed as to be largely a fiction, but the fiction itself is important as showing the spirit and rationale of the

The menials and artisans who reside in the village hold their house-sites from the proprietors, paying them small dues, perhaps in cash, or in kind, and sometimes by supplying a load or two of manure annually: if these persons leave the village, it will be a matter of local custom whether they can sell the cottage or remove the roof tree and timbers, or not. The uncultivated portion of the village is no longer 'Government waste' to be applied for when wanted and allotted by the village or Revenue Officers; it is the *shámilát* or common property of the body, who graze their cattle on it; and if there are profits from wild fruits, thatching grass and the like, they share these among themselves[1]. When this waste, or part of it, is wanted to extend the cultivation, it is regularly partitioned.

The management. Absence of a headman.—The management of the co-sharing body and its concerns was originally effected by a *pancháyat* or council of the heads of households. There is properly speaking no one headman: the families were too jealous of their equal standing to permit any one man to establish anything resembling the central authority, dignity and privilege, of a Central Indian *pátel*. But for Revenue and administrative purposes a headman of some kind becomes indispensable; and the head of the eldest or chief branch (or some other leading or capable man) is selected (subject to the approval of the Government officials) to act as representative of the body. Usually where the village is divided into sections, there is a representative of each section. In modern times such a person is called *lambardár* (p. 26).

As a matter of fact it depends on a variety of circumstances whether this official has much, or any, influence or power. Sometimes he really has to undertake a considerable personal responsibility for the revenue of his village: sometimes the sharers pay their own revenue share directly to the treasury, and the

constitution. When a body needs strengthening, or it may be owing to various accidents and circumstances, connexions on the side of the wives of the co-sharers obtain land and admission into the circle; or purchasers or mortgagees do the same; and as time goes on, their really different origin is ignored and forgotten.

[1] It may be that the older tenants have a customary right to graze their cattle on this waste so long as it is not cultivated; all these details vary according to the local custom and the position and origin of the tenants.

lambardár really has very little to do. And what with the progress of division of lands and other circumstances, the *panchâyats* have almost everywhere disappeared, or at least are only assembled on some special occasions; their regular meeting to audit accounts and so forth, is very much a thing of the past[1].

This form of village, no less than the other, has the common services of a staff of artisans, watchmen and the like; for the causes which necessitate such an arrangement are the same in both cases.

Landlord villages may or may not contain a subordinate tenant body. Sometimes the co-sharers themselves cultivate the estate. Causes of the existence of tenant bodies under the village proprietors.—The co-sharing body may cultivate the land itself—that is, may work the fields directly, with no other aid than that of their families or of labourers or menials who have no position as tenants of any class. This will depend on circumstances, for instance on caste, and whether the proprietary body established the village on abandoned or virgin soil, or whether they grew up over an existing older body of cultivators, and allowed them to remain as their tenants. In many cases this latter condition obtains; and also if the landlord families are of a non-agricultural caste, then as their caste rules may prevent their touching a plough, they will always employ tenants—whether an older cultivating body or a new set called in and located by themselves. In the North-West Provinces, speaking generally, it is more common to find the proprietary communities consisting of non-agricultural castes: they are families of either conquering or ruling races, or of the official and revenue-farming and capitalist classes, who have grown up over the older villages, so that there is generally a tenant body which represents the old landholding group.

[1] I have been asked whether a member of the community could be expelled. At present there is of course no power to deprive a man of his proprietary share; nor do I think it likely that there ever was; but if a person offended against caste or social rules in such a way as to render him obnoxious to the whole body, and he was not strong enough to form a party in his favour (as he most likely would do), then the *panchâyat* could put him out of society so far as to refuse to smoke with him or let the water-carrier supply his household (*huqa pání band*). If it were a bad case, the man might find his position so uncomfortable that he would throw up his holding (or sell or transfer it) and go elsewhere.

In the Panjáb, especially on the frontier, we have the case of villages founded by immigration or conquest of active, energetic tribes, where there were often no pre-existing cultivators. But even here tenants were often a necessity, because in bringing virgin soil into cultivation, every hand is valuable. In such villages we find tenants occupying a somewhat secondary, but still privileged, position in the village; they consist of the camp followers and dependants who always come in crowds with an adventuring or conquering clan or tribe. The descendants of such associates will now be found to claim tenant-rights on the ground that they helped in the 'founding'; or at least that they were located and given land at an early stage in the village history. In many of the frontier district villages also, the landowners despise the plough (calling themselves *sáhu* = 'the gentry') and always give their land to tenants. In some cases we hear of fighting tenants employed to cultivate (and defend) outlying lands (in Pesháwar and Hazára). On the other hand, in the Central Panjáb among the *Jat* communities (and so with many other agricultural castes), the co-sharers very commonly work the whole land themselves, with no other aid than that of their wives and families; the village menials giving their services at harvest-time. In many agriculturist villages tenants have also been introduced; but this is often traceable to the times when it was necessary to invoke all the assistance that was to be had, in order to meet the burden of Sikh Revenue assessments.

I have said nothing about the extent of shares, or about the principle on which the proceeds of land cultivated in common are distributed; that will follow immediately; it was my object first to contrast *the two kinds of village in their broad distinctive features*.

Designation adopted for each kind of village.—It is desirable to find some brief designation by which to refer to the two kinds of village, and I have indicated the one in which the landholdings are separate units, and there is no sharing of a whole estate, by the term RAIYATWÁRÍ village[1].

[1] The individual cultivator, whether independent as in Western and Southern India or holding under a landlord as in Bengal, is generally

The other form may be provisionally called the LANDLORD- or JOINT-VILLAGE, because there is always an individual owner—or more frequently a co-sharing body—holding the landlord right over the whole [1].

Internal constitution of the village.—We must now proceed to say something of the internal constitution of the village and of the origins to which we may, in some cases at any rate, be able to trace them.

Of the first class (*raiyatwárí*) there is nothing more to be said in regard to the constitution. The several holders of land are distinct in interest, and the only bonds which unite them are the common locality, the common services of a group of artisans and menials, and a common subjection to the *pátel*; these have been already sufficiently noticed.

Idea of right to the land in the case of the individual holdings in the village.—It may further be remarked, that the peasant's right to his separate holding is recognized in terms which imply a somewhat inferior claim. The reason of this will appear further on. Here, I can only say that although in the beginning of this century the idea of private rights in land had often become feeble, this was not necessarily the result of any decay in the village constitution; but only of agrarian oppression and over-taxing in unsettled times. There is no doubt that the idea of a right in land, on the ground of first clearing and establishing tillage, has at all times been cherished in India; but when

called *raiyat* (or *ryot* as it is phonetically written). This is accurately *ra'íyat*, an Arabic word meaning 'protected' or 'subject.' The term should be remembered because it has come to be used (often in compound terms) to designate those forms of Revenue Settlement and Revenue management generally, in which the individual holding is dealt with, and not any kind of estate small or large, treated collectively. Thus we speak of a 'Raiyatwárí Settlement' or a 'Raiyatwárí Province,' meaning one where the most usual (but of course not the only) form of tenure of land is that of the raiyat's separate holding.

[1] It is worth while noting, as showing how things may be looked at from different points of view, that while in Bombay the vast majority of villages are *raiyatwárí*, there are in certain districts a few villages whose origin is to some extent traceable, and which are unmistakably in the landlord form. So that the Bombay people have the spectacle of both forms of village before them: yet they call the *raiyatwárí* village *sanja* = joint or associated, and the landlord-villages *bhágdárí* or shared; because in the former case the absence of all landlord-right over the whole village, enjoyed in shares, is remarked; and the village is regarded as associated or 'united' on a common basis of equality and a common control of one *pátel*.

all kinds of conquering rulers have claimed to be proprietors of the soil and have for generations past employed Revenue contractors or local land-officers, all of whom reduced the theory to the most rigid form of practice by habitually rack-renting the landholders, by putting in this man and turning out that, from year to year, simply with a view to securing or enlarging the Revenue, it is hardly to be wondered at that the idea of private right in land should in some places grow weak, and the people be more anxious to be allowed always to relinquish land that they could not manage profitably, than to have a title which would also carry a certain fixed responsibility. We shall hereafter see that in the *raiyatwárí* provinces this right of relinquishment (though now seldom resorted to) is still a feature of the Land Revenue system.

It is quite possible also, that a village anciently in the *raiyatwárí* form may pass under the power of some superior, whose family divide it among themselves in shares, and thus the village becomes a landlord village and may remain so for several generations. But if the family fall into poverty or their influence is lost, there may remain no more than a faint memory of the 'shares,' and the village will again become practically *raiyatwárí*. This change has in all probability actually happened in very many of the Dakhan villages[1]. In parts of Madras also, there are villages in which there is no doubt that they were once owned by co-sharing families still known as *mirásdár*, whose rights have long passed away. It is however quite impossible to hold that all *raiyatwárí* villages were once owned in such shares, and that *all* are merely a decayed form of something originally different.

Constitution of joint or landlord villages. Three methods in which land is divided among the co-sharers.—As regards the internal constitution of landlord- or joint-villages, there is much more scope for difference; it will be found, as a matter of fact, that the principle on which the co-sharers allot the land (or the profits and produce of the land in the case of an undivided holding) is not always the same. Speaking generally, there are *three principles of sharing*, one of which, at least, has several interesting varieties.

1. **The ANCESTRAL or family share system.**—The first is the principle of *ancestral fractional shares*; that is to say, of each member of the co-sharing body taking the fraction of the whole which his place in the family 'tree,' or genealogical table, points out.

2. **Special CUSTOMARY system of sharing: (*a*) sharing in equal lots made up artificially of various strips of land.**

[1] See *L. S. B. I.* vol. iii. p. 256.

(*b*) **Sharing by ploughs.** (*c*) **Or with reference to shares in water.** (*d*) **Or shares in wells.**

In all these cases, the estate is still regarded as a whole, and there are shares in it; but the *shares are obtained by classifying the soils and making up a suitable number of lots*, which are distributed among the families owning the village. Or the *number of ploughs* possessed by the body of colonists or tribal-settlers furnishes a basis for allotment; or there are *water-shares*—because the land is abundant, but the valuable thing is the water of a hill stream, and this being limited, must be utilized according to a particular rule. Or again a number of *wells* are sunk, and allotment depends on the amount contributed by each family to the well (p. 10).

3. **System of De Facto Holdings.**—The third principle is where there is no specific rule of sharing; nothing but a *de facto holding* is recognized. Each household has cultivated according to its ability; at any rate, what it now holds is the measure of its interest. This may be an always existing custom, or may be due to the loss of a system of shares that once existed.

It will here probably be asked, how do these people come to be co-sharers on such different plans? The answer is that all joint or landlord villages—whatever theory of their origin may be true—must necessarily have been formed in one of three ways:—(1) They are bodies who have succeeded jointly (according to the law and custom of inheritance) to a village at first held by some one man—the common ancestor; or (2) they are bodies made up of a certain number of families belonging either to an immigrating or conquering clan which has settled and allotted the area on its own customary methods; or (3) they may be a merely co-operative colonizing group, formed under circumstances which led them to establish cultivation on the joint-stock principle. In the first case it is natural that the law of inheritance should direct the shares; in the others, some tribal custom, or some particular sentiment about equality, or some peculiarity in the soil and climate, will naturally suggest a special method of allotment.

How a single landlord right grows up.—The growth of

a village community from a single ancestor or founder may best be illustrated by taking the simplest possible case of an imaginary village, and tracing for it a course of development such as *very many villages have actually and literally passed through.* It is immaterial whether we take the case of an old-established village of (probably non-Aryan) landholders, over whom some superior family gained the lordship, or whether we suppose a grantee or an adventurer founding a new village, and locating as cultivators, a body of his own dependants, tenants, &c. But I will take the former case. The first stage is that some relative—possibly a distant cousin of the Rájá's—or some other person who has to be rewarded, gets *a grant of the village.* In the first instance, the grant is not intended to deprive any existing landholder or diminish his right; it merely makes over to the new landlord the State-share of the produce, and other State rights in the village. But the grantee is gradually able to bring the whole of the adjacent *waste* under cultivation as his own. This fact alone may put him in possession of an area exceeding that of the old cultivating body. But even the older lands gradually fall into his hands; he will proceed to buy up one field, oust the insolvent holder of another, and so on, till he has got such a strong hold that he regards himself as owner of the whole place. In time his descendants forget that the cultivators had any rights independent of the lord, and they succeed in making them forget it too. Here then is a village (at first) under a sole landlord; and the Revenue books call this the ZAMÍNDÁRÍ KHÁLIS tenure. The example we have selected is of the landlord originating *in a grant.* When we come to speak of origins, we shall see some other ways in which a village may fall under the power of a single landlord, both anciently and in comparatively recent times.

And then the right of a joint body of co-sharing descendants.—Let us now suppose that fifty or sixty years have passed away, and that there has been a period of tolerable quiet, in which wars, plundering incursions, or famine, have not disturbed the landlord and his family. The original founder or grantee is long dead, and his sons, grandsons (and possibly some connexions admitted by gift or favour) have succeeded him by inheritance.

Estate managed in common.—Whether Hindus or Muhammadans (and being of a superior caste they are probably one or the other) they will have succeeded to the village-property jointly. They are all jealous of equal right and dignity as descendants in common of the same head; and for a long time they will not divide the estate: they appoint one of their number as the manager (or possibly employ a paid agent), and at first there is probably a *pancháyat* or committee of heads of houses, to control the common affairs. Each family will have a certain area of land as its own special holding (*sír* in Land Revenue language) for which it pays nothing[1]. The rents (of the area held by tenants) are collected, and these, together with any profits of waste-products and 'manorial' dues, will be devoted to paying the Land Revenue: if more than enough for the purpose, the surplus will be divided according to family shares: if insufficient, the necessary balance will be distributed accordingly, in the same fractional shares, among the members.

[There are other cases in which a body of co-operative colonists (not being a family descended from one ancestor) may cultivate in common or on the joint-stock principle, but these we are not now considering.]

An undivided community of co-sharers like this, may long continue, either from a jealous sense of equality and a desire

[1] **Meaning of *sír* land.**—If one of the sharers holds land besides his *sír*, it will be as tenant of the body, and paying rent to it. This opportunity should be taken to explain that *sír* land is an important matter in the North-West Provinces, Oudh, and the Central Provinces. It exists in all the numerous cases where the landlord body is distinct from, or supervenient on, a body of tenant cultivators (or cultivators who have become tenants). Each co-sharer has a certain home-farm for his own especial benefit. In the Panjáb we hear much less about *sír* because there the villages are so much oftener held by families, or tribal groups, who themselves are the direct holders of all the village land or the greater part of it; so there is no distinction. In the provinces first named, certain privileges attach to the *sír*, and accordingly the Land Revenue Acts and Tenant Acts define what is legally *sír* and what is not. (1) When an occupancy tenant-right is allowed, it does not extend to the *sír* lands. (2) When land is assessed, *sír* land is allowed a certain reduced rate (now ten to fifteen per cent.) below a full actual rental value. (3) If a man loses his proprietary right (under certain circumstances defined in the laws) he retains possession of his *sír* land as an occupancy tenant, with a certain privilege as to reduced rental.

that no one should, by becoming separate, get a start and perhaps buy up the other shares and so become the principal landowner; or there may be local circumstances making joint cultivation more convenient; or perhaps the greater part of the land (excepting the home-farms) is in the hands of resident tenants, and there is no object in dividing. Whatever the motive or cause for the continuing union, the joint-holding itself results simply from the customary principle of the succession of all the heirs together, which is in itself an archaic survival.

These undivided bodies of village landlords constitute the chief form of the tenure called in the books ZAMÍNDÁRÍ MUSHTARKA—the undivided landlord-village community.

The families separate more or less completely.—But the time comes when jealousies or quarrels arise, or there is some other motive, and a separation is agreed to. At this point we must make a little diagram, to show the several degrees of direct male[1] descent from the original landlord, founder or grantee. By the use of different kinds of type and by numbers, the grades of descent are made clear to the eye: the members supposed to be still surviving are enclosed in squares.

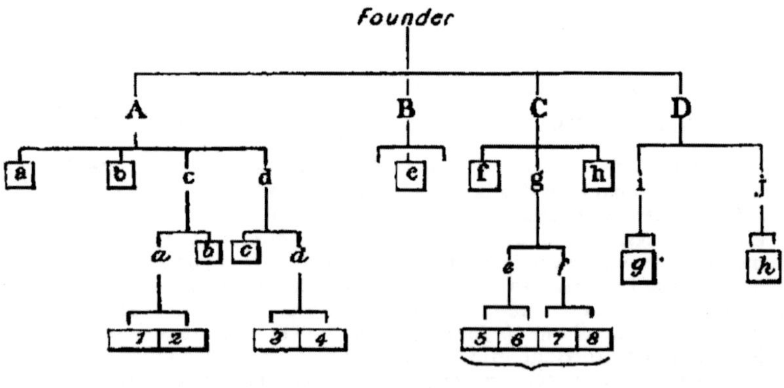

The family with its surviving members, agree to partition. Let us note that it is very probable that, at first, only the *four*

[1] Females are not usually allowed to succeed, or only in default of male heirs: sometimes daughters get a share till marriage. Widows of a sonless sharer hold for life only.

sons (A, &c.) will separate—constituting the *pattí* or main shares[1], each called by a local name—very likely that of the original owner; and inside the separate *pattís* the descendants will still remain joint. But let us now suppose that the partition is general. The principle of division of the land (and the payments with which it is burdened) will be the ancestral one, i. e. according to the fractional share indicated by the tree or diagram.

The shares of A, &c. are $\frac{1}{4}$ each. a, b, c, d, will take each $\frac{1}{4}$ of $\frac{1}{4}=\frac{1}{16}$. e, will take the whole of his father's fourth, i. e. the entire *pattí*. f, the successors of g, and h, will each take $\frac{1}{3}$ of the *pattí*, i. e. $\frac{1}{12}$ of the whole. And so—coming to the last degree—1, 2, will have each $\frac{1}{2}$ of $\frac{1}{8}$ of $\frac{1}{4}$ of the *pattí* A: and so on throughout. Very likely as 5, 6, 7, 8, are smaller shares, they will agree to continue holding their lot in common or jointly.

Nomenclature of shares and subshares.—The main shares (A, &c.) are *pattí*; the second grade (a, b, &c.) are *thôk* or *túlá*[2], the third (*a*, &c.) are *berí*. Below that the holding is *kháta*. Any person on the family 'tree' (i. e. not being a tenant or a casual owner of a plot[3]) is called (generally) a *khátedár*—a holder of a *khátá* or part of a *khátá*.

In order to express the fractional shares, since in the early arithmetic no system of 'vulgar fractions' (expressed by a numerator and denominator) was known, it was usual to refer to the whole as 'one rupee', and the fractional shares are so many 'anas' and 'pies' (*pái*); or the land measure was used, and the whole was one *bíghá* and the parts were so many *biswa*, *biswáńsí*, &c. (p. 12).

But as the ordinary divisions of money and land measure would not go very far in a division where the shareholders are numerous and remote in descent from the common ancestor, for the purpose of tenure shares, a variety of further subdivisions are to be found, e.g. the 'rupee' is not only divided into 16 *anas* and the *ana* into 12 *pái*, but the *pái* is divided into 20 *kiránt*, &c. And so the *biswáńsí* is made into a number of *reń*, *pheń*, &c., till we get tiny fractions representing each a few square yards.

[1] Sometimes there is a still earlier or larger division above the *pattí*, and called *tarf*. This may be due to two leaders having originally founded the village, or some other remote cause of primary division.

[2] There are some varieties of local nomenclature, and sometimes the meaning of the terms is inverted: the *thôk*, e. g., may be the larger division above the *pattí*.

[3] In some villages, there are individuals, not belonging to the existing proprietary families, so far privileged as to be regarded as holding their lands in ownership, but not with the status of a shareholder in the whole state (p. 131).

In the ancestral share villages the Revenue burden follows the share irrespective of the relative value of the land.—It is important to remember that under this principle of division *each co-sharer pays a portion of the Revenue burden exactly corresponding with his fractional share of the estate.* To say, therefore, that a man pays 4-*anas* revenue (one-fourth of the whole assessed sum) means also that he owns a 4-*ana* share (or one-fourth of the estate). It may be that one fourth-share is better or more productive than another; but still all pay alike as long as the system is maintained.

In managing a village so divided, there is only occasional need for any common council or united action. Each divided co-sharer takes his own rents, and pays his own Land Revenue, according to the proper fraction: he pays through the *lambardár* of his *patti* or section; but it is now the practice to get permission to pay it to the Tahsíl treasury direct. His only concern is then with any common expenditure (*malba*, p. 28 note), as well as with any questions about the building-sites, grazing ground, &c., which are still joint.

Pattídárí.—A village wholly divided in this way *on the ancestral principle,* and so that the revenue liability as it appears in the *báchh* or list of the distribution is a fraction corresponding to the land-fraction, is said to be on the PATTÍDÁRÍ Tenure.

'Imperfect' Pattídárí.—But very often the division affects only part of the land; not only the waste, but a portion of the old cultivated area also, is retained undivided, frequently because it is all held by occupancy-tenants and there is no object in dividing it (the rents are devoted *en masse* to paying the village Revenue, which may indeed, in some cases, be entirely covered by them). This is called 'imperfect' *pattídárí* tenure.

Ancestral shares rarely remain unaltered.—It is also comparatively rare to find that the present holdings correctly correspond to the fractional shares; sometimes they do so roughly; in other cases the land shares have altered, but all other profits are still shared on the correct fractions; and so the *principle* is adhered to by the villagers.

Sometimes, out of family pride, they will have this scheme recorded at Settlement as customarily binding, though neither the holdings nor the actual payments correspond to the fractions; but they have a sort of hope that they may one day return to a correct distribution. In some cases, at Settlement, villages actually consented to return to the ancestral shares—making a new start, either by a re-allotment, or by making up to those who had less land, by a grant out of the culturable common waste [1].

It is perhaps unnecessary to explain that shares are especially liable to get altered in places where the circumstances of climate and soil make such a difference between the holdings, that they become really unfair when each has the same fractional share of a heavy Land Revenue to pay. One sharer then fails to meet his liability and hands over part of his share to a solvent neighbour; sales, mortgages and the like, have their part in the change. But the chief cause of all is the long prevalence of rack-renting at the hands of Governors and land officials. Here, rather than lose the land, the family have to meet the Revenue demand as they best can, and every one pays and also cultivates according to his means. It may have been also necessary to call in outsiders to help; and these may have been secured by admission as co-sharers, or by altering the holdings to suit their convenience.

In the Panjáb, and I daresay elsewhere, a very large number of villages have, owing to such causes, *lost all remembrance of ancestral shares*, and now hold simply by the accident of possession, and pay in proportion to the holding; they accordingly fall into another class of village constitution: in Revenue language the village has changed from being *pattídárí* to being *bháiáchárá* (p. 87 note).

Villages held in severalty still retain many features of a close community.—Before leaving the *pattídárí* village I may remark that though the shares may have been allotted, and the land wholly (or partly) divided, the body of co-sharers is still treated as one; the whole estate is assessed to one sum of Land Revenue; the members are together jointly and severally liable for it. They often have some common lands and common interests that hold them together; and many features of a self-contained community are preserved.

Sometimes the Division was made from the first.—It should be added, also, that though in the illustration I have selected the division was preceded by a period of joint holding, that is by no means always the case with *pattídárí* villages. Some of them

[1] For an example see *L. S. B. I.* vol. ii. p. 673.

have been divided for generations past, and may have begun with some kind of division on family shares, from the very first founding. This, notably, is the case with villages officially called *pattidárí* in the districts on the north-west frontiers of the Panjáb.

And sometimes in a complex form.—It is also worth while noting that when a separation takes place, it is not always so simple a matter as my illustration supposes. For a body of co-sharing descendants may own much more than one village; or they may have begun with one and expanded or extended into several. When they divide, in order to secure the shares being equal in value or advantage, as far as possible, they will ignore the village or *mauza* limits, and make the *pattis* and shares up of various strips and plots scattered about through several villages, one at a considerable distance from the other. The survey at Settlement marks these sections in each village; and tables are drawn up collecting the plots forming each estate, together; and the assessment is then on the *mahál* or aggregate of plots held under one family title, but otherwise exactly the same as if all the shares had been locally in one village. A common term for this scattered allotment is *khetbat*; and where the division is by means of compact shares, it is *pattíbat*.

Villages shared on other principles.—I must now pass on to consider villages still held by more or less closely constituted communities (who regard themselves as collectively landlord of the entire area) and yet either (2) share on some other principle than that of ancestral shares; or (3) hold by mere possession or *de facto* holdings (see p. 76).

True Bháiáchárá or holding by artificial equal lots.—The most interesting form of (2) the sharing on a non-ancestral principle, is that which was originally called BHÁIÁCHÁRÁ or 'custom' (*áchárá*) 'of the brothers' (*bhái*). Here the whole area available was studied and was classified by the *pancháyat* into good and bad, better, best, &c.; and then a suitable number of lots were made, each consisting of specimen strips of each kind of soil, scattered over the whole area. Each lot so made up would be called the *bháiwádí-bígha*, or *tauzi-bígha*—an artificial land unit, which had no relation to the ordinary or standard measure; then, according to the requirement of numbers in the families, a certain number of such units would be made over[1] to each section and subsection—who would form the *tarf*, *patti*, *thók*, &c., as before.

Sometimes other plans were adopted; for instance, it might suffice to let the unit of bad land be much larger than the unit of the best; so that when a distribution of burdens was made, the same rate would be applied to a larger (real) area of poor land, and to a smaller area of the best. Whatever was done it was always with the desire of equality—adjusting the share to the burden to be borne.

Custom of bhejbarár.—And this desire was further evidenced by the frequency with which, in certain parts of the North-West Provinces and elsewhere, a system known as *bhejbarár* was adopted[2]. This consisted in a periodical valuation of the different holdings *in statu quo*, and determining on a new distribution of the Revenue burdens (with and without some exchanges in the land-holdings themselves), to suit the condition and present value of each shareholder's lot.

By ploughs and other methods.—Very often, a simple plan of division was to assume, roughly, a certain area to represent what a plough with a pair of oxen could till, and then to count up the number of ploughs possessed by the body, and assign (by lots drawn or otherwise) an extent of 'plough units' corresponding to the number of ploughs owned. This would often happen where the village was formed by an associated or co-operative body.

Sometimes cultivation would be established by sinking a number of wells, each of which would command a certain area—an area usually much in excess of what the well could actually continually keep moist, but including all fields that could, under any circumstances, get a certain amount of water from the well; then the shares would be reckoned according to the 'wells' without any reference to the area of land actually in possession. Or the 'well,' i.e. the entire area watered by it, might form a lot to be subdivided.

Principle of de facto holdings.—(3) In some villages, the

[1] By drawing lots for them, or by some other device.

[2] As a matter of fact, I believe, this system originated in days of heavy Revenue assessment, when such an equalization of the burden was inevitable in almost any form of joint village, whether originally *bhdiáchárá* or *pattidári*; but it was characteristic of the former.

body may have come to regard itself as united landlord, and yet *no system of sharing* is traceable. This may be a constitution originally adopted because land was fairly equal in value and abundant, and so each family took what it wanted or had means to cultivate. *Kásht-hasb-maqdúr* (cultivation according to ability) is the phrase then used to describe the system: or a man says his holding is his *dád-illáhi* (the Divine gift), meaning that he cannot account for the extent of his holding or its origin. In these cases it is always doubtful whether we have a really joint-village, or only a *raiyatwárí* form, which is now treated as joint under the general Revenue system [1].

May be occasioned by loss of an earlier share system.—Often too, such a constitution has gradually come about through the *loss of an earlier system* of definite shares. I have already noticed how seldom *accurate* ancestral shares are maintained: the same causes carried further, may result in a total (or nearly total) loss of all memory of original shares—*de facto* possession is alone recognized. But sometimes there is positive proof of this loss in the fact that the feeling of joint ownership in the whole may remain, and that some profits, and even the waste land, may be divided on the old principle (see pp. 82–3).

Imperfect Bháiácházá.—If, in any of these non-ancestrally shared or *de facto* holding villages, a portion of the land is held undivided, we have the 'imperfect' form (as adopted in the text books) just as we had in the *pattídárí* (p 82).

In these cases the share of the Revenue always proportioned to the holding.—It will be observed that, unlike the case of *pattídárí* villages, the Revenue burden is *here always paid in proportion to the share or to the* de facto *holding*.

Summary of these non-ancestral forms.—To summarize

[1] Two prominent examples of this may be noted. The villages of Ájmer and those of the Kángra (hill) district in the Panjáb are returned as *bháiá-chárá*; both being simply treated as joint-villages at Settlement. In Ájmer, really, the villages were pure *raiyatwárí*, as in Central India. In the Kángra hills no villages at all existed, but separate farms were aggregated together and an area of waste made over to them.

In these cases the joint responsibility is never enforced, and the gift of the waste and the example of neighbouring villages led the people to acquiesce. Such a plan was tried, but had to be given up, in parts of the Central Provinces; but local conditions were there quite different.

these villages which are held *otherwise* than on ancestral shares, we have—

1. Villages shared on the true *bhâiâchârâ* principle of equalized artificial lots or holdings.
2. Villages shared by ploughs, well-shares (or by any other method), but the allotments are still regarded as *shares* of a jointly owned whole.
3. Villages once *pattidârí*, but owing to the changes and chances of time and the effect of heavy Revenue burdens, the old share system was upset, and the *de facto* holdings have become stereotyped completely.

To these we must now add:—

4. Villages where only *de facto* holdings, on no known principle of sharing, have all along been recognized, but still the villagers have come to regard themselves as a joint body [1].

Summary of the whole group of landlord villages.—And then finally, to summarize the *entire group* of *joint* (*or landlord*) *villages under all forms of constitution*, we have—

Revenue burden proportioned to fractional share in the estate (more or less nearly and in principle.	1. Single landlord villages (*Zamíndârí-khâlis.*) 2. Held by a joint body undivided (*Z. mushtarka*). 3. Divided on ancestral shares (*pattídârí*). 4. 'Imperfect' (part undivided, form of 3).
Revenue burden proportioned to the actual holdings.	5. Shared on other principles, or on no principle (of the four kinds above noted —all now officially generalized under the name *bhâiâchârâ*.) 6. 'Imperfect' (part undivided, form of 5).

[1] **Official (generalized) use of the term bhâiâchârâ.**—It has unfortunately become the custom in Statistical tables to lump all these four cases under one heading—'*bhâiâchârâ*.' The loss of historical tenure-details, thus occasioned, it will require no very vivid imagination to realize. Probably the cause of this generalization was that from a revenue point of view, all possessed one (important) feature in common. The revenue burden was *always proportioned to the holding*, and not (as in ancestrally shared villages) to the fractional share.

Origin of the forms of village.

It is common to find in histories and text-books, that these two forms of village—the *raiyatwárí* and the *landlord* form—are generalized together, and a description is given of *one* (supposed) universal type of 'village community'; and from want of access to details, even eminent writers have been content to take the matter for granted, and to proceed to account for such a type, with reference to the analogy of European forms, such as the (supposed) German 'mark,' the Russian 'mir,' or the Swiss 'allmend.' I trust I shall not be supposed to speak with the sligliest disrespect of these writers; but it must be remembered that the historical jurist is very often compelled to construct his system on a very slender basis of fact; he is rather concerned to show, on principles which it is his great merit to have discovered or elucidated, that given (or even assuming) certain facts, the way things will develop is in this or that direction. And it seems to have been taken for granted, when the landlord-villages first became known in North-Western India, that we had here a form of primaeval village-tenure, from which all other forms were descended. To state the matter very briefly, it was supposed that a joint or undivided tenure came first in point of time, and that the *pattídárí* and *bháiáchárá* (or divided tenures) were later stages in the general process of development from the early joint-holding to modern individual proprietorship. And if any attention was given at all to the enormous area covered with *raiyatwárí* villages, it was supposed that these represented a decayed form of the other. And indeed the case of the Dakhan and Madras villages already alluded to (p. 76) was sometimes quoted to suggest that the old *mirásí* families represented not only an earlier, but a universal, form of joint-family holding which decayed into that now prevalent.

It is impossible in the space at my disposal, or indeed with reference to the purpose of this book, to go into theoretical discussions. I must therefore pass over the important question raised by M. Fustel de Coulanges and others, as to the validity of the evidence for the communal German 'mark' and other such institutions, on which the case for the joint or common tenure, as the original form in India, was largely made to rest. I can only briefly indicate—

1. That there is reason to believe that the earliest tribal movements in India resulted in the distribution of territory into areas for clans and tribal sections, which were further subdivided into village, or even smaller groups[1]. But the family-holdings inside these small groups were separate; the jurisdiction of the village- or hamlet-headman alone held the group together.

[1] Notice, e.g., the interesting case of the *Bhil* tribes noted by Sir W. Hunter, *Brief History of the Indian People*, 20th ed. p. 43.

There is no evidence of any pre-Aryan, or other really primaeval, holding 'in common,' or of a joint holding of land, as a general practice.

2. That whatever be the date of the 'Laws of Manu'—representing the custom as established in Northern India, the only kind of village known to that author is the *raiyatwárí* village under a headman with an official free holding of land. The only title to land known, is the right by first clearing the jungle. It is to me quite incredible that if a really earlier and universal form of village existed, in which the right was a common right, marked by periodical exchange of holdings, and that the families exercised their joint ownership by virtue of inheritance or birthright [1], that not the faintest trace of such a common-holding or such a claim or title to land should be found in Manu.
3. That in a large number of cases we can positively trace how the joint-village has grown up over an older (*raiyatwárí*) village, or is newly founded on virgin soil on the same principle, owing to the proud feeling of the families of higher, military, religious, or dominating caste in general, which founded it or obtained the superiority.
4. That in cases like the (supposed very ancient) vestiges of a common holding in Madras, however numerous, the facts are at least perfectly explainable on a hypothesis which is conformable to what is observed elsewhere, namely, the growth of special landlord families or joint-colonist groups, and does not necessitate a supposition that *all* villages were once held 'in common.'

Bulk of early cultivation must have been non-Aryan.—I will only remark briefly on these four heads, that we have evidence of a series of racial movements and tribal immigrations in India which occurred, in general, before the intellectually and otherwise superior race of Aryans descended from their first settlement beyond the Indus (and in the Himálayan valleys) and marched across the Panjáb to occupy Northern India from the Jumna eastward.

Whatever may be the correctness of the classification of races, and the actual affinities of any particular tribe, there can be little doubt that the distinctions implied by the terms 'Tibeto-Burman' group (Assam and the Eastern and Central Himálaya), 'Kolarian' (Vindhyan hill system and South-West Bengal), 'Dravidian' (West and South India, but probably extending northward also), correspond with actual distinctions of race. We have some evidence of what sort of villages were formed of old in Assam and the Himálayan districts. We have also the curious fact that though both Kolarian and Dravidian have almost ceased to exist as separate races, and have merged in the general Hindu population, still some of their

[1] It will at once be admitted that in all 'joint' or landlord villages, whether primeval or not, the holders claim their right as '*mirási*' or some similar word implying inheritance or birthright.

tribes found refuge in the secure but fertile fastnesses of the Chutiyá Nágpur country (South-West Bengal); so that there, the old forms—the tribal union, and the village grouping—have been maintained, in spite of some encroachments by later landlords, in a way that would not have been possible elsewhere.

We can, there, still trace customs which show that some of the people we call Dravidian had a superior village organization—notably a powerful headman, with an allotment of land held[1] in virtue of his hereditary office; and indeed with all the features which are calculated to produce the *raiyatwárí* village in its modern form. And it can hardly be doubted that these features (of which indication can also be found in other parts of the country) were really the marks of Dravidian land-holding in general.

When we reflect that the Aryan immigration was that of a non-agricultural people, whose two upper castes (military and religious) regarded agriculture with loathing[2]; that it had therefore only a residuary (upper) caste, the *Vaisyá*, and its mixed lower strata (*Sudra*) to take to cultivation at all; when, further, we recollect that the Aryans came in very limited numbers, hardly more than sufficient to form armies and take the ruling and official position over States already peopled with non-Aryans, and that they gradually multiplied by admixture with the better sort of the indigenous races, it may certainly be considered at least a very natural order of things, that the joint or landlord village should have grown up as the result of a local lordship, or at least by the founding of new villages at the hands of the superior families, or by the location of conquering tribes proud of their birth and ancestral connexion, and that the joint village (see remark at p. 80) should be the result of the joint succession and the ancestral connexion in these families, rather than a primaeval institution which goes back beyond all the earliest customs that we can actually trace.

Leaving, however, a subject of which only the fringe can be touched, I propose briefly to state how some of the joint villages are known to have originated.

Landlord villages derived from three principal sources.—1. Single founders, Grantees, Revenue farmers.—If we first roughly and generally classify the known origins of landlord bodies, we shall observe three great sources from which some

[1] There is an allotment for the chief (afterwards the Rájá, p. 34), one for the headman, &c., and one for the priest and for religious worship: the remainder was for the cultivating body who accompanied the headman and his family. The privilege or right to these lots was fully understood; but there is no trace whatever of a common holding or of the headman being proprietor of the whole village.

[2] The poorest Rájput, long driven by necessity to cultivate with his own hands, will try and avoid the indignity of touching the plough, if he can help it.

joint-villages have been derived. One is the growth, in or over an existing village, of some one man who obtained a grant, or elevated himself by energy and wealth, or who developed a position out of a contract for revenue farming; such a grantee —or any adventurer,—may also found and establish a new village in the waste, with exactly the same results.

2. Dismemberment of ruling chiefs' houses.—Closely connected with the first head, is another under which many high caste, or quasi-aristocratic village-bodies, descended from a common ancestor, may be grouped. I need hardly enlarge on the fact that under the continual succession of wars, invasions, and internecine struggles, which mark the history of every province, royal, princely and chieftains' houses were always gaining the lordship of territories, and again losing it;—gathering head, founding and acquiring dominions, and in time losing them, while the houses lost rank and were broken up. And when any of the greater conquests like those of the Mughal and the Maráthá powers occurred, the petty Hindu and other principalities, all over the country, would go to pieces; cadets of families would break off and assume independence; and territorial rule would be lost; but the family would contrive to cling, by timely submission, and by favour of the conqueror, to relics of its possessions, no longer as *ruling chiefs* but as *landlords*. This fact is universal, and accounts for more varieties of land-tenure in India than almost any other. We have already seen (pp. 40–1) how the Rájás, subdued under the Mughal arms, would be accepted by the Emperor as a kind of revenue-agent (though he still called himself Rájá), and thus he ended by becoming landlord where he was once ruler. The same circumstances enabled scions and cadets of noble houses, or petty chiefs whose power was destroyed, to keep a footing in the individual villages of the old territory.

The rule of primogeniture which holds estates together in times of prosperity becomes relaxed.—So long as a family of superior rank has some territorial position, it usually retains a rule of primogeniture, so that the estate as a whole remains intact: but when the ruling position is lost by defeat in war or by other misfortune, the members separate, and each clings to some small area

—whether it is a group of two or three villages or a single village. Gradually such families—their claim to consideration grown dim with time—are assessed to a full revenue by the ruling power, and fall, more and more decidedly, into the rank of peasant co-parcenary bodies, with perhaps vague recollections of a distinguished origin, and with caste pride which may long enable them to refuse to handle the plough themselves, and so to rely on their tenants.

These two heads of origin account for the bulk of landlord villages in the North-West Provinces and Oudh.—In the North-West Provinces and Oudh, there are a few interesting cases of the *tribal* settlements—to be mentioned next, but putting these aside, a majority of the villages that are really joint (and have not merely become so under the Revenue system) may fairly be traced to one or other of the two origins hitherto dealt with, viz. their founders were

(1) Grantees, Revenue-farmers, and the like; or (2) Scions of once ruling or territorially powerful families that broke up and became local landlords.

3. Tribal groups; colonist associations. Tribal settlements especially marked in the Panjáb.—The third principal source of joint-villages is the local conquest, or (possibly) the peaceable settlement, of clans and tribal groups—Jats (or locally, Játs), Gújars, Rájputs and others, whose place of origin and course of movement are difficult to ascertain except from traditional indications. But in different parts, we find extensive groups of villages evidently of this origin; and in the Panjáb we have it exemplified on the large scale, and in a double form. All along the North-West Frontier we have tribes settled at comparatively modern dates, of a peculiar character, and with special institutions; while, throughout the central plains, extensive areas have been peopled at a much earlier date, by Jat and Gújar clans on an apparently large scale. I have mentioned that instances of this kind are not wanting in the North-West Provinces and Oudh; and there it is frequently interesting to notice that in such cases, the villages are held not on the 'aristocratic' *pattídárí* principle[1], but by methods of equal

[1] For, strange as it may seem, we have instances of tribal groups settling without a Rájá or chief—only an equal aggregation of families with the council of heads to manage common affairs.

holding, sharing by ploughs, &c., (p. 84) (*bháiáchárá*). Very often, as we shall see in the case of the Panjáb frontier tribes, though there is a strong landlord or proprietary spirit, and a sense of union among the tribal groups that were aggregated into villages (and sometimes settled in large areas divided at once into family shares without any village grouping), there is a peculiar method of allotting lands, which on the whole cannot really be brought under the definition of either *pattídárí* or *bháiáchárá*, as these terms are generally understood in Northern India.

Illustrations of cases under either head. Landlord Family originating by grant.—I may now offer a few illustrations of these village origins. Taking the first source—that spoken of as, in a wide sense, origin 'by grant'; we have several varieties to notice. In the first place, the circumstances of the early Hindu (and other) conquering kingdoms must have always occasioned the necessity of finding provisions of land for distant relatives or inferior connexions of the Rájás, and for various persons not important enough to receive official posts or regular territorial allotments in the State organization. As the Rájá had a right to a share of the grain (as well as to other rights) in each village, and had all the waste land at his disposal, the natural thing was for him to make the necessary provision by issuing a grant. Such a grant might be made over an existing village (probably of pre-Aryan or mixed caste cultivators) or it might be to found a new village in the waste. Not only minor members of the Rájá's house, but soldiers, courtiers or servants to be rewarded, would obtain similar grants. Sometimes grants were given (*sub rosá*) for a consideration in money. In Oudh such grants can be frequently traced under the name of *birt* (Sanskrit *vṛitti*). I have already described (pp. 77, 78) the effects of such a grant and the consequences which ensued from it. Numerous villages throughout the North-West Provinces (where the co-sharers are of higher caste and descended from a common ancestor) originated in this way.

Modern instances of grant in Central Provinces. Estates in villages.—Under this head, too, we must not omit to take notice of the effect of *modern grants*, as exemplified in the case of a large number of villages in the Central Provinces, which were often held by a non-Aryan or mixed population, and were naturally of the *raiyatwárí* type. When the Land Revenue Settlement was made under the North-West system, the desire was to make the villages, as they stood, into joint-estates; but circumstances did not admit of this; so, as the system *necessitated a landlord responsible for each village* (cf. p. 151), the position was conferred by grant on the village headmen and revenue-contractors whom the Maráthá Government had established. These persons were called in official papers *Málguzár*; hence the Settlement with them is often alluded to as the *Málguzárí* Settlement of the Central Provinces. Accordingly here we have an example of landlords by grant; and as the original grantees pass away, their descendants will form co-parcenary bodies—probably *pattidárí*. The grant here was a limited one; that is to say, extensive sub-proprietary and occupancy rights were secured to the tenants; but with that we are not at present concerned.

Village landlord bodies descended from Revenue-farmers Revenue officials, and auction purchasers.—Village proprietary bodies whose origin is by descent from a Revenue-farmer, are obviously closely analogous. In the North-West Provinces a very large number of villages can be traced to an origin not much earlier than the present century, by descent from such a Revenue-farmer, or from some person who stood security for the village revenue and who purchased the village and became owner when a default occurred. In early days, also, when the immediate sale of an estate was ordered if any failure in the Land Revenue payment occurred, numerous villages fell into the hands of auction-purchasers who became landlords with a 'parliamentary title.' The sales were, indeed, often purposely brought about by fraudulent devices; and such was the injustice done, that a special commission (in 1821) was appointed to rectify matters. A number of sales were set aside; but still many villages could not be recovered.

While a number of these village bodies are not more than a

century old—yet with all the marks of the so-called 'primaeval communities,' they will very likely talk of their rights 'by inheritance,' as if they were of great antiquity. It will be remembered that in the early days of our rule, the Revenue system dealt always with some one man in each village. Hence there was an abundant supply of farmers, sureties, or single co-sharers of wealth and importance, ready to develop into landlords. It was only when Regulation VII of 1822 was passed, and a record of rights was made, that the recognition of the whole co-sharing body as jointly entitled to the proprietary position, followed. This source of origin is naturally rarer in the Panjáb, because the province was not annexed till after the British Revenue system had been improved, and the idea of joint bodies of owners was familiar.

By mere growth and usurpation without grant.—An exactly similar result would happen when there is no formal grant of the State rights or sale, to begin with, but where some particular family rose to a dominant position by mere energy and pushing; and so again where, in the numerous forays and petty local incursions, individual chiefs conquered and seized villages and managed to retain them; or where single adventurers set out from their own country to seek a new home, and founded new villages.

A remarkable instance of this may be quoted from the Siálkot district in the Panjáb. In the village of Siálkot, some generations back, a young chieftain named Dhíru (who claimed to be a Chauhán Rájput, and one of the Chattá family[1]) came from his ancestral home in the Ganges plain, in search of a new location; he found a place in Siálkot. Having married twice he had eighteen sons; as these grew up and found abundant land that was waste (and also doubtless acquired other lands in various ways) they gave rise to a number of co-sharing bodies forming separate villages: these men once had their heads and family-chiefs, over groups, but the Sikh Maháraja reduced them; and now no less than eighty-one separate villages have arisen from this one centre: all are of course strong landlord villages—probably *pattidárí*. Not very far off, a small number of Bhattí tribesmen settled, and have now formed a group of eighty-six villages, of which Pindí-Bhattián is the centre, a place considerable enough to be shown on the maps.

[1] The Chattá is one of the noble families described in Sir L. Griffin's *Panjab Chiefs*.

Illustration of landlord rights arising from a lost ruling or territorial position.—Turning now to the case of landlord villages arising out of the break up of territorial estates, or the disruption of a Ráj or other rulership, I have already (p. 91) stated how this comes to pass. And it is obvious that it may either result in tolerably *large* estates, or else go so far as to leave the members of families in possession only of single villages or even less. Some further remarks will be made in Sec. II (Landlord Estates): here, therefore, I will only give some cases of *village estates* arising out of such disruption, and ask the reader to refer also to Sec. II which follows. In the Rái-Barelí district of Oudh, there is a remarkable group of estates—some of them being single villages, others being larger groups—but the whole originating in the dismemberment of the family territory of a celebrated Rájá of the *Bais* caste called Tilok Chand. In quite another place, the Gujrát district in the Panjáb, will be found a number of villages of *Chib* Rájputs which are also traceable to a dismembered 'Ráj' that lasted down to the Sikh times and was then destroyed. The Rájá and his barons and their territorial rule completely passed away—the descendants of the stock remain as bodies of village proprietors. On the Malabar (west) coast of India, the Náyar *janmi* landlords (as they are called) are only the descendants of territorial chiefs who lost the ruling position, and still adhered to their land, claiming it (as usual) 'by birthright.' But instances of this class can be found all over India.

Illustrations of clan or tribal settlements.—Under the third head, we include all cases where a certain area of country is occupied, more or less exclusively, by villages belonging to one clan or tribe. This may be a large area, as in the case of the great *Jat* (in the Panjáb the *a* is short) and *Gújar* settlements; or it may be in comparatively smaller areas, like the *Goráha Bisen* settlements in Oudh (Gonda District), or those in the Hardoi district, or the Pachahra Játs of Mathurá (North-West Provinces.)

Impossibility of determining that there was any considerable body of settlers; often large groups of villages originate with a single family.—One thing, however, is to be observed; it is a mere question of available space and a sufficient lapse of time whether a now extensive clan-location should be attributed to any considerable tribal movement; it may often be due to a few families settling down and afterwards multiplying and separating. I have already given, in another connexion, an instance of groups of eighty villages and more, all originating in one single founder. And in the North-West Provinces, there is a highly interesting case of the expansion of a single family into a large group of villages covering an area of 28 sq. miles (it is only recently that separate villages have been formed; the whole area was originally divided at once into family shares). The place is known as Kharaila-Khás in the Hamírpur district[1]. The Pachahra Játs of Mathurá also settled about 200 years ago on the left bank of the Jumna, apparently only as a few individuals; they now form quite an extensive colony.

North-West frontier tribal settlements. Classification of soil for purposes of division, on a principal of equality.—But on the North-West frontier of the Panjáb, the districts have been almost entirely peopled, within historic times, by tribes who evince a strong sense of territorial right by conquest, and always speak of their 'inheritance' in the land[2]. But they did not settle in groups holding the land *in common*. Where, in places, joint-stock or common cultivation is practised, it is not due to any archaic (supposed) communistic ideas, but to suit special conditions and local circumstances. Speaking generally, we find that the frontier tribes always made a division, and one that was not by any means always founded on fractional ancestral shares. Sometimes they divided *the land*, and sometimes, when the water of a canal or hill-stream was the important requirement for cultivation, *shares in the water* were arranged. In some tribes, we observe the formation of village groups; in some cases we find a whole tribal area divided out at once

[1] For some details see *L. S. B. I.* vol. ii. p. 134.

[2] Whenever a family is found claiming its lands on the ground of birthright or inheritance (*mirás, wárisí, wirásat*, &c.), it is a certain indication of landlord claims.

into family or individual shares and not first into villages[1]. But there are always allotted *shares*, sometimes *per capita*, sometimes by families or households. Very frequently the whole territory was first classified and formed into certain different groups or lots (*wand*, *vesh*, &c.), and the shares would be made up of strips or plots out of each lot; here the plan directly points to a desire for equality of advantage in the holdings.

Periodical exchange of holdings.—We find also in these places a not yet entirely extinct custom of periodical redistribution of holdings among the families (and at first among the lesser sections of the entire tribe—as if little kingdoms were to exchange territories *en bloc*).

This appears to me to be primarily due to the desire to secure equality, by giving each a turn at the good or the bad; such equality not having been altogether secured by the making up of the shares in the way above stated. It is, however, held by some to be an indication of an early stage of property in which the right is supposed to reside in the clan or tribe collectively. It should be remarked, however, that this periodical exchange (*vesh*) is I believe never (certainly very rarely) found in places where cultivation is only possible by aid of irrigation, and where consequently fields are all laboriously built up and embanked, so as to utilize the water from the hill-streams during their seasonal flow.

These frontier villages are quite a thing *per se*, and their occupation is of comparatively late date, and in one case as late as the fifteenth or sixteenth century.

Extensive Tribal locations in the Central Panjáb.—The Jat and Gújar settlements in the Central Panjáb are much more ancient[2], and it is now impossible to account for specific origins. Most persons, looking to the whole circumstances of the case, will probably conclude that they represent really *large* tribal allocations. Although the areas have, in the course of time, received a certain admixture of villages of other castes (and of

[1] The village division usually follows it at a later date; see examples in *L. S. B. I.* vol. ii. pp. 134, 135, 668. These were all very large areas, not divided into villages but at once into a number of family, or household, or individual, shares.

[2] For some details as to the tribes in the Panjáb plains (which were never occupied by the Aryan immigrants), and the relations of Alexander with them, see *L. S. B. I.* vol. i. pp. 122, 141.

other origins) there is no mistaking the general prevalence of one particular race. But there are also many local groups of villages which represent the expansion and subsequent division of families during many generations, all deriving their origin from a few ancestral chiefs, the locale and form of whose territorial rule have long been forgotten. In some villages there are now several different elements combined;—evidently representing a state of things naturally brought about by the necessity for united effort against enemies or severe taxation, in the past.

In a considerable number of Panjáb villages (not speaking of the frontier districts) the *pattidárí* or ancestral principle is wholly or partly preserved: but a still greater number have been called *bháiáchárá* (in the official sense) because the share system has been upset or even wholly lost. There are some cases of the (true) *bháiáchárá* form where the land is held in artificially equalized lots; and many in which the holding is by 'ploughs' and by 'wells' (pp. 84–5), the last two being frequently met with.

Present condition of Panjáb villages.—Long periods of disorder and severe Revenue assessments have here resulted, as always, both in mixing the landholders—necessitating the admission of good workers of other castes and families to maintain the village, and in breaking down artificial systems of sharing; substituting *de facto* holdings, and payments corresponding thereto (pp. 83, 86). But under all circumstances the Panjáb villages, though much invaded (in some districts) by money-lenders, who have bought land against loans not repaid, or mortgages unredeemed, still show a good deal of the strength of union. They are not allowed, as under the North-West Provinces law, to completely partition the village estates, i.e. to break up family holdings into entirely separate estates. The custom of pre-emption is recognized by law, in its rather strong local forms; and wherever the co-sharers are well to do, they have the opportunity of getting the 'first refusal' of every plot of land that is being sold in their village, and so preventing its passing into the hands of strangers.

Colonist villages.—It must not be forgotten that besides clan groups of villages, and those which owe their origin to individual founders and their multiplied descendants, many villages owe their foundation to *associated parties of colonists*, who having reclaimed the waste by their co-operative efforts, are very likely (though not connected by common descent in many cases) to have a feeling of union, and very possibly a sense of joint ownership to the tract which they have colonized. We have instances of this class of village in the South-east Panjáb; and the Settlement Reports of Sirsa and Rohtak give interesting accounts of the formalities observed on founding the village-residences in a central position, and in drawing lots for the landholdings[1].

Early Colonist villages in Madras.—From a distant part of India comes another example of the same kind. Among the villages of the usual *raiyatwárí* type in Madras, there are local, and sometimes numerous, cases, where some of the landholders claim to belong to families that had once held the whole villages in common or in shares: and accordingly they speak of their *kániatsí* (afterwards called *mirási*) rights. In such villages, however, the old families have now lost their original position; only the shadow of joint rights remains.

Without going into any controversy regarding the origin of these villages, it is an undeniable fact that, locally, they are connected almost entirely with the district (once the kingdom) of Tanjore, and the district of Chingleput[2]. Now the latter was the centre of the ancient territory called 'Tondai-mandalam,' and there are historical and traditional data, universally accepted as having a foundation in fact, which account for there being here landlord-villages; inasmuch as a Hinduized Dravidian kingdom like that of the Cholá princes, would not only make grants to Bráhmans but would produce other leading families who would found, or obtain the lordship of, villages. But more especially there is evidence of a great colonization of *Tondai-mandalam* (principally in or about the eleventh century A. D.) by means of an energetic caste called Vellálar; and in virtue of their colonizing services, a special right to the land they cultivated was recognized. That they should largely have adopted the joint-stock cultivation (*pasang-karei*) is just what we might have expected[3].

[1] *L. S. B. I.* vol. ii. pp. 678, 687.

[2] When I speak of these districts, I do not of course mean to confine myself to their exact modern limits; the Trichinopoly district was also part of Tanjore; and the Chingleput *mirási* villages extend, I believe, into North Arcot.

[3] Under this method, no permanent allotment was made; each year it was determined (doubtless by the common council) what fields each would plough up; and the proceeds were thrown into a common stock and divided according to the share of each. Sometimes a modified method (called *kareiyídú*) was adopted. Here the land was allotted for a short term of years, after which an exchange or re-allotment was made. This method is admirably adapted to cure inequalities, because each family gets its turn at the good and bad holdings. In some of the villages we have also traces of a permanent division into shares (*Arudikarei*).

The after history of Tanjore, and its fate under the Maráthá oppressors, amply account for the gradual decay of such joint-villages, and for their falling into the *raiyatwári* form. The old *mirási* families would still have a memory of their superior right; and among the other landholders, some would be the old resident tenants brought in probably, at the founding, by the superior families (such are called *úlkúdi*), and others (*parakúdi*) would be the later cultivators employed from time to time and not connected with the village foundation, or not hereditary residents in the village.

A superior right or overlordship occasionally arises over landlord-villages.—In concluding a notice of the landlord- or joint-village, it may be mentioned that by the effects of subsequent grant, or conquest, even a co-sharing body with a landlord claim may come, in turn, to be subjected to some new superior. In the Panjáb and elsewhere, we find such villages with two landlord groups in them—a family of 'superior proprietors' ('*alá-málik* as they are called) taking certain rents or dues from the village proprietors. This is only another instance of how, in India, one set of rights *grows up over another*; the complication that would, in modern times, ensue, being obviated by the fact that, in early times, all varieties of right were met by division of the grain produce among the different claimants.

Section II. Landlord Estates (other than village estates).

The space we have devoted to village tenures is not disproportionately large, when we reflect on the fact that village-estates, and villages made up of groups of individual landholdings, constitute a very large majority of the landed interests in most of our Provinces. And even where some form of landlord estate on a larger scale is the prevalent tenure, still it will be villages that form the component parts of the estate; and their rights, though now subordinate rights, are still in existence, and cannot, at least in many cases, remain unnoticed. Moreover a great deal of what has been said regarding landlord-villages—

the growth of families by grant and usurpation and the effect of the disruption of petty kingdoms—applies equally to the larger estates. Very commonly the greater estate is a lordship arising in the same way, only that starting from a source of higher rank or being more directly connected with the ruling power, it has extended over a larger sphere, perhaps to a *pargana* or even a whole district, instead of a single village.

If we glance over the list of provinces, we shall note that they vary considerably as to the degree in which landlord-tenures (other than village communities) prevail. Landlord estates (some great and many smaller ones) are the general characteristic feature of BENGAL and of OUDH. They occur to a certain extent in the NORTH-WEST PROVINCES; but they are rare (and of quite exceptional origin) in the PANJÁB. The estates owned by landlords in the CENTRAL PROVINCES occupy a considerable proportion of the total area of the province; but they are of a special character and not landlords in the Bengal sense. Parts of ÁJMER and BERÁR are held by landlords who were formerly territorial chiefs. In BOMBAY there are a variety of (practically) landlord estates, but mostly in the Gujarát districts, and on the West Coast. In MADRAS, the Northern districts show some great Zamíndárís of the Bengal type, and there are also some landlord-estates in other parts; but nowhere, except in the North, do they form a characteristic feature of the districts[1]. In ASSAM a few estates are held by landlords. In BURMA there are few or none, unless waste-land grantees are included.

Cases where the Government is direct landlord.—I may preface this account of landlord-estates in their general varieties, by noting that in some cases (and apart from older historical theories of the State ownership of land in general) the Government is the direct owner or 'actual proprietor' of the soil.

It will be enough to simply enumerate the kinds of property so owned:—

1. **Property of former Government; and escheats.**—Houses, lands, or gardens, that were part of the personal estates of former rulers or Princes, and passed to the British Government on the acquisition of the Province (commonly called *nazúl* lands). To these I may add also lands escheated owing to failure of heirs; and estates forfeited in past years for State crimes and rebellion.

2. **Lands sold for arrears of Revenue and bought in, &c. Lands not under Zamíndárs and exempted from the Regula-**

[1] The *janmí* landholders of Malabar may form an exception, but they are special to this district.

tions. Alluvial lands. Policy in Bengal to retain such lands. Lands (chiefly in Bengal) of which a Settlement has been refused, or which have been auctioned for arrears of Revenue, and have not found a purchaser, have become Government property. Cases of this kind rarely occur in other provinces; and where, in former years (when sales for arrears of Revenue were more frequent), lands did come into the hands of Government in this way, the policy was always ultimately to find owners for them. There are also 'Government Estates' in Bengal, in some cases, because there was no proprietor to whom the permanent Settlement applied; in others because the territory was exempted from the (Permanent Settlement Zamíndárí) Regulations and declared to be directly under Government management. Sometimes considerable areas of alluvial island (*char* they are called) formed by the changing action of the rivers, become Government property, when, under the circumstances, the law does not regard them as 'accessions' to either of the riparian estates.

In the older reports, such estates were called *Kh̲ás* (special, private), i.e. directly held by Government. In Bengal it is thought politic to retain their management, partly because sometimes they are large areas (the '*Raiyatwárí* tracts' of official returns) in which the actual *raiyats* or cultivators are much better off as tenants dealing direct with the Government officers, than they would be under some middleman proprietor; and partly because the charge of such estates enables experience of land-management to be gained, as well as a knowledge of agricultural conditions, which (in the absence of a survey and all statistical returns) could not be gained in any other way.

3. **Waste lands not included in any estate are always the property of Government.**—It may be necessary again to mention, in this list of Government estates, all unappropriated waste lands (p. 57) which are still awaiting disposal under the Waste Land Rules.

4. **Lands acquired for public purposes.**—It is hardly necessary, however, to make a fourth head for the lands which are acquired for special public purposes under the Land Acquisition Act (1870), and with which, ordinarily, the Land Revenue Administration is not directly concerned.

Landlord rights of private persons.—Coming now to private rights of this class, the greater landlord interests—varying in size from a whole *pargana* or *táluka* (and even a still larger area) down to a group of a few villages or less—will generally be found to have arisen in one of these ways :—

a. The present landlord derives his right from a position as Revenue-farmer, or a land-official under native rule.

b. From a former territorial chiefship or rulership.

c. From a State-grant of some kind.

(*a*) Estates arising mainly out of Revenue-farming.

The Bengal Zamíndár.—The typical instance of this class is the Bengal *Zamíndár*, who was acknowledged as landlord by the Permanent Settlement under Lord Cornwallis in 1793 (to be described hereafter). Only a small percentage of the existing estates are large enough to have an area of 20,000 acres and over; for those first constituted were much broken up, partly by failure to pay the Revenue, which caused their sale piecemeal; partly by the effect of partition between joint heirs.

A curious instance of this is afforded by the old estate once called 'Haveli Munger' (Monghyr district). A couple of brothers in the days of the first emperor had obtained the official position of district officer or *chaudharí*. Then they became Zamíndárs or Revenue-farmers; and as the family multiplied, the whole estate was divided up into *tarfs* or family lots: some of these passed by sale out of the family, others remained as separate *táluqs* or smaller estates, and were ultimately brought under the Permanent Settlement as so many small independent Zamíndárís.

But a great number of holdings separately dealt with as Zamíndárís were, owing to local circumstances, always petty.

Origin of the regular Zamíndárs.—Speaking of the larger district Zamíndárs in general, the persons who acquired the estates had been of varied origin; but they had gained and consolidated their position by being allowed to farm the revenues. Some of them were the old Rájás or territorial chiefs of the country (p. 40); others were district officers; so that really the Bengal Zamíndár illustrates all three of the heads of origin above enumerated.

Extent of the estates.—Whatever the estate was, its extent was determined by the list of *parganas*, villages or lands mentioned in the warrant by which the Zamíndár was appointed to manage the Revenues. The limits of such areas were known only by custom, with reference to local landmarks and written descriptions.

Beginning of the landlord title to the estates.—The origin of official Revenue-farming is uncertain. There was no one date at which a system of the kind was formally promulgated. Rájás and territorial chiefs were probably from quite early times recognized as managing their old estates subject to a fixed contribution or tribute to the Imperial Treasury (p. 41). It may be broadly said, however, that farming became general as a system, in Bengal, from the reign of the Emperor Farukhsíyar (1713 A.D.).

Zamíndárs originally not landowners but Revenue agents. Subject to official appointment by warrant and no power of alienation. Process by which the position became hereditary and turned into landlordship.—That originally the Zamíndár was not in any sense a local landowner (except as far as he had private lands, or had, as Rájá, some kind of territorial interest) cannot reasonably be doubted. His position depended on an official warrant which ran for his life only, and that on condition of good conduct and subject to the pleasure of the ruler. This warrant contained nothing that indicated any grant of landed rights; nor was there any power of alienating any part of the area. But still the position of Zamíndár was such, that a century before British rule sufficed to develop it into a practical landlordship. The position became hereditary (as it would naturally tend to be in the case of a Rájáship, where the title itself was hereditary). The opportunities for such a farmer to become actual owner of the estate were many. Then there was, as I have said, a large area of waste, and each Zamíndár was fully entitled to cultivate this (by his own located tenants), so that he really became owner of it. Areas so appropriated were called *khámár* (and by other names in Bihár). There was also a certain nucleus of private land (*nij-jot* or *sír*). Lastly there were ample opportunities of buying up land, getting it in mortgage, or seizing it for unpaid arrears of rent. Each Zamíndár could also get certain land exempt from revenue (representing a deduction on his total payment) as *nánkár*, i. e. land for his private subsistence (lit. 'bread making'), and this he would naturally absorb as his own.

Reason for former difference of opinion as to the rights of Zamíndárs.—The reason why so much discussion about the real claims of Zamíndárs at one time arose, was that one set of writers kept their attention fixed on the original intention of the farming system and its first features, and the other appealed to the existing results as they had been produced by the practice of a century and perhaps more.

Other interests in Bengal practically placed on a level with Zamíndárí estates.—In Bengal, the same policy (of this presently) which resulted in a formal recognition of ownership (including a full right of alienation) in favour of Zamíndárs, also conferred a similar right on many small landholders of different origin, who in the end became landlords in the new legal sense.

Proprietorship was always a limited one.—Only let it be remembered that the proprietary right conferred was by no means an unlimited or absolute title. It was always intended to be limited by the maintenance of all practical interests (by whatever name designated) which existed, though in subordination to the Zamíndár. At first, as we shall see, those interests were, in many grades and degrees, insufficiently protected, because the subject was not understood; but as time went on the law was improved.

Persons who became landlords under the Permanent Settlement, other than regular Zamíndárs. Bengal taluqdárs and other landlords.—A few words will now be necessary to describe the other persons (in Bengal) who became owners, though not belonging to the official class of Zamíndár in the earlier sense. In the first place, in the outlying districts of the East, North-east, and South-west, there were no regularly established Zamíndárs, but local chiefs, and sometimes the state officers in charge were treated on the same footing, and these were accepted as landlords under the Permanent Settlement.

But even in the old-established districts, certain persons had been protected by State warrant under the designation of *taluqdár*. That meant that they were not in a position to be called Zamíndár, but their estate (*taluq*) was allowed a fixed or favourable assessment; and the management of it was left to the holder (who was thus freed from the exactions of land officers or of the neighbouring Zamíndár). In some cases the *taluq* had existed before the Zamíndárí, and for this or for some other reason, it was recognized as *Huzúrí* (paying direct to the *Huzúr* or State Treasury). In other cases, a *taluq* holder was recognized as entitled to a fixed payment, but he had to pay through the Zamíndár, who was thus able to exercise a certain control. Such *taluqs* were said to be 'dependent.' Often the Zamíndár himself created such *taluqs*—granting fixed or favourable terms to some old landholder whom he felt it necessary, or politic, to conciliate in this way. At the time of Settlement, rules were made as to which *taluqs* should be separate and which remain as subordinate interests under the great landlord. Those that were allowed a separate Settlement (and they were numerous) became themselves (smaller) Zamíndárís.

Other petty landholders.—In some of the Bengal districts, there had been no great Zamíndár, and the conditions under which land had been settled and cultivated were peculiar, so that the persons recognized as Permanently Settled landlords were of a peculiar character, and often were no more than petty landholders who would have been called *raiyats* under any other system.

As an instance, the district of Chittagong may be cited. Here the country was originally a dense semi-tropical jungle ; it had been settled in patches (wherever facilities for cultivation were greatest) by little groups of cultivators under leaders called *tarfdár*, who were responsible for the Land Revenue. The occupied lands had been measured at the time: so that the *tarfdárs* were recognized as 'actual proprietors,' and, in this instance, according to the areas measured in 1764. The unmeasured land (subsequently tilled and called *nauábád*=new cultivation) did not come under the Permanent Settlement; and the holders of it are under a different system of temporary Settlement, and are practically (but not *eo nomine*) proprietors of their holdings.

Landholders in Bihár.—In this connexion I must refer to the Bihár districts (Northern Bengal). It will be remembered that in Bengal generally, the growth of the Zamíndárs had obliterated the village rights, and the importance—except for purely local purposes—of the village grouping. This was facilitated by the fact that in the Central Zamíndárí districts the villages had never (as far as can be traced) been otherwise than of the *raiyatwárí* type; no strong or high-caste landlord families had grown up in or over them to claim the the village-area in shares. The headman (*mandal*) soon lost his influential position, and became merely the subservient nominee of the Zamíndár; and the *raiyats* easily fell into the general status of tenants. But in the Bihár districts, and still more in the adjoining Benares districts (which a year or two later were also brought under the Permanent Settlement), village landlord-bodies had grown up. In Bihár their origin was due to the local predominance of a peculiar caste called *Bábhan*, of the military order (and probably of mixed—possibly Bráhman—origin). These bodies had however fallen, to a greater or less extent, under the power of the neighbouring Revenue-grantees and officials, and these latter were settled with as Zamíndárs over the heads of villages.

But these village-bodies still retained cohesion enough, even in this secondary or tenant position, to secure certain *málikána* or cash allowances as a compromise for their lost rights; these allowances the new landlords were bound to continue.

Zamíndárís in Madras.—Turning now to other Provinces, MADRAS is naturally the first to engage our attention. It is only in the North (and exceptionally elsewhere) that Zamíndárs had been recognized by the Mughal ruler[1]. Generally speaking, however, the Northern Zamíndárs were not so much farmers of Revenue, as tributary territorial chiefs; and a notice of them more properly belongs to the next group.

Some great landlords in the North-West Provinces.—In the NORTH-WEST PROVINCES certain Rájás and other territorial magnates were recognized as landlords when, by the exercise of Revenue-farming rights under the Oudh kingdom, they had established a virtual title to such a position; but the villages under them were protected (in many cases) by separate Settlement engagements which fixed their payments to the overlord.

[1] In Madras a few proprietary estates called 'mootah' (*mutthá*) may still be found; they are relics of the attempt to introduce a general Permanent Settlement, under which, in the absence of real Zamíndárs, parcels of land were put up to auction as landlord estates. Most of these artificial landlords failed and disappeared.

The Policy adverse to their recognition. Compromise by means of a 'double tenure' allowance.—There is nothing that calls for remark about these landlords; except to say that in the North-West, their interest was often of such a character as, in the eyes of the responsible officials, did not amount to a full landlord right. Whether this was so or not was indeed a question of fact, but it depended much on the policy of the day; and some severe (and not always discriminating) strictures have been passed on the conclusions adopted. The result was rather to minimize the concession of landlord rights, and to prefer the recognition of what was called in the North-West Revenue language, a *taluqdárí* or 'double' tenure; this meant that the village owners were recognized (and settled with) as the actual proprietors, but that a sort of overlordship or *taluqdárí* interest over them was recognized, and this took the shape of a money allowance paid through the Treasury[1].

The Oudh Taluqdárs.—In Oudh, I have already incidentally mentioned the local chiefs—representatives of the old Hindu kingdoms (of which Oudh anciently was a centre). It is only necessary to add that the landlords who had been called *Taluqdárs* by the Native Government, were not always Rájás, but sometimes bankers and capitalists, grantees and military officers; and in one great estate, at least—that of Balrámpur, the Názim or district officer became *Taluqdár*[2]. Under the first Settlement after the annexation, it was intended to recognize the village estates in preference to the *Taluqdár* landlords; but the (incomplete) work of the Settlement was swept away by the Mutiny; and after the amnesty, the *Taluqdárs* were recognized and settled with—all, that is to say, but a few whose lands were permanently confiscated, in which case the estates were conferred on others[3].

[1] The amount at first varied; but speaking generally, the '*Taluqdárí* allowance' is ten per cent on the Land Revenue.

[2] This was a very remarkable family; the high official who founded it was a man of great genius and power, and soon carved out for his family a fine estate; he was in fact within a short space of becoming a formidable rival for the Ondh throne itself. As to the term *Taluqdár*, see note at p. 41.

[3] In this way the Rájá of Kapúrthálá, a native Prince in the Panjáb, received a grant of a great estate in Oudh as *Taluqdár*.

The *Taluqdárí* estates of Oudh differ from the Bengal Zamíndárís in several ways. The Revenue Settlement is not permanent—only in a few cases, as a special reward for loyal service, was the assessment declared unalterable. Certain rules about the non-division of the estate, and the succession by primogeniture, were applied to the first-class estates. The rights of the village bodies under the landlords were protected by law, as will appear hereafter.

Use of the term Taluqdár elsewhere than in Oudh.—The reader will not have failed to notice that in other provinces besides Oudh, the terms *taluq* and *taluqdár* are made use of. In Bengal, *taluq* often indicates a holding in the second grade, inferior to a full proprietary estate; elsewhere its widespread use—and its present application to a variety of tenures—arose from the fact that the Mughal and Southern Muhammadan Governments had been in the habit of applying the name as a general and conveniently vague indication of 'dependency' on the central authority, in the case of any kind of local chief from whom it accepted tribute, but otherwise left in possession. In the North-West Provinces (apart from the special rights of the Oudh landlords) '*taluqdárí* right' and '*taluqdárí* allowance' refer to the cases already noted, where a limited overlordship has been held to be established, and where that superior right is held to be satisfied by a cash allowance.

The Bombay Khot.—One other class of landlord estate, which arose out of Revenue-farming, may be mentioned; it is peculiar to the Konkan or Upper Coast districts of Bombay. In this Presidency generally, the later system of Revenue-farming, cruel and oppressive as it was, had been carried out chiefly by the agency of the Land-officers (*desmukh, despándyá*, and other titles) without developing landlord estates. But in the coast districts, local farmers of villages (or groups of villages), called *khot*, had grown into such a position—probably owing to some original connexion with the villages of a different kind,—that after much discussion, legislation was had recourse to, and the *Khots* were recognized as virtually landlords; but the old village landholders (*dhárekar*) were protected in their rights[1].

[1] Bombay Act I, of 1880, deals with Khot estates. The holders claimed all the waste and Forest land; but this was disallowed. Only by way of compromise, it was allowed that when State Forests were formed, a certain part of the net proceeds should be paid to the Khot.

(*b*) Landlord Estates arising out of former territorial possessions or Ruling Chiefships.

Estates of this origin, as a class, cannot be sharply severed from those last considered; for though the influence and the opportunities of the Revenue-farmer's position were there referred to as the direct origin of the right in the existing estate, the position of Revenue-farmer itself was often secured by the old territorial connexion which the grantee had as Rájá, Thákur or local chief. Indeed, some of the now permanently settled Bengal landlords (e. g. those in the Chutiyá Nágpur districts) were never Revenue-farmers at all, but simply local chieftains with whom the Mughal ruler had not cared to interfere. In Orissa the few Zamíndárs that exist are of the same character: for in the hill country, the Chiefships were recognized in the superior rank of Tributary States, rather than as Zamíndárís.

The Tributary or Feudatory State and the (subject) Zamíndárí often distinguishable only in degree, not in kind.—And this reminds me to add that when we consider the class of landlords who were once ruling chiefs, it is generally difficult to draw any real line between the subject Zamíndár (who may have a title of rank or be an hereditary nobleman, but still is a subject) and the class of smaller Feudatory States which are not subject. The only practical difference is that in the former a Settlement is made, and the jurisdiction of the Collector runs: in the latter case the tribute is settled by treaty; and the territory is not subject to the British Revenue or other jurisdiction, but only to general political control.

Madras Landlords. 'Polygars.'—The Zamíndárí estates of Madras are properly of the class now under consideration; the holders are mostly local chiefs, who were tributaries rather than Revenue-farmers to the Mughal Government; at any rate the largest estates were so. But there are some estates (*polliam*) of chiefs called *pálegára* or 'polygar,' which more especially represent territorial chiefships, and admirably illustrate the way in which landlord estates arise out of the disruption of a kingdom. The Vijayanagar dynasty of Southern India which rose on the ruins of the earlier Cholá, Cherá and Pándyá kingdoms, flourished for some centuries, and reached a high degree of power and civilization. But it ultimately succumbed[1] in 1565 A.D., leaving a number of its 'barons' (called *náyaka*) who still retained a local rule in their several estates. But their descendants, lacking the control of a powerful head, soon fell into lawless ways, becoming more like freebooters and marauders than hereditary rulers. There were, indeed, several varieties of 'polygar'; some of them were of less dignified origin, having begun as land officers with certain revenue functions, and partly having police duty; they too, finding themselves unchecked, threw off all restraint, and mercilessly rack-rented their lands. Notwithstanding the doubtful claim and position of many such chieftains, they would (as a class) probably have given rise to a not inconsiderable number of landlord estates, under the policy of a permanent Settlement, had not the majority of them become so accustomed to lawless independence that they could not settle down under a new order of things. In most cases they went into armed resistance and open rebellion, whereon they had to be subdued by military force and mostly disappeared. Some of their descendants still receive small cash pensions. The greater and more dignified chiefs of Rámnád, &c. (Southern and Western Polliams) have been confirmed in their estates, and are in all respects like the great Zamíndárí estate-holders of the North.

Central Provinces Zamíndárís.—In the CENTRAL PROVINCES, the 'Zamíndárí' estates had nothing to do with Revenue-farming[2], and wholly belong to the class we are now considering. They are simply the estates of the old Gond chiefs or barons of the former régime. The Rájá being overthrown, his *Khálsa* became the territory directly managed by the conquering Rájás of Nágpur. The old 'baronial' territories being in the hills on

[1] See Hunter's *Brief History*, &c. pp. 129, 130. For details about Polygars see *L. S. B. I.* vol. iii. pp. 15–21, and the Fifth Report, vol. ii. p. 93.

[2] It had, however, been customary to make over tracts of country to managers with a view to extending cultivation and increasing the revenue, and they were called *Zamíndár*. These chiefs managing their own lands were similarly denominated.

the outskirts of the Maráthá domain, were not productive of much Revenue; they were therefore let alone, the chiefs being made to pay a moderate tribute. This position was maintained under the British Government. The estates were subjected to a general kind of Revenue Settlement, which varied in form (and in degree of detail) in different districts, and according to the rank and circumstances of the chief or landlord[1].

Relics of earlier chiefships in other parts.—The province of Ájmer and the Northern part of Bombay (chiefly in the Ahmadábád district) also afford examples of this class of estates, in some rather curious varieties. In both we have remains of the old Hindu quasi-feudal system, under which the Rájá or sovereign held the *khálsa* or central territory, and his chiefs held the outlying portions (p. 121).

In Ájmer the Government has settled the *khálsa* territory with village bodies under the North-West Provinces system. In the rest, the chiefs (*Taluqdárs* as they were called when Ájmer became part of the Mughal Empire) have been recognized as landlords paying a fixed tribute.

Landlord chiefs in Bombay. 'Wántá' estates. Mevási estates.—The Gujarát country affords a still more curious instance of tenures arising from the disruption of old local chiefships. In the wars that followed one after the other (especially after the attempt of the Emperor Aurangzeb to conquer the South, and after the Maráthás rose to power at the close of the seventeenth century) the whole country became a prey to the ravages of rival chiefs. The old Rájás had long disappeared, and their *khálsa* land had become the Revenue-paying lands of the conquering power: but the subordinate chiefs—often holding the wilder or hill country, or at all events

[1] Here again is an instance of what is noted at p. 111. A certain number of these territorial chiefships were admitted to the rank of Feudatory States and so are not subject estates or *Zamíndárís* at all. Otherwise there is little real difference. Among the actual *Zamíndárís*, the smaller ones were settled quite like private estates, all subordinate rights being recorded; the larger were settled in more general terms and without detailed records. Large areas of forest are included in these estates, but under certain special conditions as to their management (see Sec. 124 A of the Land Revenue Act XVIII of 1881).

the outlying territory—were more fortunate. If they submitted, and agreed to hand over a portion of their Revenue to the conqueror's treasury, it was convenient to leave them in local control of their territories, under the usual designation of *Taluqdár*. Sometimes, however, the chiefs were not left in peace. Long before the Maráthá times, some of them were considered to be too powerful, and for this or for some other reason, their estates were sequestrated, and only a fourth or other portion left them. Estates of this origin are still known by the name of *Wántá* or 'portions[1].' In troublous times, moreover, a number of dispossessed chiefs turned into marauders and freebooters, and would then roam the country[2] and contend fiercely for the rents of different villages. Old estates broke up, and new ones were consolidated; while the roving chieftains took to levying black-mail and placing under their protection such groups of villages or stretches of territory as could be held from some fort in the Vindhyan hills. These irregular tenures, never really under the authority of any Central Government, constituted what were called the *Mevásí* estates. It is somewhat surprising to find that such possessions have survived at all; but the descendants of the chiefs to the present day hold some of the lands, under the same designation. In some cases all territorial rights had really passed away; or at any rate they were sufficiently compensated by a cash allowance—still paid to the descendants of the families[3].

[1] And even some of these (reduced) lands were made to pay a quit-rent or *udhaḍ-jama*, as it was called.

[2] This was especially the case in Northern-Central India, because the growth of the British Power, after the defeat of the Mysore Sultans, had gradually brought all but the central (Maráthá) region under its control, and so left only the Dakhan open to be the camping-ground of the rival chiefs, and the refuge for adventurers and freebooters driven out of the other States. All this is admirably explained in Sir A. Lyall's *Rise of the British Dominion in India*, 1893, p. 250 ff.

[3] Such are the *girásiyá* or (political) allowances paid in Bombay to a few families. *Girás* means a 'mouthful' or subsistence. In the Royal demesne, the Rájá's younger sons were often allowed villages as *girásiyá* chiefs, i. e. holders of subsistence grants: but the term came to be applied, in North Bombay, to the lands seized by marauding chiefs who levied blackmail, or accepted the rents of land, as the price of not harrying the village. The allowance noted in the text is regulated by (Bombay) Act VII of 1887.

In conclusion it is worth while to notice, how seldom territorial chiefships gave rise in the Panjáb to landlord estates; and yet both on the frontier and in the interior, a division into smaller or larger local chiefships was once a general feature. Neither the genius of the people nor the policy of the Sikh rulers allowed such a growth. Ranjít Singh had made the chiefs his *jágírdárs*, i.e. he expected military service and the support of effective troops in return for the Revenue he allowed them to take; and often when he thought they were getting too well off on an assignment of the entire Revenue, he would reduce them to be '*chahárami*,' that is allowed them only one-fourth.

(*c*) Estates arising out of Grants in various forms.

We have two main kinds of grant to consider, one where the *land*, either waste or abandoned by former cultivators, was given on a direct title; the other where a grant of some *Revenue privilege* was originally made, and the right to the land has grown out of it, by a process practically the same as that by which the Revenue-farmer became landlord.

Direct grants of waste or abandoned land.—Direct grants of land to be cultivated and owned by the grantee have at all times been made. Sometimes the object was simply to increase the Revenue; the usual plan being to allow a very light assessment (or none at all) for the first years (during which there is much expenditure on clearing the land and little profit) and after that to charge the full rates. Often too, such grants would be made on permanently favourable terms, as a reward for service, or to encourage settlement in a country where some special inducement was necessary.

Proprietary titles by modern grants of waste land.—Under this class will also come those grants of waste land that were made in the earlier periods of British rule and under the first waste land Rules (p. 59): for then the grants were usually of the full proprietary right and possibly free of Revenue charges also. All proprietary estates of this class represent such simple instances of direct title to the land, that further explanation is unnecessary.

Revenue grants or assignments.—But a great many

existing land titles have originated in grants or assignments of Revenue which were never intended to include a landed right at all; these demand a little more consideration.

We have already noticed the system of Revenue assignments in connexion with the question 'what lands are liable to pay revenue?' (p. 52). But here we have to notice the subject from the tenure point of view. Many estates and landholdings, even though the Revenue privilege is now wholly or partly withdrawn, still owe their origin as landed interests to what was originally a Revenue-free grant. It may save a reference backwards, if I here remind the reader that the Mughal system always contemplated two kinds of grants of Revenue. One was in perpetuity or at least for as long as the object of the grant continued in existence; and it was always intended to convey a title to the land as well: it was a *milk* grant, i.e. an out and out gift of soil and Revenue both. The land perhaps already belonged to the pious, learned or decayed noble family, for whose support the Revenue charges were remitted; in that case the land became 'freehold'; or it might be waste and the grantee would himself bring it under cultivation; or at any rate it was so held that he would have no difficulty in becoming the superior owner. Grants of the *milk* class are called *in'ám*; or more specifically, *mu'áfí* grants.

Jágír Estates.—But another large class of grants had nothing to do with the land-right. The Imperial territory was classified into two large divisions (adopted from the Hindu organization). There was the *khálsa*, administered by the Emperor's *Díwán*, *'A'mil*, and other officials, the Revenue of which went to the Treasury: the rest was the *jágír* land (which included the frontier and outlying tracts) of which the Revenue was assigned to certain State offices and military commands, as already described (p. 53).

At first this system was regularly carried out. Free grants were issued only by the highest authority. Even the Governors of Provinces could not make them, except in the most distant Provinces like Kábul and the Dakhan. The assignments were or life; and no more Revenue could be taken than was specified in the grant. But the time came when the decline of the Empire brought relaxed control and chronic impoverishment; and I have already stated (p. 54) how such grants began to be issued irregularly and even established fraudulently. Then it was that all kinds of grants became permanent because they were not surrendered on the death of the grantee. When British rule began, forged titles and pretended grants, backed only by the fact of present possession, were everywhere to be found. Under such circumstances a *jágírdár* or other grantee easily usurped the right to the land as well as the Revenue privilege. And indeed in many cases it would be very natural for him to take it; for he might have cleared, at his own expense, large areas of the waste; he would probably have some private property of his own as a nucleus, and he could easily buy up a great deal more, and so complete a working title to the whole.

When the first British Land Revenue Settlements were made, the Administration was mainly concerned with the question whether, in the numerous cases of claim by grant, the Revenue should continue to be remitted (p. 55): but in Settlements which included an adjustment of landed rights, there was the further question whether the grantee was (or had become) proprietor or not. It might easily be the case, that a *jágírdár* could show himself to have become the owner of an estate, and yet fail to satisfy the authorities that he had a good claim to hold it Revenue-free: Government would then assess the land and not continue any Revenue-free privilege, though the ownership was acknowledged.

In Bombay and Madras such grants became proprietary. —In Bombay it was found that the Maráthá rulers had often imposed a quit-rent (in the lump and without detailed valuation) on these tenures; this device avoided the odium of appearing to resume them. A number of estates having acquired in this way a fixed Revenue payment in the lump, are shown in the returns as *udhaḍ-jama'bandí* lands [1]. The proprietary right was,

[1] In that case the fixed payment is not liable to change at a revision of Settlement.

in these provinces, recognized as conveyed by a Revenue grant; and the lands were said to be 'alienated,' i. e. the State right, both in the soil and to the Revenue, had been parted with (p. 52).

When the inquiry was set on foot, detailed proof of the grant and its terms was generally waived on the grantee consenting to accept a 'summary Settlement'—which equitably determined the local limits of his grant, and imposed a moderate quit-rent or Revenue. If he chose to undergo the ordeal of a full inquest, it might be that he would succeed in establishing a valid grant to be wholly Revenue-free; but he was just as likely to fail, in which case he would get nothing at all.

The *in'ám* holdings in Madras were also settled in a similar way, and if allowed they were confirmed by title-deeds on the basis of a procedure called 'enfranchisement,' which was very like the 'summary Settlement' of Bombay. The grants to be admitted at all must have been in possession for fifty years: and if the claimant chose to prove the absolute freedom from charge and any other incidents, he might do so; otherwise all difficulty could be avoided by undergoing 'enfranchisement,' that is accepting reasonable limits for the estate, and a moderate fixed assessment (in some cases this was allowed to be redeemed)[1].

In Northern India.—In Northern India generally, there was no universal rule that either the *jágírdár*, or the smaller grantee (*mu'áfídár*), was, or had become, proprietor; it depended on the facts and circumstances in each case.

In Bengal.—In Bengal the same remark applies; the rules which were acted on at the Permanent Settlement had nothing to do with the title to the land. All grants before 1765 A. D. (the date of the grant of 'Bengal, Bihár and Orissa' to the Company) were allowed as valid, and all others were more or less set aside: the details cannot here be gone into[2].

Distinction between mu'áfí and jágír not maintained in modern times.—In Northern India, the grants in *mu'áfí* and in *jágír* are now hardly distinguished. Properly speaking, the former indicates the 'pardoning' of the Revenue charges on a man's own land, or on land that had been granted to him; and it does not involve service or keeping troops; the latter means an assignment of the Revenue of a tract of country,

[1] The Madras Commission (since 1858) dealt with 444,500 claims affecting some six and a-half millions of acres (see note at p. 55).
[2] Information will be found in *L. S. B. I.* vol. i. p. 42 ff.

always on condition of service. If any distinction now exists, the *jágír* is usually the larger political grant, and the other is the smaller personal grant. The term *inam* (*in'ám*) is more commonly used in the West and South (where 'alienated lands' are spoken of) and *mu'áfí* in the North. It would be interesting, but it would occupy too much space, to enumerate the local names by which the smaller *in'áms* or free grants are known, and the various purposes for which they were issued: these have been noticed in general terms (p. 53). The regular *jágír* or service grants were more uniform; being in all cases, to pay for service, to support troops, to provide for the administration of frontier tracts, or for the restoration of land that was out of cultivation.

Ghátwálí Tenure.—One variety, however, may be indicated, namely the grants called *ghátwálí*, where a chief was allowed to take the Revenue of a hill or frontier tract on condition of maintaining a police or military force, to keep the peace and prevent raids of robbers on to the plain country below. The curious feature is that the benefit of the grant was distributed through all the grades of the militia forces: the head chief got his (larger) share, and every officer, and every man of the rank and file, had his free holding of land. Landholdings of this kind exist at the present day in several districts.

General observations.

In concluding this notice of the greater landlord estates, a few general observations may be permitted.

Subdivision of large estates on exactly the same principle as villages.—It should be noted that though the divisions of an estate into sections (*tarf, pattí*, &c.) are more characteristic of villages, yet many larger estates, where there is *no rule of primogeniture* to keep them intact in the hands of the eldest heir [1], divide up exactly on the same principles; they break up into *tarf* and *patti* also [2]. Indeed there is really (as I have said) no

[1] Whenever it is thought desirable to keep the higher class of estates from breaking up (e.g. Oudh Taluqdárs, Ahmadábád Taluqdárs and those in A'jmer), regulations are, as far as possible, introduced establishing primogeniture.

[2] In the Ambála district (Panjáb) there are certain *jágír* families—

sharp line to be drawn between the estates that consist of one village (or of shares extending over two or three villages) and the larger class of estate embracing twenty villages or more; and whenever a larger estate is from any cause in a condition of decay, it is likely to dissolve first into a number of co-parcenary village estates.

Tendency of Revenue farming to become landlord right.—It is curious also to notice how invariably Revenue farming tends to develop into a proprietorship of the land itself, whenever, that is, the Revenue farmer is left uncontrolled, the government being weak and inefficient. In Bengal this growth had been so steady and so complete, that though repeated efforts were made to get rid of Zamíndárs, they were always unsuccessful; and at last it was found politic to consolidate the position and regulate it by law, rather than to ignore it. When, however, the Revenue farmer is confined to his duty by effective control, as in the Maráthá States, cruelly as he may oppress the people, he does not become landlord [1].

Territorial position as Ruler tends, in its disruption, to become a local landlord interest. Stages of the process.—Another very remarkable tendency is for the higher castes and members of ruling families not to pass away altogether, in the frequent event of the disruption of the whole kingdom, or of schisms in the family group, but to descend from the ruler's place and cling to fragments of the old territory either as tributaries and Revenue managers of the conquering State, or even without the aid of such recognition. At first they may maintain a position of superiority, not interfering much with the land, and content with the grain-share or rent; but as time goes on, and the suc-

descendants of Sikh horsemen who conquered a number of villages and obtained part of the Revenue or State share without getting any hold over the land itself. This right having become prescriptive, is continued solely in the form of an assignment of a fourth or other share of the Revenue to the families who have no concern with the land in any way. This family 'cash-estate,' if I may so call it, is nevertheless distributed in shares, *patti*, &c., among the branches of the family exactly as if it were a landed estate.

[1] The case of the Central Provinces *málguzárs* is no exception; they were made proprietors by the British Goverment in pursuance of a particular policy and in conformity with a particular Revenue system.

ceeding State assesses the landlord family like any one else, they descend more and more to the rank of peasant proprietors, being reduced perhaps to working the land themselves, only they still retain a family sense of union and a certain feeling of superiority. Their neighbours, all permeated with caste ideas, recognize this too; and long after any tangible privileges or distinctions have passed away, the remote descendants of the once superior families are still distinguished as *mirásidár* or by some such title.

This change to a landlord character facilitated by the old territorial and administrative organization.—The facility with which *estates* (groups of land under one title) have been formed in India, whether Rájás' estates, Chiefs' estates, *jágírs* or village-estates, is due to the ancient customs of territorial sub-division, which really are nothing else than the divisions of the conquered or occupied area allotted to the sections of the original Tribe. Each branch, according to its seniority, has a graded place in the organization, and its chief a certain territory appropriated to him.

Origin of groups of eighty-four, forty-two, and twenty-four villages locally formed.—The Hindu kingdoms were nearly always small; and when we hear of great Emperors like Chandragupta and Asoka, or extensive kingdoms like Vijayanagar, it was that they took the lead as Suzerain over a confederacy of smaller States, each of which was, as regards its internal affairs, practically independent. Not only was the kingdom itself of limited size, but the central feature of its constitution was a further division into 'feudal' territories: the best land for the Rájá, and the rest for the great officers (heads of clans); frontier and wild tracts were held by the chief selected for his special ability as *Senápatí* or Commander of the forces, and by special grantees. As to the principle on which the limits of the royal and other shares were fixed, this depended largely on value, on the natural boundaries and rivers, or on distinctions of hill and plain, jungle-land and alluvial soil, &c. But we can everywhere trace a tendency in occupied country to allot by groups of villages; we find the *chaurassí*[1], or territory of eighty-four villages, and the half of that as the *béalísí*, and so forth. The Land Revenue was taken by the chief, as by the Rájá himself, each on his own tract. The Rájá took no Revenue from the chiefs, or in their estates ; though he could demand benevolences or aids in time of war, and also a fee on succession. The real bond of union was the investiture by the Rájá and the necessity of furnishing the quota of troops for the royal service, and coming in rotation for ceremonial attendance at Court.

Inside the territories thus allotted, there was again the administrative division into villages, groups of villages, and districts[2]. All these divisions naturally provided the basis of so many different sized landed-estates, when the rule was lost. Speaking broadly, the Chief's territory or perhaps the whole 'Ráj' became the *Zamíndárí* ; and the *pargana*, under a lesser chief, became the *Taluqdárí* estate ; smaller lordships survived as single village-estates, or at most as estates consisting of groups of villages.

Section III. Formal Recognition under British Rule of Rights and Interests in Land.

Two principles or foundations for right in land.—The general outcome of the preceding brief investigation of tenures, as far as it has gone, has been to establish two principles, or two bases, on which all rights of ownership in land may be said to rest. I am speaking of rights of independent holding, and not merely of those of a tenant who recognizes that the land is not his, and that he holds under, and pays rent to, some one who is the real owner.

1. There is the right of the individual landholder—probably the most ancient form of right of which we have any proof—the right depending on the occupation of a plot of land, and the

[1] As to the prevalence of this division, there are some interesting details in Beames' *Elliot's Glossary*, s. v. chaurassi.

[2] As we read in Manu of the 'lord of ten villages,' the 'lord of 100 villages' (i. e. district or *pargana*), and so on.

subsequent clearing of it from the trees and perhaps dense jungle that covered it.

2. There is also another kind of right—that which originates in conquest, grant, or natural superiority; it frequently appears as, in reality, the shadow of what was once a territorial or ruling position. Right in land of this kind, is spoken of as the 'inheritance right'; and it resides either in one landlord, or (commonly) in a joint body having lordship over a village or a larger estate, as the case may be. It is the existence of the right of one kind or of the other, which has made the holding, or the village, or the great estate (as the case may be), the natural unit with which the Land Revenue administration deals, and which it assesses in one sum.

Necessity for consolidating and defining rights.—In order, however, that not only should the right person be made liable for the Revenue, but that the right person should be secured in a just enjoyment of the remaining profits of the estate or holding, it was necessary to place the title to land on a secure basis (pp. 64, 5).

Historical retrospect regarding right in land.—It is necessary for us to take a very brief glance backward at the history of landed right in India, in order to explain how the customary bases of rights and interests in land were dealt with under our Anglo-Indian legislation.

Right by first clearing alone known to ancient times.—Whatever may be the real date of the LAWS OF MANU—whether it be as early as 500 B.C., or whether the form in which the work now stands is as late as the fifth century A.D., we have no earlier record, as far as I am aware, of prevailing ideas on the subject of right in land; and it is remarkable that Manu says '*land is his who first cleared away the jungle, as the deer is his who first brought it down.*' Throughout the whole work not the slightest trace can be found of the superior ownership by 'hereditary' right (*mirásí* as the Moslems called it), still less of anything resembling a holding in common.

The right by first clearing, is still essentially the basis of the *raiyatwári* holding; and of that of the humbler classes, now become tenants under landlords, who claim to be privileged or hereditary tenants because their ancestors first cleared the land [1]. The superior right by grant, conquest, colonization, &c., now summarized in a number of vernacular designations, all signifying a right by inheritance, is a subsequent or at least an independent growth.

Superior right as territorial ruler not as landlord, originally claimed by royal and noble houses. Conquering rulers at a later date claim to own all the land. Manner in which this claim was dealt with by the British Government.— In early times therefore, we are not surprised to find the old Rájás and chiefs content with the territorial rule; no sign of any claim as landlord or direct owner of all land, can be traced. It is equally certain that in the days of Mughal rule, private right in land was recognized [2]. But in later days of continual conquest and change of dynasty, and especially when the great deputies of the Mughal Empire, in Oudh, Bengal, Hyderabad, &c., set up as independent sovereigns, and when Maráthá chiefs conquered territories all over Central and Western India, the claim was extended beyond the old right to the State-share, and the right to the waste; it was made to embrace the entire area. In 1765, it was certainly a *fait accompli*, that the ruler of every State in India was the superior landlord of every acre. The rulers of Native States make the same claim to this day, as applying to all land which they have not granted Revenue-free. When the British Crown succeeded, this right passed, on all principles of law, to it. But our first Governors, e. g. Lord Cornwallis, whether or not they were aware that it was not truly an ancient right but the result of later conquests and usurpations, at once perceived that it was impolitic; and while the first Regulations were not always very exact or consistent in their language, it may safely be stated that the British Govern-

[1] The landlord group may also have 'founded' the village, and so unite the claims of the first clearer with that of the superiority of caste and family as overlord: but their founding was not work with their own hands; hence in a subordinate grade, the tenant who has actually dug up the fields, also bases his right to consideration—and that more directly—on the 'first clearing' (*búta shigáfi*, and other phrases).

[2] For some authorities on this point see *L. S. B. I.* vol. i. p. 226 ff.

ment accepted the right only so far as it afforded a convenient basis or standpoint from which to declare and define private rights.

Private right as landlord recognized. To all Zamindárs, Taluqdárs and grantees expressly.—Our first dealings being with the great Zamíndárs of Bengal, it was there first declared by law, on grounds of policy as well as on a recognition of facts, that those landholders were full owners as far as might be, consistently with the just rights and interests of other parties. In Madras the same declaration was made to the Zamíndárs and other 'actual proprietors.' It was afterwards made to the Taluqdárs of Oudh; and generally either by law, or by the grant of title deeds, to all sorts of proprietary grantees and estate holders, in all parts of India.

And to village landlord bodies. And to heads of villages in the Central Provinces.—It was also made, by direct inference from the language of Regulation VII of 1822, and by the terms of the records of Settlement, in favour of all the landlord-villages of Upper India, where these were independent and not in turn subject to a superior landlord. It was similarly declared in the case of the *málguzárs* of villages in the Central Provinces. In all these cases the right was essentially a proprietary right; as full as possible, i. e. including all rights (not inconsistent with law and custom) of disposal by gift or will, sale or mortgage, but always limited by the right of the tenants, 'subproprietors' or others, entitled to share in the benefits of the land.

Government is then no longer the universal landlord.—In the face of declarations affecting so large a portion of the cultivated and occupied area in British India, it is impossible to go on speaking of the (British) Government as universal landlord (see p. 49).

Modified declaration of Right in individual holdings in the Raiyatwárí Provinces. Reason for not defining the raiyat as formally 'proprietor.'—But in the case of the individual holdings in *raiyatwárí* villages in Bombay and Madras, the case was different. Whatever may be the real theory of origin, these individual holdings represented, at the time, a somewhat weak form of right, because the cultivators had long been so harassed with Revenue burdens and local exactions, that their hereditary attachment to the land had to contend with the fear of being unable to hold it without starving; instead, therefore, of welcoming any legal fixation of their right which would have secured it, but also bound them to be responsible for the Revenue whether they cultivated or not[1], they desired to have a freedom to hold if they could, but to let go if their means failed. It was in Madras that this was first (though slowly and reluctantly) recognized: and it became an *essential feature in the raiyatwárí system* that the landholder might always (by giving notice at a proper time) relinquish any field or definite part of his holding, and thus escape the Revenue liability. In this state of things, it has been usual to avoid calling the 'raiyat' owner of his land *eo nomine*. In Bombay he is called the 'occupant,' and his right as such—hereditable, transferable and liable only to the Revenue assessment and to any other payment that may be due to some superior—is defined by law[2]. In Madras there is no general Land Revenue Act, and there is no legislative definition of the raiyat's tenure; but the question has been discussed in the Law Courts, and practically the right is the same as that defined by the Bombay Code: in common language, it is a right which is theoretically, rather than practically, distinguished from a proprietary right[3]. In other provinces, where individual right is the customary tenure, a similar plan has been followed; the Burma Land Law and the Assam Land Regulation define the 'landholder's' right, without calling it ownership.

In these cases therefore (but not otherwise) it is open to any one to argue, that there is a residuary or ultimate proprietary right remaining to the State: and that is why, in the Provinces where land is held by grantees (*in'ámdár*), these lands (in which there may be a proprietorship in set terms) are said to be 'alienated.'

[1] It will be remembered that in every landlord village or estate, *because* the owner has a secure title, he has also the responsibility for the (moderate) Revenue; he cannot get rid of the liability by not cultivating, or by throwing up the estate.

[2] And where there is some kind of overlord right, as in Bombay, the holder of it is called the superior occupant and the other the inferior.

[3] See *L. S. B. I.* vol. iii. p. 128 ff.

Section IV. Sub-proprietary Rights in Land.

Superimposition of landed rights and interests one on another.—It has been already remarked that Indian tenures are largely the result of changes and growths, the fruit of the wars and incursions, tribal and local conquests or usurpations, and of the rise and fall of ruling families: the right by conquest or 'birthright' supervenes upon the right by 'first-clearing.'

There was no systematic or political attempt, at any time, to remodel land-tenures formally; but claims grew—one set of rights was superimposed upon another. If the right in land may be assumed to have been, at first, a simple thing—a tribal group settling down in one place, forming villages, and allotting separate family holdings; in any case circumstances soon altered: a scion of the ruling chief's family got a grant of the State share in a village, and his descendants, in the course of years, were found to have appropriated (as a joint body) the whole; the Governor created a Revenue farm, or granted a *Jágír*, and a new overlord right was established; and as changes went on, the lords or noble families that first had the dominant position, in their turn fell into the second rank under a new lord who arose over them. All the former right-holders then strove to maintain some recognition of their lost position. When once a landlordship is established, the landlord himself feels bound to recognize the older claims in some way; and he allows subsidiary tenures, which are often permanent rights. Sometimes also he creates similar but new rights to provide for some part of his estate which he cannot manage himself. In any case, *various grades of right are found to co-exist*; some being very nearly proprietary, others being more and more distinctly what we should call tenant-rights. The people distinguish between 'resident' and 'non-resident' cultivators, or one kind of landlord and another; but such customary distinctions have not the effect of a definition in an Act of the Legislature.

Security of legal position to the person at the head, necessitates definition of the rights below him. Difficulty of the task.—When once the necessity of defining the legal position of *the* proprietor or other head primarily interested and responsible for the estate or holding, arose, it followed that, however defective our first perceptions of the question may have been, a legal security for all other secondary and tertiary interests was necessary also. And this was difficult, because the incidental and often haphazard character of the changes—the fact that all were due to gradual processes of growth and decline—resulted in this, that the different interests appeared in all shades and degrees of strength or weakness: *here*, was a landlord who had obliterated all rights but those of bare tenancy, below him: *there*, was a landlord whose position was so doubtful that it was a debated question whether he should be recognized at all: *here*, were strong tenants still proudly remembering that their forefathers were once great *jágírdárs* or even territorial chiefs; *there*, were others whose only anxiety was not to be bound down to the land, but be allowed to give it up directly they felt unable to pay the rent.

General plan of the legal recognition of various interests.—Broadly speaking, the way in which the matter has been dealt with is this. In *raiyatwárí* countries, the holdings were generally simple; the mass of holders farmed the land themselves, or employed tenants about whose contract position there could be no doubt: at most there would be some overlord whose rights were confined to a rentcharge with no power of ejecting the actual occupants. Therefore the Revenue law simply regarded the actual occupant of the holding, and dealt with him. But in all landlord estates, there might be many varieties. In some there might be a Rájá or other magnate who was clearly the landlord or actual proprietor of a considerable tract of country. In other cases, there would be a general claim of some magnate over a tract of country, but his direct interest was so limited that it was regarded as only an overlord interest, and was called a *taluqdárí* right, represented by the receipt of a cash payment calculated at a certain percentage of the State Revenue. In others, there might be a number of landlord villages—all of some conquering or colonizing tribe, with nobody over them, and with none but tenant rights under them. In others, again, there might be (1) the immediate landlord, or 'actual proprietor' (individual or co-sharing body); (2) certain persons who on various grounds were called 'sub-proprietor' or 'inferior proprietor'[1]; (3) old tenants, who were 'hereditary' (*maurúsí*) or 'occupancy' tenants; and (4) tenants at will.

And of the classes (3) and (4), be it remembered, that in a large number of cases they do not represent any *contract* tenancy, but merely a grade of interest which has gradually fallen, in the course of generations, to an indefinite subordinate position under a superior; we of the West can only designate it by the term 'tenant,' but our Legislators (in Bengal, e. g.) have often preferred the vaguer native term *raiyat* (p. 74 *note*). The distinction, however, may be easy to draw on paper; but when many years have passed away, an ignorant peasantry does not easily retain proof, if it even has a tradition as to its origin, as to which class it really belongs to. In all these cases it becomes a question of no small difficulty how to define and to characterize the different grades of right.

In consequence of these gradations of right, it is possible to represent landed interests in India in a kind of scale or table. Regarding the Government with its Revenue rights, and its occasional direct ownership of land, and as the fountain head of rights, as the first degree in the scale, and the actual cultivator, wherever he has any permanent right to occupation, as the last degree, it may be there is one, or two, or more, interests intervening. Thus:—

One Interest.	Two Interests.	Three Interests.	Four Interests.	
1. The Government is sole proprietor. (Khás estates, alluvial islands, &c. in Bengal).	1. Government. 2. The *raiyat* or 'occupant' with a defined title (not a tenant). (As in Madras, Bombay, Berár, &c.).	1. Government. 2. A landlord. (*Zamíndár*, *Taluqdár* or a joint-village body regarded as a whole.) 3. The actual cultivating holders, individual co-sharers, &c.	1. Government. 2. Landlord. 3. Sub-proprietors, or 'tenure holders.' 4. The *raiyat* or actual cultivator.	1. Government. 2. An overlord or superior landlord. 3. An actual proprietor or landlord (usually a village body). 4. The actual cultivating holders, individual co-sharers, &c.

[1] Or, in Bengal, 'tenure holder' is the technical term.

(1) Sub-proprietary rights.—Practically all the intermediate degrees are recognized either (1) as 'sub-proprietary' or (2) as rights of privileged (or 'occupancy') tenancy. Wherever the right is sub-proprietary, the holder is owner in full as regards his particular holding; he has, however, no part in the whole estate or its profits, nor a voice in its management. There may be locally incidental conditions and features of his tenure which vary. When the right is not so strong, it is admitted in the tenant class, but with occupancy rights in several degrees, as we shall presently note.

Local names and customary forms of tenures not proprietary.—As regards the local names representing these tenures, they are very various [1]. Sometimes the names remind us that the rights are the vestiges of an older, different position; more frequently they indicate the purpose for which the tenure is created; and still more frequently merely indicate the nature of the privilege, or the features of the tenure as regards its extent, duration, and the payment to be made. I can only here give a few selected examples of subordinate rights or tenures.

Subordinate rights in Bengal. 'Tenures' and their privileges.—In Bengal no grade of such right has been formally defined as 'sub-proprietary' in the sense above noted. But the 'tenure' of the Bengal Tenancy Law is practically of this class. Many permanent interests (heritable and transferable and held at a fixed payment and often called *taluq*, sometimes *jot*), though not entitled to independent proprietary recognition, have all along been considered entitled to protection [2]; and the

[1] It may be noted that languages retaining primitive elements have always an abundant distinction of terms for separate concrete ideas, and very few for abstract or generalized conceptions. In the Indian vernaculars, we have, e. g., a vast number of names for personal ornaments; each kind of ring, bracelet, &c. has a different name, solely owing to some difference in the form of decoration or workmanship. And so with land terms; besides local varieties of dialect giving different names for the same thing, there are also a vast variety of terms indicating not so much differences in the character and origin of the tenure, as distinctions of rates of payment and other features of mere detail. This invests the subject, complex enough in itself, with a further air of mystery which is really factitious.

[2] This will appear better from the account of the Permanent Settlement which follows.

Tenancy Act of 1885 has put the matter on a clear and definite basis as far as possible. The Act does not indeed define what a 'tenure' is, as it was found impossible to do so; but there is a presumption that the larger subordinate holdings (exceeding 100 *bighás*) are of this favoured class; and it is for the landlord to rebut it. The practical privileges of fixity of holding and unenhanceable rent-payment are secured.

As an example of such rights I can only allude to the *patní* or *patní-taluq*—in this case a modern right created by the Zamíndár. When a landlord found that he was not fond of land management, or that some one else would manage better than himself, or still oftener, when a portion of his estate needed development and he had not the means or the inclination to undertake the work personally, he would create a *patní*; this in effect consisted in giving a *permanent* managing lease for a part of the estate: the contract specifies a fixed sum representing a rough rental value (either estimated by bargain or as the total of existing rents) of the tract, and the lessee or *patnídár* binds himself to pay that amount, he of course being allowed all rights of management, breaking up the waste, enhancing rents, &c. In time the *patnídár* will probably have a large profit, and then in his turn he may divest himself of the toil of direct management or (oftener perhaps to share the work of developing a waste tract) he will create (by 'sub-infeudation' as it is called) a *patní* of his *patní*, and there be a *dar-patnídár*: and this process may again be repeated to a *sihdarpatnídár*, and even further. *Patní* tenures only began to exist in the present century; and it is in 1819 that we first find a Regulation dealing with them.

There are many other 'tenures' of which the feature often is that they are perpetual (*istimrári*) and at fixed rates (*muqarrari*); often both.

Sub-proprietors in village estates.—In Northern India (and the Central Provinces) the common form of secondary right occurs in (landlord) village-estates where the present proprietary body has grown up over an earlier group; and here and there a group of fields is held by a person or family whose right is so strong as to be recognized as proprietary *quâ* the particular plot; i. e. the holder pays no rent, but only the Government Revenue and cesses; and of course there is no question of ejectment or enhancement of rent. But the holder does not otherwise share in the general rights and profits of the village, nor has he as a rule any voice in its management. In the Central Provinces, owing to the more or less artificial character of the grantee 'proprietor' of the villages, a number of persons were allowed to hold their lands on these terms, and were here called *málik-qabza*, or *málik-maqbúza* (lit. owner of the plot in possession). The same term is made use of in some cases of the kind in the Panjáb [1].

In Oudh, where the Taluqdár's estates are overlordships over a number of villages, (often landlord village-communities), it was occasionally the case that an entire village had preserved its rights almost intact; it had been granted the management of its own entire area, and that permanently, on condition of making a certain rent-payment to the Taluqdár. The same condition of relative freedom was found to be maintained by villages in other districts also—in those cases where a territorial magnate had acquired the general landlordship. In such cases a 'sub-settlement' (*mufassal* Settlement of Regulation VII and the earlier Revenue Reports) would be made; this would fix the amount to be paid by the village to the landlord, as the Settlement itself fixed the payment by the landlord to the Government. Thus all questions of enhancement, and of change of any kind—at any rate for the term of Settlement—were obviated. For Oudh, a special Act (XXVI of 1866) prescribed the conditions under which such a privileged position was conceded. In the majority of cases the village body had not secured such a position as a whole; but the Settlement Records would still recognize sub-proprietary rights in individual plots, e. g. the grove planted by a family [2]; the old *sír* or special holding of a family in its former landlord position; the field granted by the Rájá

[1] The persons who acquired such rights were sometimes former Revenue assignees who had improved the land and planted gardens, or had other claims to consideration. In some cases they were former proprietors who had retained possession of these lands, while the rest had been seized on and cultivated by some powerful family which had supplanted them. In other cases they were old cultivators who, though not descended from the same ancestor as the proprietary body, had been called in to bear the burden of the Revenue in old days, and had never paid any rent over and above their share of the Revenue and cesses. In the Gujrát district (Panjáb), at the time of the first Settlement, ten per cent. of the total cultivated area was held by such persons.

[2] In Oudh the attachment to groves is a marked feature. See *L. S. B. I.* vol. ii. p. 243.

for the support of a household whose head had been slain in war; and many others.

Such sub-proprietors not easily distinguished from privileged tenants.—In these cases of right surviving in individual plots, it was not always easy to draw the line between the sub-proprietor' (or 'plot proprietor') and the 'tenant' privileged with occupancy rights. Doubtless, some persons who in one district would have been recorded in the first, were in other places recorded in the second, category. But practically the distinction was not of much consequence, when once a Tenancy Law made it clear what the rights of the class of 'occupancy tenant' were, and it appeared that those of the highest or most privileged grade, in practice differed but slightly from those enjoyed by a 'plot proprietor.'

The rights classed above as (2) tenancy rights, are so important and numerous as to demand a separate section for their consideration.

Section V. Tenants.

Tenant Law.—Every province has its own law regulating the subject of Tenancy. The precise circumstances of the land, and the history of the growth and decay of rights, are naturally different in each; and so the legal provisions need to be different, although a generally similar policy will be found to pervade them all[1]. I may therefore indicate the general principles on which the protection of the rights of the Tenant class has been effected.

Features of tenancy common to all provinces.—The

[1] The Bengal Tenancy Act is VIII of 1885 (in some districts the older (Bengal) Act X of 1859 is still in force, and some districts have special laws applicable to them alone); North-West Provinces XII of 1881; Oudh XXII of 1886; Central Provinces IX of 1883; Panjáb XVI of 1887. In Bombay the few provisions requisite are contained in the Revenue Code (Bombay Act V of 1879), chap. vii. In Madras there is a Rent Recovery Act (Madras) VIII of 1865, which provides all that is necessary for the protection of tenants in general. The other provinces have no need for special Tenant Laws; but such provisions as are necessary have been inserted in the Land law; e. g. in Assam Regulation I of 1886.

remarks already made about the way in which landlord and overlord rights grew up, over, and often at the expense of, other rights in land, are illustrated not only by the existence of grades of proprietors; they are far more widely illustrated by features of Tenancy in landlord estates. As time goes on, and the dominant grade of landlord confirms its position, the whole of the original landholders tend more and more to sink, along with the landlord's own located tenants and followers, into one undistinguishable mass of non-proprietary cultivators.

A certain number, no doubt, of the strongest rights succeed in asserting themselves: the landlord has probably found it worth while to conciliate some of the old cultivating body by granting a lease on terms which really attest a former superior position; or otherwise, there is distinct proof forthcoming, that a tenant has all along paid a fixed rent, or a rent which only represents a share of the Revenue burden imposed by the ruler, and that he has a permanent tenure: or there may be no sort of doubt that a tenant is an ex-proprietor. Thus there are always some tenants whose case can be more or less easily explained; and every Tenancy Act will be found to make provision for what I may call the 'natural' class of protected tenants;—those in whose favour definite facts can be asserted and proved.

But all rights are not thus definable. Where the landlord class is itself non-agriculturist, and where its origin can be largely traced to a position as Revenue farmer or grantee, or where it represents the fallen families descended from once ruling houses, we may be quite certain that a proportion of the tenants represents the old landholding class who originally had tangible if not legally secured rights in the soil, but has now sunk to the tenant level. And even where the tenants have, at some more or less distant time, been located by the present landowners, or their ancestors, still they may have been located on special terms or under circumstances which give a claim to a privileged position. Yet in all these cases definite proof of the circumstances and the origin of the tenancy may be difficult to obtain.

Difficulty of distinguishing classes of tenants.—As a matter of fact, in the North-West Provinces and Bengal, it was found excessively difficult to draw a line between tenants who represented the old landholders and those whose position was really due to contract. In the course of time rights become obscured, especially when possessed by an improvident and ignorant class: and even in the case of those later tenants who really were located by the landlords, and had nothing special about their origin, there was always this (not unimportant) feature in their favour, that they had been called in at a time when no one thought of evicting tenants because they were far too valuable;—tenants were in demand, not land.

The twelve years' rule.—Consequently in Bengal and the North-West Provinces, where this difficulty was especially felt, the Legislature in 1859 (Act X of 1859) cut the Gordian knot by enacting a general rule, that where any tenant had continuously held the same land for twelve years, he should be regarded in all cases as an 'occupancy tenant[1].' The later laws have not departed from this principle: but where the tenant has also certain special circumstances in his favour (over and above a mere twelve years' possession) he may be recognized as not only occupancy tenant, but as having superior privileges, and perhaps be called by a distinctive name.

Tenant right controversy. The twelve years' rule not always needed.—The general rule was not, however, accepted without a somewhat fierce discussion. As for years past the practical power of the landlord (under the influence of Western ideas of landlord and tenant) had been continually growing, it was naturally to be expected that some authorities would

[1] This rule is retained *totidem verbis* in the existing North-West Provinces Act. Elsewhere, it has been so far modified that holding of any land in the same village (the individual fields may have changed) gives the right: this prevented a landlord's defeating the intention of the law, by making a tenant give up his fields and take others in their place before twelve years were out. On the other hand, this evasion could not be practised with the large class who had already held (themselves or their ancestors) for more than twelve years: and this simple fact was comparatively easy to prove where it would have been difficult to establish more specific incidents of a former position; hence the North-West Provinces were satisfied to retain the narrower rule.

be in favour of the landlord, and others inclined to back the tenant. The Legislature had the difficult task of holding an even balance between the two extremes. In certain provinces the existence of what I have called the natural classes of privileged tenant was so clear, and the circumstances of the landholding interests were such, that there was no occasion for any further general provision. In the Panjáb and Oudh the 'twelve years' rule' does not apply. In the Central Provinces it is only applied in a special and limited way. In these three provinces, however, as I have already mentioned, a number of privileged landholders were recognized as 'sub-proprietor' or proprietors of their holdings. And when this class was provided for, there was less difficulty in restricting the occupancy tenant-right without recourse to any broad artificial rule[1].

The position of tenants never defined before the days of British rule.—It should always be borne in mind that there was

[1] These provinces, however, did not escape the usual troubles of divided opinion and discussion. In the Central Provinces, it was at first directed that Act X of 1859 should be in force; but under such conditional circumstances, that tenants who would have no claim except in virtue of the twelve years' rule, were put down in the records as 'condititional occupancy tenants'—meaning that their position would depend on the ultimate retention or rejection of Act X of 1859. But other tenants were regarded as so well entitled to protection that they were recorded as 'absolute occupancy tenants'—whose rights were in any case to be respected. It is with regard to these latter that the controversy arose, chiefly on the point who was to bear all the burden of proof. As it has turned out, a modified tenant law was passed (Act IX of 1883, amended in 1889) and the position of all tenants has now been adjusted. In the Panjáb, Act X of 1859 was never in force, but the first Land Revenue Settlement Records were framed on the North-West Provinces models under which the prescribed forms of register contained columns adapted to the (there legal) distinction between twelve years' tenants and others: hence, in several Settlements, the recording officials showed a number of tenants in the 'occupancy' columns by reason only of a certain number of years' holding. This, legally speaking, was not tenable. Thereon arose a long controversy about revising the entries: a compromise was ultimately effected: and the existing law allows, as one class of occupancy tenant (the rest being the natural classes), those whose names were maintained in the Records of the first Settlements (as revised). In Oudh, also, a controversy arose as to whether the provisions of the Sub-Settlement Act (determining the case of sub-proprietors), and the Tenant law provisions regarding the natural classes of privileged tenants, were really sufficient; and whether justice did not require a more extended recognition of occupancy rights. The question was settled by the revised Tenant Law of 1886, which did not enlarge the occupancy class, but gave certain privileges to *all* tenants in the matter of a seven years' term without further enhancement or ejectment.

one feature in agricultural life which made it possible to raise an argument, when it came to be a question of securing any class of tenant by giving occupancy rights. It is simply impossible to point to any time when there was any *law* that a tenant (whether under a person practically the landlord, or under the State regarded as landlord) could not be ejected, or have his rent raised so that he could not afford to keep the land; there was, no doubt, a certain popular feeling on the subject; notably that the descendant of the first clearer of the land, or one who had helped to found a village, had a permanent hereditary right: on the other hand, there was also the principle that might was right;—in the case of every despotic ruler and every land officer under the pressure of stringent demands from the Treasury Department. Whatever might result from the conflict of these two sentiments, there was this important corrective, that landlords never wanted to turn out a cultivator as long as he would work diligently—they were only too eager to keep him. Consequently, the right to 'eject a tenant' was not a matter that occurred to any one to consider; while as to 'enhancement,' if an over-zealous Collector or a greedy contractor made his demands so high that the cultivator was forced to take flight, he would readily find land to cultivate, and protection for his person, on a neighbouring estate. This must naturally have secured the cultivating class, independently of the sentiment of hereditary right above mentioned. Fortunately, also, this hereditary sentiment made the old tenants strongly attached to their lands; and they would strain every nerve to pay a high rental rather than abandon the ancestral holding. Naturally then (as without cultivators there is no Revenue), all tolerably good rulers encouraged and protected, if they somewhat highly rented, their old resident tenants [1].

Natural distinction of Tenants.—Speaking of the 'natural' classes of occupancy tenant, there is always a well-known distinction between settled or 'resident' tenants (many of whom had held their own lands—as they once were—from the first) and casual or 'non-resident' tenants. And there was a not inconsiderable class represented by *ex-proprietors*—people once themselves landlords, but who in the changes and chances of time had lost their position, but could still point to the fields

[1] Though the temptation to put a heavy rent on tenants who would rather pay than lose their dearly cherished ancestral lands was often yielded to, still oriental rulers and officials were extremely skilful at squeezing and letting go in time. They always knew how to stop before driving a good tenant to despair. Only a few villainous tyrants and land-contractors, who had a temporary chance, acted otherwise. Unfortunately, however, the tenant class came to acquiesce in a state of things that kept them in a perpetual state of bondage; living near the edge of necessity, on a bare sufficiency with no surplus, they had to work for their lives, and could have but small enjoyment in them.

that were their *sír* or special holding (p. 79 *note*). And similarly there were ex-grantees (*mu'áfídár, jágírdár*) who had claims to consideration of various kinds.

Remarks on 'ex-proprietary' tenants.—It is important to remark on this, that everywhere in India, the loss of a proprietary (or superior) position on land, and the descent from a landlord, or a co-sharing right to a tenant position, does not always, or even frequently, imply the actual loss of cultivating possession of at least a part of the land. To this day if an unthrifty village co-sharer gets into the toils of the money-lender, and first mortgages his land, and then submits to the foreclosure of the mortgage, he does not leave the land; he cultivates as before; only that now he is tenant of the purchaser, and has to pay rent in cash or kind. And the same thing always happened when a purchaser or other person obtaining the landlordship by grant or aggression, was not of the agriculturist class. He could not till the fields himself; and unless (exceptionally) he wanted a better class of tenant, he would retain the *quondam* owner or holder of the fields: very often a new overlord would be unable to get other tenants, or circumstances compelled him to conciliate the existing holders.

Tenants who took part in the founding of a village.—Another natural class of tenants with rights, is represented either by the old dependants, servants, or humbler relations, of the village founder, who came with him to the work of establishing cultivation, and helped him in sinking the wells and building the cottages (see also p. 73): these might never pretend to equality with the landlord family, but they were hereditary tenants in virtue of having shared (or wholly performed) the labour of digging out the tree-stumps and clearing the jungle. And where, in after times, Revenue burdens pressed, and tenants were called in to till additional land, and thus make up the total sum, their invaluable assistance was secured by the offer of many privileges: among others they paid nothing but their share of the Revenue, as, indeed, might be expected [1]. If after-

[1] It may be added that custom very generally recognized that old resident tenants had a right to plant trees, sink wells, or make improvements

days of prosperity enabled the landlord family to exact some small percentage payment or fee, it did not alter the nature of the case. All tenants of this kind at the commencement of British rule, represented a class that must have been established for many years if not for generations, and they were clearly entitled to legal protection.

It will now be advisable to enumerate the 'natural' and 'artificial[1]' classes of tenants contemplated by the different Laws.

Features of the Bengal Tenant Law of 1885.—In BENGAL, I must confine my remarks to Act VIII of 1885 (which, however, applies to all the oldest and most wealthy permanently settled districts). We find first of all a distinction (already alluded to) as to *raiyats* (for they are still so classed) who are 'tenure' holders (p. 130).

'Raiyats at fixed rates' are the highest class of tenant, and have practically very much the same privileges as the 'tenure-holder.' The rent cannot be enhanced, and the holder cannot be ejected except for some express breach of the conditions of the tenancy. All other privileged tenants are grouped together as 'occupancy tenants'; and the term includes (*a*) all persons who acquired the position under Act X of 1859 or other law, or by custom, prior to the passing of the Act of 1885. (*b*) persons called 'settled raiyats,' i.e. persons who have held land (not necessarily the same fields) continuously for twelve years, in the same village. The twelve years may be before the Act or after it, or part before and part after (so occupancy rights can go on growing).

All other tenants are 'tenants at will' and have only the benefit of some general protective provisions, which, however, are valuable. Some rules also are enacted regarding 'sub-tenants,' i. e. tenants of a tenant.

The North-West Provinces Act XII of 1881.—In the NORTH-WEST PROVINCES, there are, in the permanently settled districts (Benares division), certain tenants at fixed rates just as in Bengal[2].

on the land, at their own option; which was not the case with non-resident tenants.

[1] By the use of this term it is not intended to imply any objection or disparagement, but merely to distinguish the cases in which the position recognized by the Acts depends on a general rule of twelve years' occupation (or whatever it is), which makes it unnecessary to go into details as to former position. In the class of rights which I call natural, the tenant has to prove the specific facts which give him his claim; but ordinarily, in those cases, he would be able to do so without much difficulty.

[2] In fact these areas were the petty proprietary holdings which were not thought sufficiently important to be treated as separately settled estates, and yet the Revenue farmers themselves had felt it necessary to recognize them as not liable to alteration of payment, still less to ejectment.

All other tenants if they have held the same land continuously for twelve years, are occupancy tenants (no other proof of special circumstances is called for). Tenants of less standing are 'tenants at will.'

Among the occupancy tenants, one feature may give rise to a distinction; if they are also 'ex-proprietary tenants' (p. 138), that is are in possession of land that was once their *sír* or home farm, they have a privilege of a reduced rent, which is twenty-five per cent. lower than that of ordinary tenants.

The Central Provinces Act (IX of 1883).—In the CENTRAL PROVINCES, the more or less artificial creation of *málguzár* proprietors over the villages (p. 93) resulted in a wide scheme of protection for the rights of the old cultivating class. So that we have here the somewhat (to Western eyes) unique spectacle of a country where the landlords have no control over a large part of their tenantry, either as regards raising their rents, or ejecting them from their holdings. Ejectment can only be effected by decree of Court on very special grounds provided by law; and enhancement is impossible because the rent is fixed by the Settlement Officer when settling the Land Revenue; in other words, the rents can be only enhanced when a new Settlement occurs. The Act mentions specifically, 'absolute occupancy tenants,' these being a class recognized at the first Settlements as having an exceptionally strong position[1]. They cannot be ejected (practically) for any cause whatever; and their (privileged) rent must be fixed for the term of Settlement. The next class is of the ordinary 'occupancy tenant.' In certain districts all tenants (except as mentioned below) are tenants of this class. In the others, only those tenants belong to it, who had completed an occupancy of twelve years on the same land, before the Act came into force. Rights of this class are not (except in certain districts) growing up as in the North-West Provinces and Bengal. The occupancy right does not arise (in either case) on the proprietor's home farm[2] nor when a tenancy was created with an express contract that occupancy rights were not to be acquired. Tenants holding land as a *remuneration for village service*, are specially recognized in the Act. Ordinary (non-occupancy) tenants are also protected in various ways, and practically their rent also is settled by the Land Revenue Settlement operations.

The Panjáb Law (Act XVI of 1887).—The PANJÁB affords

[1] See note, p. 136. I cannot give the details as to what tenants were so recorded, but I may mention generally that it was always on the ground of specific features of the tenure independently of any general artificial rule: the class included old hereditary cultivators, those who had once a proprietary character, those who had expended capital, those who had taken part in the founding of the village, &c. (see *L. S. B. I.* vol. ii. p. 481 ff.).

[2] And in these Provinces it consequently became necessary to make some rather elaborate distinctions as to what is, and what is not, *sír* land: the improvement of the definition in the Tenancy and Land Acts was one of the chief objects of the amending law in 1889. Details will be found in *L. S. B. I.* vol. ii. p. 490.

an instance of a province where the occupancy right is almost purely one of natural growth; indeed it would be entirely so, but for the necessity of recognizing those who, whether strictly entitled or not, did get recognized at the early Settlements, and whom it would be unjust now to disturb.

In the Northern districts up to the frontier, where so many of the villages represent an occupation by conquest, there are many old landholders reduced to the position of tenants; or the new-comers brought camp-followers and dependants who helped them in their first settlement; and in many other parts there are numerous tenants who claim to have cleared their land and to have assisted at the founding of the estate. And the Panjáb villages had all of them to undergo a long-protracted struggle to maintain themselves against heavy Revenue assessments. The marks of this struggle are not only seen in the large number of villages in which the old share system has been upset, but also in the fact that tenants were called in to aid in keeping up the cultivation, without which the Revenue payment would have been impossible. These conditions are indicated by the fact that the tenants paid neither rent nor service; the utmost that was customary was some small overlord fee. 'Ordinarily,' says Sir J. B. Lyall, 'rent did not go to the proprietors in those days; the Government or the *jágírdár* took the real rent direct from the cultivators by grain division or crop appraisement' (pp. 35–6); and the proprietors got only 'proprietary dues.' These consisted of some money payment, or a small share in the grain (one seer in forty or so). The reason why so many tenants are shown as paying cash rents in the present day, is, that they really only pay (through the proprietor) the amount of the Government Revenue (which is always in cash), to which perhaps some small addition (usually calculated at so many *anas* per rupee of Revenue) is made.

The Act therefore (after allowing for cases already admitted under the earlier law and practice) simply defines as occupancy tenants, those who for two generations have paid neither rent nor service to the proprietor but only the share of the Land Revenue; those who are ex-proprietors; those who had settled along with the founder and aided in the first clearing; and those who had been Revenue assignees and had remained in possession of the land. A general power is, however, given to any one to prove any special facts other than these, which in the judgement of a Court of Justice would give a claim (on general principles of law and equity). These naturally entitled classes (secs. 5, 6, and 8, of the Act) are given different degrees of privilege, according to the general custom and sentiment on the subject; and the limit of rent-payment in each case is expressed in terms of its being so many anas per rupee of Government Land Revenue[1].

[1] Thus the 'sec. 5 tenant' cannot be asked to pay a rent which exceeds two to six *anas* (according to the kind of tenant) per rupee of Land Revenue plus rates and cesses. Those under sec. 6 and sec. 8 pay twelve *anas* in the rupee as the limit.

Features of the occupancy privilege.—The foregoing paragraphs having given some idea of the kind or class of tenants who are protected by law, a few words will be necessary to explain in what the protection consists. In general, there is a limit to the *enhancement of rent*; both as to the amount, and as to the period which must elapse before a rent once enhanced can be enhanced again. And there are conditions protecting the tenant from *ejectment.* Either provision would be useless without the other. It would be no use to provide that a tenant could not be ejected, if at the same time rent could be demanded at such a figure as to leave him no profit: nor would it be useful to restrict the enhancement, if at any moment the tenant could receive notice to give up the land.

Each Act must be referred to for details, but the following will serve as an indication of the manner in which both subjects are dealt with.

Enhancement.—There are exceptional cases (as already suggested) in which enhancement of the existing rent cannot be had at all; ordinarily, enhancement (in the absence of express agreement in due form) can only be had by decree of Court on proof of certain circumstances. The rules of enhancement are adapted, in each case, to local requirements and customs. Either the *grounds* of enhancement or the *amount* of it may be restricted according to the grade of privilege which the tenant holds.

The occupancy right heritable.—The occupancy right is declared heritable; and the rule of succession is laid down [1].

And conditionally alienable.—The tenant right is declared alienable, but subject to the consent of the landlord, or to other conditions; e. g. the landlord usually has a right of preemption.

Law of distraint for rent. Notice to quit. Rent instalments and remissions.—The Acts also extend a certain protection to all kinds of tenants, especially with a view to preventing harsh dealing in the matter of distraint for arrears of rent; and

[1] e. g., in the Panjáb, it passes in the direct male line and only to collaterals in certain circumstances of joint tenure. Widows are allowed a life-interest.

allowing the exemption of cattle, tools, and seed-grain, in the event of a sale. Various provisions may be found tending to obviate rack-renting; and always to secure the tenant having due notice to quit, and that at a proper season. The payment of rents by instalments—after the harvest is reaped, and the means of payment are secured—is a matter of great importance to the tenant: it is accordingly regulated by law, and it is often provided that if the Government has extended grace to the landlord in the matter of Revenue payment in a bad year, the benefit shall also be passed on to the tenant.

Right to make improvements.—An important protection is also given by laying down rules as to who has the right to make improvements on the land; and by determining how far enhancement may follow on such works, and how far a tenant's expenditure of capital is to be protected for his own benefit.

Rent-Courts. — Some of the Acts provide that questions between landlord and tenant, as of rent, ejectment, and other matters shall be decided by Revenue Officers sitting as Revenue Courts: but this matter will be more conveniently noticed in a later chapter on Revenue Business and Procedure.

Tenancy in Raiyatwárí provinces.—Hitherto the general purport of my remarks has been to describe the relations of landlords to their tenants in provinces where the prevalent form of landholding is that of a landlord, or at least of co-sharing village bodies regarded collectively as landlord. We have still to take notice of the case of Tenancy in Raiyatwárí countries. In both MADRAS and BOMBAY as well as BERÁR and ASSAM, there are some landlord-estates; but in general, there has been but little artificial growth of a landlord or middleman class, and consequently there has not been the same scope for the general growth of a variety of grades of interest—resulting in different kinds of 'sub-proprietor,' 'tenant at fixed rates,' 'ex-proprietary tenant,' and the like.

Even the ordinary raiyat or 'occupant' may have on his land tenants that he has himself contracted with, or old cultivators who were there before him. In Madras, the Zamíndárs, polygars and other landlords, of course have villages of 'tenants' under them; and in Bombay the *Khots* of the Konkan, the Taluqdárs of Ahmadábád, the *máliki* and *kasbáti* holders, the *In'ám* holders, and all varieties of overlord-tenure generally, represent cases where virtually there is a landlord who has tenants under him. But the law is remarkably simple, and can be summarized in a few lines [1].

Provisions of the Madras Law.—In *Madras*, the grant of landlord rights was not intended to affect any other rights; Regulation IV of 1822 expressly declared this. The only provisions relating to tenants (and they apply always—not only to *Zamíndárí* tenants) are contained in Rent Recovery Act (Madras) VIII of 1865.

Every tenant is allowed to have whatever privilege he can prove. There is no artificial rule about rate of rent or imit of enhancement. Every landlord must give his tenant a written lease (*pattá*) and can require a counterpart or an agreement; and no one will be permitted to sue in Court for rent, unless he has given such a lease, or at least he has tendered one and it has been refused[2]; or the issue of it has been waived by consent. No extra charge whatever above the rent specified in the lease, is allowed. Where there is a dispute about the rate of rent, the Act lays down the principle of decision. All contracts, expressed or implied, are to be enforced. If there is no contract, the rate is to be that of the Government assessment in certain cases, or failing that, the customary rate of the locality, or a rate ascertained by comparison with lands of similar 'description and quality' in the neighbourhood. If the parties are not satisfied, either of them may claim that the rent be discharged, in kind, according to the *váram* or old customary division between the State (or landlord) and the cultivator: and failing ruch a rate, the Collector may fix an equitable rent, having due regard to whether the landlord has improved the land, or whether its productive power has increased otherwise than by the agency, or at the expense, of the raiyat. There are certain provisions as to the right of the superior to apply to the Collector to enhance the rent, when the superior has effected an improvement, or when the Government has done so and has raised the superior's revenue accordingly.

[1] As a matter of fact, these superior tenures are so much the result of survival of old territorial or ruling claims, that the *raiyats* on the estates have remained very much on the same terms towards the overlord, as the ordinary raiyats on the survey-tenure have towards Government, only perhaps paying somewhat higher rates.

[2] And if either the landlord refuses to grant, or the tenant to receive, there may be a 'summary suit' before the Collector, so that a *pattá* may be directed to issue.

Tenants in general can only be ejected pursuant to a decree of Court on the merits : or in certain specific cases stated (wrongful refusal to accept a *pattá* (sec. 10), or being in arrear (sec. 41) when no distraint can be had). Tenants can always relinquish their land at the end of the year.

The Act gives detailed instructions as to the recovery of rent in arrear, by distraint and sale of crops and moveable property ; or by sale of the tenant's interest in the land—if by 'usage of the country' he has a saleable interest. On failure of these methods, there may be a warrant of ejectment from the land; and in a case of wilful withholding of payment, or 'fraudulent conduct in order to evade payment,' there may be an order of imprisonment, up to a limit specified, which varies according to the amount of the arrear.

The Bombay Law.—In BOMBAY the tenancy in general is succinctly dealt with in chap. vii of the Revenue Code (Bombay Act V of 1879). In the case of the estates of *Khots*, there are provisions about the tenants in the special Act I of 1880 ; in this case the old resident tenants are protected like occupancy tenants elsewhere. In all cases under the ordinary law, either the holder of the land is the direct 'occupant' paying Revenue to Government, or he is an 'inferior occupant' paying rent to some 'superior' (of whatever kind).

In the latter case, if there is an agreement, its terms alone determine the features, rentcharges, and liabilities of the tenancy; if not, then the usage of the locality is referred to; and failing that, what is just and fair under the circumstances. So with the question of duration; if it cannot be proved when the tenancy began, or that there was any agreement as to how long it is to last, or any usage in this respect, then the duration of the tenancy is presumed to be co-extensive with that of the superior occupancy. But nothing in the Code affects the right of the superior to enhance rent, or to evict for non-payment of rent, when he has a right to do so by agreement, or by usage, or otherwise.

An annual tenancy can be terminated on either side by a notice of three months before the end of the cultivating season (which may in the absence of other dates, be presumed to close on March 31).

Superior holders may invoke the assistance of the Collector for the recovery of rent (or Revenue in alienated lands) due to them : this assistance consists in applying the same measures as might be taken to recover the Government Land Revenue. And in alienated lands, the grantee may have a 'commission' issued to him, in certain cases, to exercise certain powers for the recovery of the Revenue and otherwise.

CHAPTER VIII.

THE LAND REVENUE SETTLEMENTS.

Section I. Of Settlements in General.

WE have now brought to a close our chapter on Land Tenures; we have only taken a flying view of the leading features of this wide subject, but still we have to some extent understood how it has come to pass that there are either (1) landlord estates, (2) village estates, or (3) separate holdings, to be dealt with by the Land Revenue administration. We have also to some extent realized how often it is that when some landlord interest appears and invites recognition above that of the immediate cultivator's holding we are left in doubt as to whether the apparent or claimant landlord is really the one who ought to occupy the position; and if he *is* recognized as entitled to a principal share of the profits, we have generally to take steps to secure other interests in the soil, which often have been borne down in the process by which the landlord grew up.

Consequently in all modern Settlements which deal with any kind of landlord estate, whether held by a great landlord or by a village-body owning only a few hundred acres, there is always something more to do than merely assessing the Revenue, and calling on some 'actual proprietor' to sign an agreement to pay it. There is sure to be a need for making a record (which has a certain public authority) of the rights and interests of persons other than the individual or the body who actually 'holds the Settlement' (as the phrase is). In some cases the record not only gives the local (and the legal) designation of the tenure, but also fixes the amount which the inferior is to pay to the superior; in other cases it is enough to describe the holder as a tenant of a certain privileged class; and then the Tenancy or Rent Law of the province will declare what limits are placed on the enhancement of rent and on the liability to eviction.

The Settlements of Western and Southern India which are able to deal directly with separate holdings, have no such double task; they simply record the person or family actually in possession of the field or holding, and determine the proper assessment which that person is called on to pay—an assessment which solely depends on the character and value of the land, and has nothing to do with the class of holder, or his relation to any one else.

And just as the nature of the tenures determines the form of Settlement and what rights have to be recorded, so also it affects the method of assessment. According as we have to determine a lump sum which a landlord, or landlord - village collectively, has to pay, or a separate charge for each holding or unit of survey, so different methods of valuation have been found convenient. Hence it happens that several kinds of Settlement have been locally developed. But primarily, the question which kind of Settlement should be adopted, has always depended on what kind of tenure is *generally* prevalent.

Requisites of a Settlement. Demarcation and Survey. Statistical data of agricultural conditions. Valuation of land and assessment.—Before we briefly consider each variety of Settlement by itself, we will take notice of some features which all varieties of modern Revenue-Settlement have in common. In the first place they must start with (1) a complete *survey* of the land, involving a preliminary *demarcation* of the necessary *boundary lines*; because without that, neither can there be an exact account of the culturable land, and the extent of each kind of soil which requires a different rate of assessment; nor can there be any correct record of the rights of all parties, landlord, co-sharer, sub-proprietor, occupancy-tenant, or whatever they are, in case the system requires a record of rights. And (2) in any case there must be a correct list of the revenue payers and their holdings, and a schedule accounting for every field and plot of land in each village. These are supplemented by other statistical tables and returns, which illustrate the past history and present state of the village. Lastly (3) there must be a *valuation of the land*, the ascertainment of revenue rates, the totalling up and adjusting of them to give the sum payable by the estate or holding; in some cases subsidiary proceedings as to the distribution of this total among co-sharers, and the adjustment of tenant rents, are necessary.

It is true that one form of Settlement was made without a survey, without a detailed valuation of land, and without (at first) any record of rights, and without any Statistical information: but the experiment—forced on us, as it was thought, by the necessities of the time—has never been repeated. No other Settlement dispenses with the general requirements above stated.

Three main kinds of Settlement.—As a matter of fact, there have been three main kinds of Settlement, following (as will have been already anticipated) the fact noted, that we have always to deal either with landlord estates, with village estates (or *mahâls*), or with separate holdings. Each kind has one or two local varieties, depending partly on peculiarities of the agricultural conditions, and partly on the features and incidents of the prevailing tenure of land in the Province. I will at once give a comprehensive list of the varieties, which will afterwards be briefly explained and described.

1. Settlement for single estates under ONE LANDLORD.—
Usually large estates, but not always (p. 122).

Varieties:—

(1) Settlement with Zamíndárs, i.e. Permanent Settlement of Bengal and North Madras.

(2) Settlement (Temporary) in Bengal of estates and districts not subject to the Permanent Settlement.

(3) With Taluqdárs in Oudh.

2. Settlement for estates of proprietary bodies, usually VILLAGE COMMUNITIES. (These are sometimes called *mauzawár*, or more correctly *mahálwár* Settlements).

Varieties:—

(1) Settlement of the North-West Provinces (including Oudh for villages that are not under Taluqdárs)
(2) Settlement of the Central Provinces (called the *Málguzárí* Settlement).
(3) Settlement of the Panjáb.

3. Settlement for INDIVIDUAL OCCUPANCIES **or holdings.**

Varieties:—

(1) The Raiyatwárí system of Madras.
(2) The Raiyatwárí system of Bombay and Berár.
(3) Special systems (in principle *raiyatwárí*, but not officially so called) of Burma, Assam, and Coorg.

Permanent and temporary Settlements.—But as a matter of fact there is another classification which is more conveniently adopted, and which has reference to the fact that certain Settlements are 'Permanent,' i.e. were made once and for all, at rates never to be increased or diminished; and others are made so that the assessment should be revised after a certain period of years: in Revenue language they are 'Temporary Settlements.'

And the Permanent Settlement which was the first system to be tried, was the only one made without any demarcation of boundaries, without any survey of land, without any attempt to value the land in detail or to record rights (see p. 148).

Consequently it is more convenient to consider the Settlements with reference to this distinction. It will be found that the Settlements with great landlords in Bengal and Madras come under the first: and those with Oudh Taluqdárs under the second: all the Settlement systems of the North-West Provinces, Central Provinces, Panjáb, &c., as well as the systems called *raiyatwárí*, are all 'Temporary' and have the demarcation, survey, and record of rights carried out; although it may be here repeated that the *raiyatwári* Settlement does not profess to inquire into (or determine) rights, as the other Settlements do.

Special kinds of estates in provinces which as a whole belong to a certain class.—It may be necessary to explain that where a Settlement is as a whole Temporary, or on one or other of the systems above tabulated, there may be particular estates dealt with differently[1].

For example in the North-West Provinces, though, in general, village Settlements are made, certain landlords have been settled with as Zamíndárs for an entire estate of many villages. A still better example is Bombay. Here the great bulk of land is held in simple occupancy holdings (in *raiyatwári* villages). But there are a few landlord villages (called *narwá* and *bhágdárí*), some *Taluqdárí* and other landlord estates, and the (practically landlord) estates of Khots[2]. In these cases there may be special arrangements made for each estate, and often special Acts regulating the matter. So too, in any province, particular estates may be allowed, as a reward or favour, a permanent assessment. This is the case with a few of the Taluqdár's estates in Oudh, and with certain chiefs in Ájmer.

The Middleman.—In writings relating to the Land Settlement we so often find reference to the 'middleman' proprietor, that it may be well to call attention to the general features which this term indicates. The distinction between Settlements of Classes 1 and 2, on the one hand, and those of Class 3 on the other (p. 148), has arisen, really, out of the fact that in the two former, there is some kind of middleman between the actual cultivator and the Government; and this middleman is, more or less fully, the proprietor and 'holds the Settlement.' In the latter there is ordinarily no such person; the occupant pays direct to the State, the Revenue assessed on the particular fields he holds. In Bengal, the Zamíndár had obtained such a firm position as middleman, that (as we have seen) it was considered not only just, but a matter of State policy, to give

[1] Independently of the fact that a part of the province may be entirely settled under another system. Thus the Benares division of the North-West Provinces is permanently settled (p. 161) because it was, at the time, part of Bengal. So there are parts of Madras permanently settled because, at the time, a system similar to that of Bengal was applied (before the general *raiyatwári* system was ordered).

[2] In Bombay, for example, the returns show (approximately) thirty million *acres* held *raiyatwári*, about two and a-half millions held by overlords (relics of territorial chiefship); rather more than two and a-half millions held by *Khots* and other (Revenue-farmer) landlords.

him a secure position; and this experience, backed by the 'landlord and tenant' ideas natural to English gentlemen of the eighteenth century, produced the feeling that there ought always to be some one person to whom the State should look for its Land Revenue, and to whom the State should in return give landlord rights to enable him to meet that responsibility and keep himself and his tenants in well-being. At a later time, the circumstances of the provinces in the North-West suggested an extension of this idea to the village bodies; but there the middleman is really rather an ideal being; he is represented by the jointly responsible body as a whole, of which the individual co-sharer is only a member, and does not deal directly with the Government. It is then the nature of the middleman proprietor and not the size or the extent of the estate, that distinguishes Class 1 from Class 2. And when the necessities of Madras caused Sir T. Munro so strongly to urge the new departure—the *raiyatwári* method with no middleman (Class 3), there were not wanting, at the time, many people who foreboded ill of the scheme. It then became the distinctive mark of the two systems, that in the one the Government would never deal with a middleman, while in the other it would never deal with any one else.

And this distinction led to a special feature which distinguishes landlord Settlements (of all kinds) from *raiyatwárí*. In the former, the landlord has a legal proprietary title (p. 125), but also a fixed responsibility. He is bound to the land and to the payment of the Revenue on it for the whole term of Settlement; he cannot at his option relinquish the estate. Hence in early Settlements especially, he always signed an agreement for the term; and there is in fact a contract between him and the State. In *raiyatwári* Settlements, the occupant is held by no lease and signs no agreement. He cannot indeed have the Revenue rate assessed on his holding raised during the period of Settlement; but he can at the close of any year and before the next cultivating season begins, relinquish his holding (or any recognized part of it) and so free himself from responsibility whenever he pleases.

Discussions as to the merits of systems.—In past days it was often the custom to enter into discussions as to the relative merits of the several systems. In reality nothing can be more fruitless. Each system in actual working has developed, and been found to need improvement in detail; but it entirely depends on the nature of the tenures whether one system should be adopted or another. The only question that can reasonably arise is where there is some doubt as to the real character of the prevailing tenures. If, for example, we have a district where, as a rule, there are no great estates, only villages, then it may be a question of fact whether, in a sufficient number of villages, there exists a landlord class, who can be conveniently dealt with as one, jointly responsible, body, or not; if there is, the village system will answer; if not, it is very likely to fail. In the Jhánsí district (North-West Provinces), for example, in the light of modern knowledge it is perfectly clear that the villages were really *raiyatwárí*, as in the Central Provinces; yet the attempt was made to apply the North-West Provinces joint-village system, and the result was failure. So some authorities believed that in the Dakhan, the traces of old families or brotherhoods of co-sharers in many villages, would warrant the village system being there applied; but it was decided that these traces were too shadowy, and the present condition too generally *raiyatwárí*, to make any village system workable. In the North-West Provinces, again, it was not unfrequently a matter of doubt whether there was any great landlord really in such a position as to be entitled to a Settlement, or whether the village bodies under him were not entitled to be independently dealt with. All these were questions of fact; and owing to the obscurity of the indications, and the inclination of the authorities towards the (aristocratic) landlord view, or the democratic (supporting the peasant or village class), so the application of one system or the other was determined; and the decision may be criticized. But to compare the systems themselves—to say the one is intrinsically better or worse than another, is absurd.

Duration of Temporary Settlements.—Let me also here save future explanation by saying that though a term of twenty to thirty years has been very often adopted for 'Temporary' Settlements, it has never been thought wise to fix this or any other period, by law. The duration of each District Settlement is determined with reference to the whole of a variety of circumstances, by the Executive Government, in each case. A fairly long term is obviously requisite in order to enable profits to be fully realized and the benefit of improvements and extensions of cultivation to be enjoyed; but too long a term subjects the State to great loss in case a rapid development (e.g.) of canal and railway lines is taking place, or there is a material alteration in the prices of produce. Dates have also to be fixed so that periods may expire one after the other, and not all at once; for in the latter case the Settlement Staff could not cope with so much work at once, and many districts would have to wait a long time before the revision could commence.

Initiation and close of Settlement work.—In general, it may be convenient to note, a Settlement (or a revision of Settlement) is set in operation by an order notified in the official *Gazette* of the Province; and this will state whether all the work of a Settlement is to be done, or only an Assessment, or a new Record of Rights (if the system requires it). A Settlement is said to be complete, either when a certain notification to that effect is issued, or when a certain sanction to the work is given, as the Land Revenue Act of the Province may prescribe.

The initial notification usually contains orders appointing the Settlement Officer (p. 30) and his Assistants, and if necessary investing them with powers under the Act.

Cesses and Local Rates.—Before leaving the subject of Settlements in general, it may be convenient to explain that though all the older 'cesses,' in the sense of illegal exactions and informal additions imposed as a means of increasing the Land Revenue, have been for ever abolished, there are certain rates over and above the Land Revenue, which are justly levied according to law, for local purposes. The Land Revenue is Imperial Revenue; a portion of it indeed goes to meet the general expenditure of each province; but there are purely local charges, such as District roads, Village schools, and District Public Works, the payment of village officers, and the like, which are justly chargeable solely on the local proprietors; hence in the Revenue Records may often be found the old division—in a new sense—of 'Revenue and Cesses.' There are local Acts in each Province, under the Permanent Settlement as well as the others, for the levy of such cesses.

Here reference may be made to Bengal Act IX of 1880 (Cess for Roads and Public Works); Acts III of 1878 and IX of 1889 for the North-West Provinces; Act X of 1878 for the Central Provinces; Act XX of 1883 for the Panjáb; Act II of 1880 (or III of 1889) for Burma, &c.

Famine Insurance.—One of the local rates imposed was to enable Government better to meet the expense of famines when they occur. This gave rise to the popular notion of a 'Famine Insurance Fund,' which it is supposed Government should husband —perhaps investing the annual proceeds of the rate like a trust fund—and spend it only on Famine Works. But such was never intended, nor would it benefit the public. The rate was provided to be spent on any object or any kind of work that tended to place the Government in a better position generally, to meet calamity when it occurs. One of these objects has been the reduction of the public debt; but there are many others; and it is a matter of good financial policy and convenience in each year, to determine what shall be done; any expenditure usually incurred, may be suspended or diverted to other purposes that are more pressing, without any mis-application or illegal disposition of the rate.

Section II. Landlord Settlements.

The Permanent Settlement.

As applied to Bengal.—The celebrated Permanent (Zamíndárí) Settlement of Bengal was made (in 1789–1793) under the auspices of Lord Cornwallis. It does not apply to the whole of Bengal even as it was in 1793; there were certain tracts to which for special reasons it was not adapted. There were also parts of districts which at the time were waste, and were only occupied long after the Settlement was concluded. It also does not apply to those districts which became British territory at a date subsequent to 1793. In these a different and Temporary system (p. 149) prevails.

The Permanent Settlement, as a system, has but little to recommend it either for study or imitation; but historically it is both interesting and important. On its arrangements depend the titles to the majority of the estates in the most populous and wealthy of the three Presidences. Its principles have also largely affected other systems; and under it was gained the experience which enabled the Government to organize the work of district administration in other provinces. The

Collector and his Assistants (p. 23) as first appointed in Bengal, became the model for the District government of Madras and then of Bombay, and indeed of all the provinces that were afterwards annexed.

Sketch of administration previous to 1789.—The Bengal system acquired its peculiar features partly under the difficulties and circumstances of the situation (p. 46), partly under the influence of a deliberate policy. When the province of 'Bengal, Bihár and Orissa'[1] was granted to the East India Company in 1765, at first no attempt was made to conduct the administration by British officers. A well-meant but ineffective supervision of the existing native official staff was provided for; but in truth the old Imperial system was so broken down under the corrupt and feeble Government which marked the days of the decline of the Mughal Empire, that in 1772 the British Government felt forced to undertake the direct administration of the Civil and Revenue departments, and the District Supervisors were accordingly made Collectors[2]. Very shortly afterwards Warren Hastings was appointed Governor-General, and he at once set on foot measures for transforming the Company's 'merchants' and 'writers' into District Officers.

Attempts to improve the Land Revenue Administration.—At first the staff was small, and various plans were tried, now of leaving 'Collectors' in each of the (then very large) districts (or *zillas*), now of locating them in groups at certain important centres to form Revenue Councils or Committees. No new Land Revenue Settlement was made, but the attempt was made to secure a better control of the collections by a system

[1] 'Orissa' then meant only the country corresponding (roughly) to the Midnapore district. The *Díwání* of Bengal, &c., granted by the Imperial rescript, meant the Civil and Revenue administration which was conducted by the *Díwán*, as the Criminal and Military (*nizámat*) was by the *Názim*.

[2] I take this opportunity to correct an error, which was inadvertently left at page 393 of vol. i. of my *Lana Systems of British India*. Lord Clive finally left India in 1767, so that the sentence as it stands is unintelligible. It ought to have been 'a proclamation assuming the administration was issued on the 18th of May, 1772; and although Clive had previously (in May 1766) taken his seat as *Díwán* or Minister of State at the annual assembly for fixing the Revenue, held near Murshidábád, our direct Revenue control did not begin till 1772.'

of five years' leases (or farms) of the Revenue of Districts or parts of Districts. Under these arrangements, many of the existing Zamíndárs were set aside; for even if they accepted a farm it would be solely as a matter of contract and without reference to their existing rights or privileges as Zamíndár. The plan failed and some injustice was done; it was soon found necessary to restore the Zamíndárs, and leases were accordingly issued to them, year by year, for the sums roughly estimated to be due with reference to the old accounts. The state of affairs soon attracted the notice of the Home authorities[1]. A 'Regulating Act' was passed in 1773; and this gave certain powers of local legislation, and established the general framework of local Government. But it did not attempt any change as regards the Revenue. The amelioration of this important branch of Administration was first directly attempted by the Act of 1784 (24 George III. cap. 57). This Act led to the re-establishment of the Zamíndárs, and directed a full ascertainment of their proper 'jurisdictions, rights, and privileges.' To carry this direction into effect, Lord Cornwallis came out in 1786, as Governor-General and Governor of Bengal[2]. He had with him Mr. John Shore (afterwards Sir John Shore and Lord Teignmouth), an officer who, in spite of the immense difficulties of the task, had thoroughly mastered the Land Revenue question and knew more about it than any one else at the time. Various and prolonged inquiries were made, chiefly as to the Revenue accounts and the sums that the Zamíndárís ought to yield, and also regarding the history of the Zamíndárs themselves[3].

[1] See on this subject Sir A. Lyall's *Rise of the British Dominion in India*,' p. 145 ff.

[2] The Act did not in any way direct a 'Permanent Settlement' to be made, as is sometimes supposed. It only sought to put an end to injustice to the Zamíndárs and to repeated changes—now farms, now annual leases—in the Revenue management. It was not till six years afterwards that the Settlement was proposed to be made permanent.

[3] To this period belong the celebrated minutes of Mr. Shore (1788–89). These are to be found in the *Fifth Report on the affairs of the East India Company* presented to the House of Commons in 1812 and since reprinted. One valuable minute, which is not therein included, is given in Harington's *Analysis*, vol. iii.

The Decennial Settlement.—Rules were at first drawn up for making a Settlement for ten years with the Zamíndárs. These rules were concerned chiefly with prescribing the principles on which the Collector should fix the lump sum for which each estate in Bengal, Bihár and Orissa [1], respectively, was to be responsible.

Consolidation of the position of the Zamíndárs.—But it was considered insufficient merely to agree with the Zamíndárs for the amounts to be paid; it was determined that they must be recognized in a secure legal position as landlords with a heritable and transferable estate, in order that they might be able steadily to realize the Revenue, and enjoy a substantial profit. Government, however, reserved to itself the right to enforce punctual payment of the Revenue according to the customary instalments, and to sell the estate at once if there was any default in payment. In conferring a landlord title on the Zamíndárs, and in recognizing their rights, not according to a theoretical view (however correct) of their original position, but according to existing facts after a century's growth and development, Lord Cornwallis was in entire accord with Mr. Shore and most of the Civil Servants. But the Governor-General further considered that it was not only desirable to confer the landlord title, but also to declare that the assessment fixed for ten years should be invariable or 'permanent.' In this he was opposed by Mr. Shore; and, indeed, the arguments of that able adviser were never really answered [2].

This Settlement was not, however, made (as is sometimes supposed) in a hurry or without much consideration. Except as regards the declaration of permanency,—for Lord Cornwallis might have let the original ten years' lease run out before further action,—

[1] See note as to Old Orissa at p. 155.

[2] I cannot go into the question, which is explained more fully in *L. S. B. I.* vol. i. p. 405. Lord Cornwallis based his reply on some mistaken views —especially the idea that the *raiyats'* rent was in general dependent on agreement with the landlord. He, however, probably thought that in some way the permanence of the assessment was bound up with the security of the title to the estate. This was a very natural feeling, but it is not really logical; a man's title to his estate is no more compromised by a revision of his Revenue-payment than the property of a capitalist is by a change in the Income Tax.

the whole proceeding was marked by careful inquiry and much thought. The Governor-General deliberated about it from 1786 till 1790; and when a report on the proposal was made to the Home authorities, the Court of Directors again kept the question in suspense for two years, and only in 1792 did they give their somewhat reluctant consent.

In March, 1793, a proclamation (embodied in the Statute Book as Regulation I of 1793) was issued, confirming the Zamíndárs, and declaring the Settlement 'permanent.' Regulation VIII, of the same year, republished (with amendments) the Settlement rules above alluded to.

Reasons for the absence of survey and other details.—The reasons why this Settlement was made without any survey or record of rights, were various. A survey at this time would have been, under any circumstances, a matter of the greatest difficulty; but it was also thought that any attempt to pry into the interior concerns of the estates would be prejudicial to the interests of the new landlords and excite their distrust. As for the raiyats, it was hoped that the landlords would come to terms with them, and that their rights would be sufficiently protected. It was not, moreover, intended to make any detailed valuation of lands according to different classes of soil and their productive value, so that the want of detailed maps and area schedules would not be felt. There were already official lists of the estates, and of the villages and *parganas* which each included.

The Assessment. Adjustments needed owing to change of system.—Holt Mackenzie afterwards described the Permanent Settlement of Bengal as a 'loose bargain, . . . intended rather to tax the individual than the land.' All that could be done was to determine a lump sum for each estate with reference to the rules above spoken of. The old Revenue *Kánúngos* (pp. 25, 6) had still their official records of past collections (as well as their local experience) to aid the Collector in finding out the proper sums; and the totals were revised, in the rough, with reference to general considerations of the prosperity of the estate, the value of its waste area, and its capacity for extension. But there were important adjustments to be made; in former times various deductions had been allowed from the total Revenue payable. For example, as the landlords managed and paid the police, certain lands (called *thánádárí* lands) were freed from reckoning, in order that their revenues might cover these charges; there were also certain allowances for pensions for which the Zamíndár was made responsible. In future, as Government would relieve the landlord of such public charges, the police lands were resumed and assessed, and the allowance for pensions was struck off. So too, as the landlord was to have all the balance after paying the Revenue—a balance which would continually augment as the estate developed, and land and produce rose in value—there would be no need to make the old provision of *nánkár* or land (held free of charge) for the Zamíndár's subsistence. On the other hand, all cesses and extras on the Land Revenue (p. 39) were abolished; and as the landlord would no longer be liable to such additional demands, he in turn was strictly prohibited. under penalty, from levying such charges on the landholders. who now became legally his 'tenants.'

The sáír or sáyer.—It should be mentioned that in the old days, the Land Revenue (increased periodically by the *abwáb* or cesses) was called the *Mál.* But besides this the Zamíndár had to account for the *siwái*, or 'other heads' of Revenue—which consisted of the *sáír* (or in Bengal writing *sáyer*) profits from waste land, grass, fruits, fisheries, and various tolls, duties and rates, on roads, ferries, markets and bazaars, and on pilgrimages, marriages, &c., not to speak of excise duties. The Settlement dealt with these (1) by handing over to the landlords (as part of their own profit) all the legitimate *sáyer*; (2) by abolishing altogether the tolls on pilgrims, marriages and other items of the kind which were oppressive or unjust (in some cases compensation was allowed for the abolition). (3) The excise duties and such road and ferry tolls as were proper to be maintained, were separated entirely from the Land Revenue, and taken under the direct management of the Collectors.

Protection of other rights in land. Separation of taluqs.—I have already indicated (p. 106) that the Government extended the privileges of the landlord-title and permanent assessment not only to the old-established district farmers and to local chiefs and heads of districts who had held something of the same position as regards the Revenue of their districts, but also to smaller landholders in districts where there were no Zamíndárs. But with a view to the protection of rights in other cases, the Regulation directed the Collectors to consider the case of smaller estates called *taluqs* (p. 107), and to *separate* from the Zamíndárís (under certain rules) such of them as appeared to be entitled to be dealt with as independent estates. The advantages of separation were very great, because not only would the now independent landlord be freed from all possibility of unauthorized exaction, but his tenure would be secure from being lost (as it might have been had it remained subordinate to a Zamíndár) in case the Zamíndár's estate should be sold for arrears of Revenue. Some of the *taluqdárs* were clearly entitled to this 'independence' as having existed before the Zamíndárí; but the rules recognized several other reasons. One of them, for instance, provided that a dependent *taluqdár* who could prove that he had been subjected to unlawful exactions by his Zamíndár, might be separately settled with. As a matter of fact, an immense number of small estates were allowed to become separate; and in this way a considerable number of older interests were protected. Indeed, petitions kept coming in so fast, that it had to be provided that after a certain date no further applications for separation would be received[1].

'Resumed' lands.—Another cause of many separate landlord estates has also been incidentally noticed before, in another connexion (pp. 55, 118). When the whole question of rights to hold land Revenue free was gone into, and the invalidity of a large number of the claims appeared, it followed that the claims were disallowed, and the land was 'resumed' as the technical phrase was, i. e. assessed to Land Revenue (the question of the ownership

[1] It is largely owing to this fact, but also to the naturally limited size of holdings in Bihár and some of the Eastern districts, as well as to the breaking up of many Zamíndárís by sale piecemeal for Revenue default, that the number of small Zamíndárís in Bengal is now so greatly in excess of the moderate-sized ones, while really large estates are quite in a minority.

of the land itself, if that was in dispute, was referred to the Law Courts). When such holdings were liable to resumption, the Government generously enough left the smaller ones (not exceeding 100 *bíghás* in extent) to the benefit of the Zamíndár, if he chose to resume (under a legally provided procedure); but the larger ones were assessed permanently, and became so many separate 'landlord estates.'

As early as 1782, attempts had been made to adjust these troublesome claims; but the two Regulations of the Permanent Settlement really brought the matter to a definite issue. These were Regulations XIX of 1793, dealing with what were called *bádsháhí* (royal) grants, viz. those emanating from the royal order, and Regulation XXXVII dealing with those (non-*bádsháhí* as they were called, or *hukámí*) which had been issued by local and subordinate authorities.

Permanent Settlement of Benares.—It will here be convenient to notice that the Permanent Settlement was extended to the districts of the Benares province, which, though acquired in 1775, was not settled till 1795. The tenures here consisted of landlord-villages with a rather strong clan or tribal connexion; in many cases, chiefs and heads of sections had also obtained the lordship over various groups of villages or estates made up of parts of different villages.

The great Rájá of Benares was at the head of the whole, but he was not in a position to be dealt with as Zamíndár or direct landlord of the entire Province; and as no idea of dealing with village bodies had yet occurred to any one, the Settlements were made either with some one elder or chief co-sharer in the village, or else with persons who were heads of families, and local magnates who had acquired estates or established chiefship over groups of villages.

A very interesting report on the co-sharing village bodies[1] was prepared by Mr. Duncan the Resident in 1796: the joint ownership seems to have puzzled him exceedingly; he evidently could not understand how there could be more than one landlord in a village.

[1] A number of them (as might be expected) were *pattidárí* as connected with local chiefs and noble families, and others were *bháiáchárá* or constructed on the equal-lot principle (p. 84).

In order to include in one place what has to be said of the Benares Settlement, it may here be mentioned that in 1834 the Permanent Settlement districts of Benares—now Benares, Ballia (including part of the old 'Azamgarh district), Gházipur, Jaunpur, and the Northern part of Mirzapur—were separated from Bengal and henceforth belonged to the North-Western Provinces. Of late years they have been all completely surveyed, and a record of the subordinate rights of all co-sharers, &c. has been made; so that as they are under the ordinary Land Revenue Law of the North-West Provinces, they are in all practical respects on just the same footing as the rest of the province, with the one feature that the Revenue is fixed for ever, and that individual co-sharers (and others) have a more or less nominal superiority as the Settlement holders and actual Zamíndárs.

Lands subsequently settled permanently.—The Bengal Settlement extended to occupied lands or estates, which included a large and often indefinite area of waste land (see p. 57). But still there was much waste not so included; and at first, the occupation even of this land was tacitly allowed, only that it became liable to a (permanent) assessment under the name of *taufír*. Other estates also—the 'resumed' lands above spoken of—were also gradually assessed permanently.

Lands which did not come under the Permanent Settlement. Waste lands after 1819.—But when, in 1828, the question of waste lands was more seriously taken up, and the right of Government was asserted, it soon came to be perceived that when these lands were granted by the Collector, or were otherwise allowed to be cultivated, there was no legal obligation to grant them a permanent Settlement; for the Permanent Settlement Regulation VIII of 1793 only applied to the occupied estates existing at the time.

In the older districts where the waste was already either appropriated lawfully or had been dealt with under the law of 1819, very little could be done; but in the great tracts of forest land on the delta of the Húghlí River (The Sundarbans) and in the Eastern districts, large areas of waste were secured. In Chittagong, for example, the old settlers and their *tarfdárs* (who became landlords—p. 107) had been located by measurement, and in 1764 the area held by them had been roughly determined; so all the other lands (*naudbád*) were not subject to the Permanent Settlement. Similarly in Sylhet (now in the Assam province), a large area was recovered: there were many claims and some troublesome and protracted litigation in connexion with these lands, but ultimately the greater part have been recognized as not under the Permanent Settlement[1].

Non-permanently settled estates in Chutiyá Nágpur and in districts subsequently acquired.—It may also be added that owing to local peculiarities, parts of the Chutiyá- (or Chotá-) Nágpur districts were not permanently settled; and a portion of the 'Santhál pergunnahs' district was expressly exempted. All districts acquired in 1803 and afterwards, are (as already stated) not under the Permanent Settlement.

Measures subsidiary to the Permanent Settlement.

Effect of the Permanent Settlement on raiyats.—I have already given an account of the position of tenants or *raiyats* under the Zamíndárs (pp. 130, 139); but it is desirable here to state more directly, how the Permanent Settlement at first affected them.

I have recently mentioned that a number of the older and stronger claims to land were recognized by separating them as small independent estates (p. 160). A certain number of interests were also protected by the fact that the landholders had claims sufficiently strong to induce the Zamíndárs to recognize them as permanent tenures—often with fixed rent payments. All these cases were expressly provided for by the Regulation VIII of 1793 (secs. 49–52).

The Pattá Rules.—But for the bulk of the raiyats, many of whom were old 'resident' village landholders, nothing was thought of but to require that each should get a 'pottah' (*pattá*) specifying the area, as well as the terms and conditions of his holding. Various changes were made in the rules, but

[1] For details as to Chittagong see *L. S. B. I.* vol. i. pp. 489, 554, and for Sylhet vol. iii. p. 443; and in the present work in the section of this chapter on the Settlement of Assam.

without much success. The grant of *pottahs* could not be enforced; some tenants did not like to take them for fear that they would be held to admit, thereby, an inferior position; others, because being illiterate, they never would be certain what they were putting their names to; and in some cases when such leases were accepted they proved only engines of extortion. For while on the one hand, the tenants had to be protected, the authorities were also anxious about the Revenue; and Zamíndárs complained while they themselves were under a strict law of punctual payment, they could not get proper rates of rent and regular payments; and therefore had not the means of meeting their instalments of Revenue. At various times Regulations were enacted, which though perhaps well intended, really pressed hardly on the tenants. Two of them, Regulation VII of 1799, and Regulation V of 1812, long known as *Qanún haftam* (seventh) and *panjam* (fifth), wrought great mischief[1].

Effect of the 'Sale Laws.'—But perhaps the greatest trouble arose out of the Sale Laws. It has been already indicated that if the Revenue was not punctually discharged by a certain time, the Collector might put up the estate for sale—either the whole or a part, as might be necessary. But if a purchaser was to be induced to come forward and buy the estate, paying such a sum as would clear off the arrears and represent a fair auction value of the property, he must get the estate with a clear title and free from existing leases and burdens; otherwise an outgoing defaulter might so burden the estate as to leave it worthless in the hands of a successor. Hence the first Sale Laws provided for the voiding of all mortgages, leases and contracts of tenure, except a very few. Consequently the newcomer was able to demand new rental rates from all but a very exceptional class of tenants and landholders, without restriction. This completed the misfortunes of the tenants.

At last, in 1859, matters were ripe for the enactment of an improved Sale Law (Act XI of 1859); and almost at the sâme time the Legislative Council passed the first General Tenant Law (Act X of 1859) granting occupancy rights and limiting the power of enchancement (p. 135).

Land Registration.—As there was no survey and record of

[1] For details see *L. S. B. I.* vol. i. p. 634 ff. Regulation VII dealt with the power of distraint for arrears. Regulation V was expressly designed to benefit the tenants, but owing to certain defects, it acted just the other way.

rights, it became necessary to have a register of estates, and of changes in the ownership, by sale, gift, or inheritance; because these affected the person to whom the Collector was to look for payment of the Revenue. The first laws for registration failed to work; and even when tolerable quinquennial registers were secured, still they did not show any subordinate rights. A sort of register (though not legally binding) of the latter was, however, made, where a 'cess' was levied by law (p. 153), with a view to maintaining roads and public works; for this 'cess' had to be levied not only on estates, but on all landed interests over a certain value. Afterwards a further improvement was effected when the Sale Laws were amended, so as to give protection (by a certain procedure of registration) to subordinate tenures and interests which were to be maintained while other burdens were made voidable by the auction purchaser.

Bengal Act VIII of 1876 is now the law of land registration. Separate registers are maintained for all Revenue-paying and Revenue-free estates, arranged by districts and *parganas*, so that every acre can be accounted for. 'Estates' are compulsorily registered (i. e. are subject to a penalty for neglect). 'Tenures' (and other interests) can be registered optionally; but there are certain disabilities which exist in case they are not registered, notably with reference to their liability to be voided on sale of the estate (under which they are) for arrears.

Survey.—A separate Act has enabled a general survey to be made[1]; but this extends only to showing the local limits of estates and villages; and though it may be directed to show limits of holdings and 'tenures,' this has not yet been attempted, nor has a record of rights been legalized in connexion with survey. Act VIII of 1885 has made a certain provision on the subject (chap. x); but this can only be applied under the express conditions enacted. The want of a cadastral survey is increasingly felt. The absence of it must foster law-suits as well as delay their disposal; and it renders impossible those

[1] Bengal Act V of 1875. In alluvial and riverain lands (*deárá* survey as it is called) a special law exists (IX of 1847): to these lands Act V does not apply.

useful agricultural statistics which are available in all other provinces[1].

The Permanent Settlement in Madras (Zamíndárís).—We must now turn to the Landlord Settlement in Madras. The

[1] A survey has been ordered (as a commencement) for the Bihár districts; and it may appear strange that this has been denounced with an impatience that shows more sentiment than reason. The objection really rests on the desire to keep up the old-world relations of Zamíndár and Raiyat, under which everything was in the loose and unordered condition dear to oriental managers: the Zamíndár was then able to do what he liked and to be the absolute master; the peasant was his slave. No doubt there is also a brighter side to the picture; the Zamíndár puts on his books a very high rent—in Bíhár it is most often levied in kind—but he works it elastically, and only takes the full in good years. This system may have its advantages; but it is too much dependent on the good feeling of the landlord; and it may be questioned whether it can long remain compatible with modern conditions and modern law. The objectors also strangely forget some facts, and almost ludicrously pervert others. It is easy for them to rely on the Zamíndárs' dislike, but that arises from the very natural feeling above noticed, and still more from fear of the heavy cost which will fall chiefly on them. It is also easy to stir up the ignorant tenantry—who do not in the least understand the matter—by appealing to their traditional dread of 'measurement,' which in the old days was a process directly intended (by whatever device) to make out that they were holding more land than they were paying rent for. Very exaggerated pictures are drawn of the probable extortions of native surveyors; forgetting that there is no more reason why a survey should be oppressive in Bihár than it was in the neighbouring Benares districts, or in every other part of India where it has been successfully carried out. Indeed it should be less so, since the experience there gained will enable the present survey to be made in the best manner, and with the avoidance of earlier errors of management. It is also apparently forgotten that not only every civilized country in Europe, but every other province in India, has found a survey and a record of rights to be indispensable. And when it is urged that a survey will stir up questions and give rise to endless litigation, it seems to be overlooked that if such an anticipation is well founded, it at least indicates that boundaries, holdings, and questions of right must be, at present, in such a state of uncertainty, and so dependent on expedients and makeshifts as well as on the good-will of landlords, that sooner or later the condition of things must become intolerable.

The only real objections—or rather difficulties—to be met are, the question of cost, and the more serious question of maintaining the records and maps when made, in a state of continual correctness. But equitable arrangements as to cost are not beyond the power of Government to devise; and it is not a matter of optimistic opinion, but of simple fact, that in other provinces records can be, and are being (every day with increasing success), kept correct. In spite of the difficulties about the Orissa records—made many years ago, they are exactly similar to what have been felt, and now overcome, in Northern India. And as to the benefits of survey and records wherever they have been made—as in Khúrdá and other great estates—there can be no possible doubt. It is skilfully kept out of sight, that the condition of the petty landholders of Bihár is deplorable; and certainly no real reason is given for the belief that it can be improved without recourse to what every other province has found to be the only safeguard.

earliest acquisitions of territory were made much about the same time as the grant of Bengal. For many years no form of regular Settlement was adopted; but when the districts ceded by Mysore, and the Carnatic districts, were also added, notwithstanding that a Settlement had been begun on other principles, the Central Government determined to apply a Permanent Settlement (on the Bengal model) to the whole.

It was only, however, in the northern districts that there were Zamíndárs or chiefs who had a similar position; there were also certain lands reserved for the benefit of the Native Court of Hyderabad (known as *Haveli* lands) and there were the polygars' estates (p. 111).

The Zamíndárís were settled without difficulty; the *Havelí* lands were free to be sold to persons who became the landlords; a few of the greater polygars were settled with just like the northern Zamíndárs; and the case of the other polygars has already been explained (p. 111). No other real landlord-estates existed; consequently it was impossible to settle the districts generally, without making artificial estates or parcels (*mootah*=*mutthá*) of lands, and selling the landlord right by auction! This resulted in a miserable failure; in a short time the purchasers broke down one after another, and the attempt to carry the Permanent Settlement any further, was abandoned[1]. The result is that we have now between one-fifth and one-third of the Presidency held in great Zamíndárís or as *polliams*; and there are many smaller relics (scattered through the districts) of inferior Zamíndárís and *mootahs*. The rest is all under a separate system[2]. Inside the great Zamíndárís there were no serious difficulties as regards subordinate rights; the law reserved intact, every kind of right that could be proved to exist; and every feature of tenure or privilege, as regards fixity of rent or holding, can be secured on the sole condition of sufficient

[1] *L. S. B. I.* vol. iii. p. 14 ff.

[2] The *gross* area of all kinds of landlord estates, appears to be about 19½ millions of acres (this, however, is a total territorial area including much that is uncultivated), the *raiyatwárí* lands appear to be close on 30 millions of acres—but that is the Settlement area, i. e. takes in only the village (occupied and cultivated) area.

evidence of the facts or custom. There is no artificial twelve years, or other similar rule. Rent-free holdings in the Zamíndárís were all maintained. The Permanently Settled estates are still governed by Madras Regulation XXV of 1802. This is supplemented by Madras Act II of 1864 which provides for the recovery of arrears of Land Revenue, and by Act VIII of 1865 which regulates the Zamíndár's dealings with his tenants (p. 144). The grant of the landlord title and the conditions of it are evidenced by a *sanad* or title-deed in each case (p. 65 *n.*). The absence of tenure difficulties may be due to the circumstance that the Madras landlords were mostly territorial chiefs who had not exercised that close dealing with the land which in Bengal resulted in so many subordinate grades of right.

It should be noticed, in conclusion, that there is no rule (as there is in Bengal) that landlord estates sold for arrears, must be again permanently settled with the purchaser. When therefore, on the failure of the numerous artificial estates and other new Zamíndárís, in the beginning of the century, some other arrangement had to be made, there was nothing to prevent the lands being simply treated like any other *raiyatwárí* lands. This is the reason why even in the districts that are mostly made up of estates under the Permanent Settlement, there are some considerable tracts of *raiyatwárí* lands.

The Temporary Settlement of Bengal.

So much for the Permanent Settlement with landlords. In Bengal, to which we must once more return, the existence of a number of scattered estates belonging to Government, or lands which from other causes were not liable to the Permanent Settlement law (pp. 162, 3), did not attract attention. For a long time these estates were informally managed without the aid of a separate law. But on the acquisition of Katák and the other Orissa districts, as well as those now forming the North-Western Provinces, the Settlement of so large and important a territory called for special measures; and after the usual period of tentative arrangements, Regulation VII of 1822 was passed. This law (which is the foundation of all the systems of Temporary Settlement with landlords and village bodies) will be more conveniently brought to notice in connexion with the North-West Provinces Settlement system. But it is here to be mentioned that this Regulation (with its amending regulations notably Reg. IX of 1833) is still the law under which Temporary Settlements are made in Bengal; but Bengal Act VIII of 1879, and now Act VIII of 1885 (chap. x), have made important additions to its provisions: they have given power to Settlement officers, not only to record, but to adjust and enhance, rents. In the Orissa districts, and some others to which Act VIII of 1885 does not extend, the Bengal Act VIII of 1879 still applies[1].

The Settlement may apply to the Revenue or to the Rent payments. Mode of assessment.—The 'Temporary Settlements,' properly so called, are made for estates in which there is a recognized landlord or proprietor of some kind, who is responsible for the Land Revenue payment. But very much the same procedure is also adopted in fixing rents for lands in which there is no *Land Revenue* payable, because there is no landlord except the Government itself. The Land Revenue assessment is ascertained in Bengal, exactly as in the North-West Provinces; viz. by calculating the actually paid rent-rates on the estate; these form the 'assets' of the proprietor; and a percentage of the total assets represents the Land Revenue demand[2]. The method of valuation for fixing rents is described in Sec. III, and it is unnecessary to repeat the details here. Whether there is a landlord whose rental receipts have to be calculated, or whether it is a Government estate where a rental has to be fixed for actual payment by the tenants, the work is very much the same. In either case the

[1] The Chittagong Hill Tracts, the Santhál Pergunnahs and the Western Dwárs districts, have special laws of their own; and in the Chutiyá Nágpur districts there is a special Tenant Law, although Act VIII of 1879 applies also.

[2] The percentage of total assets may not be the exact Revenue, because some minor additions or deductions have to be made on other accounts; but the statement is sufficient for our immediate purpose.

Settlement officer has to *ascertain the correct rental value* of land.

It may be indeed, that in a Settlement with an existing proprietor there may be no occasion to do more than discover and record existing rents (without any enhancement proceedings) for the purpose of calculating the Revenue rates; but in some cases the proprietor will ask to have the rents raised and adjusted, and then, under Act VIII of 1885 (as well as under the earlier law), the Settlement Officer has power to take action: he can enhance rents under the conditions stated in the Act, and adjust rates of rent where they have not been settled between the parties.

In principle the procedure of Temporary Settlement, including the demarcation of boundaries, the survey, and the record of rights under the Bengal law, is virtually the same as that followed in the North-West Provinces system, next to be described. The forms of record of rights and other matters of detail may be learnt from the Settlement rules made by the Board of Revenue[1] and the Bengal 'Settlement Manual.' There would be no object in giving any further detail here. Only one point may be noticed: in Bengal (Temporary) Settlements with a middleman or proprietor, the proportion of 'assets' taken as Land Revenue, is seventy per cent. This is much higher than under the North-West Provinces Settlements; but in Bengal, the 'proprietors' who hold the Settlement are usually middlemen of a class for whom thirty per cent. of the assets (together with the entire profits from subsequent legal enhancements of rents, and all extensions of cultivation during the long period of Settlement and other profits not calculated) are an ample remuneration.

Orissa Temporary Settlements.—The most extensive of the Bengal Temporary Settlements is that of the Orissa dictricts, but as this is not a 'landlord' Settlement, I reserve a notice of it to the next section.

Settlement with the landlords of Oudh.

Oudh Settlement not permanent, and reserved to the next section.—There is one other settlement dealing with great

[1] These are printed as Appendix I to Rampini and Finucane's Bengal Tenancy Act (1885).

landlords, namely the Oudh Taluqdárs; but it has hardly anything in common with the Landlord Settlement of Bengal. It is not permanent (except in the case of a few estates, as a reward for special services); there is a complete survey and record of rights; and the component villages under the landlords are so much considered, that virtually the Oudh Settlement is regarded, and will be here described, as a modified form of the village Settlement system, in the next section.

Section III. The village (or Mahál) Settlement System.

Just as the Permanent Settlement of Bengal is the typical form adopted where great landlords had to be dealt with, so the Temporary Settlement as developed in the North-West Provinces, is the typical form made use of in provinces where for the most part *village communities* with landlord rights are dealt with; that is to say where the joint body of co-sharers is regarded as the landlord and as responsible for one assessed sum of Revenue[1]. This system can also be easily applied so as to make the Settlement with a landlord who happens to have acquired rights over a group of villages or a whole pargana; its features remain unaltered; that is why we consider the Oudh Taluqdári Settlement (p. 170) preferably under this head. The same system was applied to Ájmer, to the Panjáb and to the Central Provinces, with only local modifications in each.

The 'North-West Provinces.'—The remarks already made will have familiarized the reader with the NORTH-WEST PROVINCES, as extending from the Bihár frontier of Bengal as far as the Jumna river. The bulk of the districts were occupied by villages of the landlord type (pp. 71, 92), some of them in the hands of single landlords, others held undivided by a number of

[1] The map may here be referred to, which shows the Permanent Settlement in red (the Temporary Settlement in Bengal being yellow); the 'village' Settlements are blue; and the *raiyatwárí* Settlements in different shades of green—showing a certain connexion of principle under a variety of form.

sharers, and others being (divided) *pattídárí* and *bháiáchárá* communities (p. 84).

Early history of the Settlements.—The earlier Regulations (1802–5) were still under the influence of the single-landlord ideas derived from Bengal and from Europe. And at first the villages were nearly always settled with one Revenue farmer or with some other (single) leading person. Indeed these Regulations (1802–5) read very much as if we were still in Bengal with landlords and 'actual proprietors' to deal with in each case. Moreover it was at first declared that the Settlement would be made permanent; only that this was prohibited by the Home authorities. Fortunately, however, light broke in on the scene, and that chiefly through the exertions of Holt Mackenzie, who may be regarded as standing in the same relation to the North-West Provinces system as John Shore did to that of Bengal[1].

First proposals for the North-West Provinces Settlements. The first design briefly was this: to make a ten years' Settlement, in such a way that experience would be gained and the work improved as it went on. There was to be a first Settlement for three years, then a second for three years more, and then a third for four years, which it was hoped would prove satisfactory enough to be confirmed for ever. Consequently when the time came for making the last or four years' Settlement, it was desired to make it with every care and precaution, and a special Commission was appointed, with Holt Mackenzie as its Secretary. This Commission was soon found indispensable, and became permanently constituted as the Board of Revenue (p. 19). Briefly, the results of the inquiry were to show:—(1) That village proprietary-bodies existed, and that it was impossible to let single co-sharers, farmers, headmen and others usurp the place of sole owner[2]. (2) That a survey and record of all rights whatever, were indispensable. (3) That a Permanent Settlement as a general measure could not be thought of. The whole subject was discussed in a long and able minute by Holt Mackenzie which bears the date July 1, 1819.

The passing of Regulation VII of 1822.—At the same time as these inquiries were being made in the North-West, the

[1] There, however, the parallel ends: for the Permanent Settlement of Bengal could have no development, while the North-West Provinces system, which in its initiation is associated with the name of Holt Mackenzie, was continually improved till it attained its modern form under the care of James Thomason.

[2] And in the early days after annexation, it must be recollected, not only was village farming general, but rich men were called on to stand security for village payments. Defaults frequently occurred, and indeed were often fraudulently brought about on purpose; the old sale-law was the only method of recovery then in use, and the consequence was that villages fell by hundreds into the hands of Revenue farmers, sureties and the like, who bought them at the auction and became landlords (p. 94).

question of the Orissa districts acquired in 1803, also came up: the result was that Regulation VII of 1822 was passed to apply to both.

Its application to Orissa.—The Orissa Settlements (under the Bengal Government) were accordingly made pursuant to this Regulation. These Settlements cannot be described in this book, though they are full of interest; but justice could not be done to the subject without going into a number of details which would be out of place. But I may here once for all say, that the Orissa Settlement was made without any reference to any theory requiring a landlord or middleman. In fact it is neither exactly a landlord Settlement, nor a village Settlement, nor a *raiyatwárí* Settlement; but when the survey was made and the details of holdings were ascertained, the Settlement Officers simply *had respect to actual facts; they recorded and secured all rights as they found them existing.* Some features of each of the three systems may therefore be traced. A few of the local magnates or chiefs were recognized as landlords, and their assessment was allowed (as a favour) to be permanent [1]. Beyond that there are no 'Zamíndárs'; but various persons had acquired rights of one kind or another over villages or plots of land. The Settlement therefore took the country, village by village; the rent or revenue payable by each kind of landholder was determined, and his rights recorded: there might be the old *tháni* or resident cultivator, there might be a village headman with certain rights; or a small 'estate' belonging to a *chaudharí* or a *Kánúngo* or to a grantee of some kind. The Settlements then made have been extended from time to time, and will not expire till 1897.

Regulation VII of 1822 in the North-West Provinces.—Let us then return to Regulation VII of 1822 as applied to North-Western India.

In some cases, as I have stated, it was necessary to acknowledge a great landlord or Zamíndár, or to acknowledge one so far as to give him a *taluqdárí* allowance—as it was called (p. 109).

[1] I mean those who were subjects; I am not speaking of the chiefs in the Hill Country who are recognized as ruling 'Tributary states.'

In the former case the assessment was on the whole estate, but it was for a period of years only. If the villages in the estate had preserved their constitution and were not bodies of contract tenantry, a 'sub-settlement' (*mufassal* Settlement was the term used in 1822) would be made, which fixed what the village was to pay to the landlord; only that in that case it would be fixed at a higher figure to allow for the overlord's profit. In cases where the *taluqdárí* or double tenure was found, the villages 'held the Settlement' direct, but the *taluqdárí* allowance was provided for by making the assessment so much higher as to include the amount (ultimately fixed at ten per cent. on the Land Revenue). This was payable through the treasury, and was not collected by the overlord.

Joint and several responsibility of the village bodies. By means of a representative lambardár.—Where the village itself was the only landlord, the section on village tenures will have made the form of ownership intelligible; so that it need here only be briefly stated that the entire body was settled with *as a jointly and severally responsible unit;* and that for each village or each *pattí* or section, a sharer of standing and respectability undertook the primary liability and signed the Revenue-engagement on behalf of the whole body. Such a person was called *lambardár* (p. 26). The burden of the Revenue is distributed (with the advice and under the supervision of the Settlement Officer) among the co-sharers, according to the principles of sharing and constitution of the estate (i.e. either by ancestral shares or in proportion to the share or holding). (p. 87.) This process is called the *báchh.*

'Perfect' Partition of estates.—In case a section of the village or even a shareholder (above a certain limit) does not like the joint responsibility, he is allowed, by the North-West Provinces law, to apply to be completely separated, i. e. to have what is called 'perfect partition' which sets up a separate estate with separate Revenue liability. Perfect partition is not as a rule allowed (except at Settlement) in the Panjáb.

Amendment of the Regulation.—The Regulation of 1822 was excellent in principle, but it could not be efficiently worked, partly by reason of some assessment difficulties which will appear presently, and partly because of the deficiency of local establishments and the burden of work thrown on the Settlement officers, who had to inquire into and decide rights at the same time that they were assessing the Revenue. Two amending laws were passed in 1825; but the more important amendment was that of 1833 (after a special Committee had sat to inquire into the whole matter). It is hardly too much to say that it was the passing of Regulation IX of 1833 that enabled the first Settlements to be made with fair success.

Under this Regulation, Native Deputy Collectors were appointed; the principle of assessment was revised; and the majority of judicial cases were transferred from the Settlement Officer's Court [1]. At the same time also, the village Statistics were reformed; the Settlement Officer was empowered to fix rents for tenants, and the village maps and accompanying field-registers came into general use.

The work of Settlement considered as partly judicial, partly fiscal.—The principles thus established have never been departed from: and although details were from time to time altered so that it became necessary in 1873 to draft a new and comprehensive Land Revenue law (Act XIX), it remained a distinctive feature of the system that the Settlement involved two branches of work, (1) quasi-Judicial and (2) Fiscal. The first was concerned with the ascertainment and record of rights, the second with the valuation of land and the assessment of the Revenue demand and the adjustment of rents of tenants [2].

[1] Leaving the Settlement Officer only the duty of recording undisputed rights or at least of summary inquiry on the basis of existing possession: if there was still a dispute and arbitration was not resorted to, the case would be tried in the Civil Court, and the Settlement Records would be filled up in accordance with the final decree.

[2] **Thomason's Directions to Revenue Officers.**—As experience supplied the necessary data, a valuable book known as 'Directions to Settlement Officers' was completed by Mr. Thomason (who became Lieutenant-Governor); and this was supplemented by 'Directions to Collectors.' In 1858 when some new Settlements were being made, certain modifications were introduced by what were known as the 'Sahâranpur Rules.' An important survey change (the use of the plane-table) was introduced also. To embody these improvements a new edition of the Directions was issued in 1858. This work long remained a standard

The work naturally divides itself into stages—Demarcation, Survey, Record of holdings and rights, Assessment, and concluding proceedings.

Demarcation.—The first stage (preliminary to the survey) consisted in setting up the outer boundary marks of villages and estates (pp. 11, 147) and interior marks indicating the limits of holdings, shares, tenancies, &c. Legal powers to enter on land for survey and measurement purposes, as well as to require the erection of marks, were duly given by the Regulation, as they are also in the Land Revenue Act.

The persons entitled to record were those in possession. A disputed boundary was settled by a summary inquiry on the basis of possession; if possible, arbitration was resorted to; if not, the aggrieved party had to go to the Civil Court[1].

Survey.—Then followed the Survey: this was not a mere topographical survey, but resulted in producing for each village the SHAJRA or large scale map, showing every field with a red ink number, and accompanied by a descriptive list or index of all fields called the KHASRA.

At first the survey was made by two independent agencies. A professional survey staff made the 'Revenue survey' of the district as far as the outer boundaries of the villages; the interior details were furnished by native surveyors on the Settlement Staff. But for the later Settlements (in the North-West Provinces and Oudh) what is called the *Cadastral Survey* was introduced, i.e. the entire work was done, village by village, by professional surveyors under the Survey Department. This was much more costly, but the work was absolutely reliable, and will never have to be repeated.

Modified Cadastral System.—Chiefly on account of economy, a modified system has been adopted in the Panjáb and the Central Provinces (and probably elsewhere). Under this system, the work is once more divided, but in a better way. A scientifically trained staff lays down (not the outer boundaries of villages which can only be used for check and comparison, but) certain base-lines and fixed points of importance, which serve as absolutely reliable data for the detailed interior survey; and for this work the Settlement

text-book in the North-West Provinces and the other Provinces. It is still referred to as the exponent of principles, though its details have become superseded by later Acts and Revenue Circular Orders.

[1] In some provinces the various grades of Settlement Officers were vested with special powers, *as Civil Courts*, to decide all classes of land suits. This depended on the nature of the Settlement work and the possibility of the Officers having time to dispose of the cases that arose.

staff and the local *patwáris*[1] (p. 27) suffice. They fill in the field to field details, as well as roads, wells, tanks, groves, inhabited sites, and other features of the village area. This system is much cheaper and quite satisfactory in working[2].

Mode of preparing the village map.—In order to make the village map, (1) a list of persons holding land is drawn up (each person being classed as tenant, co-sharing owner, &c., and against a tenant's name is noted the owner he belongs to). (2) The fields are measured and mapped; and *pari passu*, each field, with details of its area, soil, and crop, &c., is entered :—

(*a*) in a permanent *khasra* or field index in which each plot is numbered as it is on the map.

(*b*) in a list which begins with the name of each holder, so that all the fields under one holder (of whatever class) are brought together.

From these data all other Settlement Records of rights and holdings, afterwards to be mentioned, can be compiled. As the lists of fields and the holders of them are made out, every kind of right—whether of a co-sharer in the estate, or of a rent-free holder, or of a tenant with some kind of privilege—is brought to record. Either the right is undisputed and is entered at once, or it may be necessary to file a suit to determine it. In that case the entry cannot be completed till the result of the suit is known. The records always proceed on the basis of undisputed rights or at least of those actually in possession.

The principles of assessment. The Land Revenue is a fraction of the total estate 'assets.' And those are chiefly the rental receipts.—The next part of the process is the ASSESSMENT. The details of the subject can only really be

[1] To give an idea of the staff, I may instance the Panjáb, with which I am familiar. In other places where the population is denser, the staff would be stronger. A Settlement Officer (probably with one or more superior grade Assistants) takes in hand four *tahsíls*; each *tahsíl* will have about eighty *patwáris*. One Inspector (*Kánúngo*) looks after every six *patwáris*: and in each *tahsíl* are four superior officials of the grade of *Tahsíldár* for supervising the details of Settlement work.

[2] The advantage of making the map by the same agency that has afterwards to keep it correct, is obvious.

learned (and this is true of all systems whatever) by practice in the field, by performing the different calculations, and learning how to make use of them, under skilled direction. Only the general idea or principle of the procedure can be set forth in a work of this kind. I have already stated that though the basis of the Land Revenue is the old 'Rájá's sixth,' modern systems have departed almost entirely from any attempt to value a share of the produce in money. Only traces of such a design are still observable in one or two Settlements. In the case of the village (or *mahál*) Settlements which we are now considering, the assessments are based, in all cases, more or less directly, on the actual rental value of the lands in the village. There is some difference as regards the mode of procedure in the North-West Provinces, Oudh, Central Provinces and Panjáb; but the underlying principle is the same, and the Revenue is technically said to consist of a fraction (usually fifty per cent.) of the 'assets' of the estate as annually received. The 'assets' mainly consist of the total rents actually received, together with the calculated rental value of lands held by the proprietors themselves, or allowed by them to be rent free; to these may be added any other sources of profit, such as valuable waste lands, income from grazing, fruits and wild produce, &c. The rental assets are of course the principal thing.

Modified methods of ascertaining these in different Provinces.— I will first briefly state the general ideas on which the practice of assessment is based, and then explain separately and a little more fully how the work is carried out in each Province. The 'rental value' spoken of is now based on rates of rent actually paid in each village, i.e. as paid at the time of Settlement, without reference to what they may subsequently become by the effect of legal enchancement. That is the North-West Provinces plan pure and simple. In the Central Provinces, this plan was modified under the necessity of securing a more perfectly *equal incidence of rents*; because while in the North-West Province, the rents ultimately paid after the Settlement are largely matters of agreement (or at least of decision in the Rent Courts) between landlord and tenant, in the Central

Provinces, all rents are fixed by the Settlement Officer for the ensuing term of Settlement, and this officer has therefore not only to determine existing rents as a basis of calculating the Revenue, but rents suitable to be actually paid during the whole term, by the tenants. In the Panjáb, again, so much of the land is held by the proprietors themselves, or is in the hands of tenants who pay in kind, that a direct process of calculating cash rentals cannot be followed; and it is necessary to ascertain a fair rate for all lands of a given class, on the basis of some specimen holdings which are found here and there to be paying real cash rents, or which pay grain rents of such a kind that, when valued in money, they will fairly represent a real rental value. And these *representative values* are applied (with suitable local variations) to all the lands of the villages.

Origin of the method.—With regard to village assessments generally, it will be remembered that the system we are describing was necessitated by the impossibility of repeating the old Permanent Settlement practice of merely bargaining for lump sums fixed on general considerations, without any reference to the actual valuation of the land. Obviously the only alternative to fixing a lump assessment empirically, is to ascertain the sum payable, with reference to the annual value of the estates according to their position and the kinds of soil they contain; the modern methods of valuation were only gradually discovered and perfected.

Attempt to value the net produce of each kind of soil.—In order to make a land valuation under Regulation VII of 1822, they began, at first, with a laborious attempt to find out the gross produce of land, and to value it in money; then deducting from this value the cost of production, they arrived at a net value. But this would not work. So many accidents and peculiarities affect different localities, that unless a calculation for each individual field could be made—i. e. for millions of fields, no correct, and certainly no equal, valuation would result.

Modified in 1833: method called 'aggregate to detail.'—A new departure was accordingly determined on, in 1833. And from that time up to the present day, the practice of assessment has gradually improved. As might be expected, there were distinct stages of this growth.

For the first Settlements there was a rough method of calculating a general sum total, which it was thought might fairly be taken from an entire pargana or other local area; this sum was tentatively distributed over the village lands, and was modified till it gave acreage-rates that appeared justifiable. But that method was soon abandoned, because attention was more and more drawn to the *rents paid by tenants as a natural standard of the value of different lands.*

Attention gradually drawn to rental value of land. At first theoretical rents (rents as they ought to be) were considered.—But some years ago, the rents were still very much customary rents, i.e. they did not represent anything like a competition rental value of the soil. As, however, time went on, this feature began to disappear; land came to be more in demand for a largely increasing population; the rents paid gradually became more and more proportionate to the real value and advantage of different soils in different situations. But the difficulty was to find out what the rents really were, in all cases; for those recorded in the village accounts of past years were either incorrect, or the information was altogether wanting; and even when a rent-rate was found out, it was at first considered that this might be far below what the land would probably be made to pay, directly the Settlement was over. So it became customary to calculate full *rent-rates, such as it was supposed would be obtained* in the years immediately following the Settlement.

The assessment so obtained might be correct in theory, but its working success depended largely on whether the landlords succeeded, either by aid of the Settlement officer's friendly interposition, or by the action of the Rent Courts, in getting his tenants to pay rents at least up to the standard of those calculated by the Settlement officer. And the result was that unequal results were obtained, in spite of the great care and intelligence that were undoubtedly brought to the work. In the latest Assessment rules (issued in 1886) the practice has been so far modified, that the rents taken as the basis of calculation, in making out a village rent roll (in which each acre of each kind of (cultivated) soil bears its proper rate) should be *actually paid* rent-rates without any theoretical increase for supposed future enhancements.

Practical steps towards obtaining correct village rent rolls.—Let us now shortly sketch the process of the rental asset valuation in the North-West Provinces. In the first place, the area under Settlement has to be divided into tracts, blocks, or 'Circles,' in which the general circumstances of climate, and physical or economical conditions, are similar.

Assessment 'Circles.'—In one circle there will be the advantage of proximity to market, facility of transport, and a ready demand for all kinds of produce: another may be marked by low-lying unhealthy situation, or may be dry upland with precarious rainfall. In one circle, water can only be found at considerable depths, and irrigation is costly or at least laborious; in another, the entire area is moistened by river percolation. The same soils may occur in all the circles: rich soil in certain fields, stiff clay, sandy loam and the like, may re-appear in each; but the conditions which affect the whole circle may necessitate different rent-rates for the same soil in each circle.

List of soils to be adopted.—Then again, it must be determined what *soils* should be distinguished; the object is always to have as few as may be, and those really distinct, and easily indicated by the agricultural population, who almost invariably have local names for each kind the practical distinctness of which they recognize. And there may be *degrees* of goodness of each kind. Still the number of different rent-rates necessary to cover all the soils and all the degrees of goodness of each soil, can be reduced to a very moderate limit, and yet furnish an appropriate value for every assessable acre in the village.

Zones of Cultivation practically made use of.—There was, in the North-West Provinces, a circumstance which facilitated this classification. It was observed that villages often had their cultivation in three broadly distinguished belts or zones (in vernacular *hár*). The first was the homestead zone, that nearest the village and easily accessible to manure and irrigation: long working and the supply of manure and water usually obliterated other distinctions, and one rate (and that the highest) would represent all land in this condition. The next zone was the 'middle-land,' in which perhaps natural soils had to be distinguished. The third was the 'outside' zone; here soils had to be distinguished, cultivation was poorer and more precarious, and water and manure were only occasionally available[1].

Tables of rent for each kind of soil in each village. Standard rent rates for kinds of soil in each circle. Called 'the prevailing rates.'—The existing and past rent rolls of the villages were scrutinized, and abstracted in the office, so as to give a table of rents for *each kind of land*; local inquiries and inspections to test and verify the rates were also carried out. In this way certain *standard rates* were ascertained, by adopting the rates of carefully selected average fields of each principal class of soil. These rates were such as were known to be fair, and were considered to be average or sample rates, being uninfluenced by any exceptional or purely local circumstances. Such standards were called the 'prevailing rates' of the circle.

'Corrected rent roll.' Villages above and below the average.—Now it is obvious that if by a judicious comparison of rents actually paid, we have obtained a series of rates representing each kind (and degree of kind) of soil recognized, and those rates represent neither very high nor very low rents, we have a scale of rates, which when applied to the soil areas of a village, ought, so to speak, to represent a fairly accurate rental value of at least some villages in each circle. Those will be in fact all the *average* villages. Even then, the valuation total will not equal exactly the rental account as shown by the most accurate village records. For in each village, there are lands held (of the proprietor's goodwill) rent-free; and there are also the *sír* lands or home farm (p. 79) of each co-sharer, either unrented, or paying nominal sums. As Government does not profess to exempt these from paying Revenue, the proper rental value has to be put on such lands. The rent roll of the village so

[1] Care was taken to inspect the villages minutely and mark on the map the limits of the three zones, so that each 'number' or field in the map could be arranged in a list showing its zone, its soil difference (where that was needed), and the appropriate rent-rate set against it.

supplemented, will, however, fairly correspond, as regards rates, to the actual rent roll of the tenant holdings; but (as I have above stated), this will be for average villages. In each circle, however, there are sure to be villages above or below the average; villages in which special features, confined to the village—such as caste of cultivator, number of tenants paying grain-rents [1], large proportion of land not rented and in the hands of the proprietors themselves—make it impossible to say that rates derived from the total of actual tenant rents shown in the books, represent a fair valuation. In such cases a specially 'corrected rent roll' has to be prepared; and this may be done, by referring to the prevailing or standard rates of the circle, or else getting 'village rates' as they are called, i. e. rates for the particular village, which are either rates derived from the average incidence of the total recorded rental (for full paying lands) on the total paying area, or are rates observed to be paid on neighbouring and similar holdings.

In some cases the recorded rents may be incorrect.—But there is yet (unfortunately) another cause why the recorded rental roll of the village may not answer to a roll prepared according to prevailing rates; it may be that the village papers are incorrect, or even fraudulently understate the real (or actual) rents paid; in that case no one can complain justly, if the Settlement officer sets aside the village records, and applies, as he is empowered to do, the 'prevailing' rates of the circle.

Allowance made in valuing Sír lands.—In speaking above of the application of rates to land which does not pay rent because it is the proprietor's home farm (or *sír*), I should mention that it has been customary to make some allowance for the benefit of the owners; the land is not valued at full (tenant) rates for similar soil, but (under existing rules) at from ten to fifteen per cent. below those rates.

Rent Rate Reports.—It must also be mentioned, that the 'prevailing' rates, &c., intended to be made use of in calculation, have to be reported to the chief Revenue authority for sanction

[1] Which itself is an indication of some exceptional precariousness of the crop (pp. 35, 37 note), such as flood, drought, or depredation by wild beasts.

before they are made use of. The reports give all the data and statistical information (in a suitable form) on which the rates proposed were ascertained.

Rental assets not quite the whole; some addition may have to be made for other profits.—The total rental-assets of a village being thus ascertained, there may be some addition to the total to be made on account of 'manorial' profits (as it is often the custom to call them), and possibly to allow for some valuable waste which is not assessable acre by acre at full rates, but still should not be allowed to be wholly disregarded.

Proportion of the assets which represents the Land Revenue.—Of the total assets, the Government at first took sixty-six per cent. as its Land Revenue; but in those days the assets were very loosely estimated; and moreover the Settlement holders were very often farmers, *sadr málguzárs* (as they were called), and others, whose right and responsibility were adequately recognized by the remaining thirty-three per cent. left them. But in later times when the real proprietors were settled with, and assets were more accurately calculated, the rule came to be (and still continues) that from forty-five to fifty-five per cent. should be taken—fifty per cent. being the standard; anything above or below that requires to be specially reported and expressly sanctioned.

The jama'.—The percentage of the total assets is not always mechanically taken as the village assessment, for there may be some further local peculiarity of circumstance or some feature of past history which can be best allowed for by making a small lump addition to, or diminution in, the total. In any case the total assessment as finally sanctioned is called the *jama'*. It is distributed as already stated (p. 174) among co-sharers; so that ordinarily the several co-sharers pay their own quota through their *lambardár*, and the joint responsibility has but rarely to be enforced.

Adjustment of rents to suit the Settlement rates.—It will be noticed that in the North-West Provinces, although the rents used as a basis of calculation are as far as possible rates in actual (present) use, there is nothing to prevent the landlords from enhancing their ordinary tenants' rents in future, so long as the Rent Law allows it, or the tenants agree. At the Settlement only certain privileged tenants are entitled to have their rents actually fixed for them by the Settlement Officer, the rest depend on voluntary settlement with the landlord, and with recourse to a suit for enhancement under the Rent Law, if necessary. But as a matter of fact in past Settlements, the officer in charge did a great deal, as friend of both parties, to bring about an adjustment [1].

This refers to the past.—This account of the assessment refers to what has been done in all modern Settlements up to the latest series. In the future it is hoped that revisions of Settlement will be effected with greater facility. That ultimately no new demarcation, survey, or land valuation and soil classification will be required, is probable. It will only be necessary to revise the existing rates on some general principle of a percentage addition; and only in the less developed estates will it be necessary to provide for the assessment of new cultivation [2].

System applied to Oudh.—The system just sketched out was applied to Oudh, only that there, the Settlement was only occasionally with the villages; in most cases a single Taluqdár landlord was settled with (in one sum) for an estate comprising a greater or less number of villages; and these were in different stages of preservation as regards their rights in the second degree. The Taluqdár's Revenue payment was based on the aggregate of the sums leviable as rent from each village. Attention was therefore paid more to individual villages and their rent according to what past payments had been, and what they now might be with reference to local circumstances, and less to general rates of rent for soils, prevailing throughout circles. It might be that some whole villages under the Taluqdár were entitled to a 'sub-settlement' (p. 132); and then the payment they had to make was fixed so much higher as would allow

[1] Otherwise if the tenants are strong they resist the just demands of an easy-going landlord; or if weak they are made to pay rents that may approach a rack-rent.

[2] In *L. S. B. I.* vol. i. p. 355 ff., I have given an outline of the proposals made and of the discussions which have taken place, regarding the future procedure of revision Settlements.

for the Taluqdár's profit as well as the Government share [1]. In most cases, however, there were only sub-proprietors of plots (p. 132) whose Revenue payment was fixed so as to allow at least for the minimum legal profit. A Taluqdár can never get *less* than ten per cent. profit after paying the Revenue; how much *more* he gets on the whole estate, depends on the number of villages entitled to sub-settlement and the number of sub-proprietors and occupancy-tenants.

Applied to the Central Provinces. Equal incidence of Rents how to be secured.—The modification of the system, as applied to the Central Provinces, is chiefly if not solely caused by the necessity of securing to the utmost degree possible, an equal incidence of rents. The result of the somewhat artificial creation of proprietors over the villages was, that a large measure of protection had to be accorded to the tenantry (pp. 94, 140). And this is given effect to by legal provision that the rents of all occupancy-tenants shall be fixed for the term of Settlement by the Settlement Officer; and as the Act gives power to settle all other rents also, and certain conditions arise in consequence of such fixing, it is admissible to say broadly, that in practice all rents are fixed at Settlement and for the term of it. The Settlement Officer's task is therefore not merely to fix rates for the purposes of Revenue calculation—rents which may be more than realized by the landlord afterwards; he determines rents which are actually payable, and at the same time serve as the basis of assessing the Land Revenue. Hence it is especially important that the incidence of the rates should be, as far as possible, equal in all villages. It was perceived that this object could best be secured, if by some process we could reduce all soils, so to speak, to a 'common denominator,'—that is, if we could ascertain the relative value of one soil to another, and thus

[1] If the village were independent, it would get fifty per cent. of the assets (the Government taking fifty per cent.—p. 184). But as it is holding under a landlord, reference to the lease, or to past custom, may show that the landlord is entitled to twenty-five per cent. (it can never be less than ten per cent.); in that case the village would be assessed at seventy-five per cent. of the assets, of which fifty goes to Government and twenty-five to the Taluqdár. If the village terms were such that they got less than twenty-five per cent., they would not be entitled (under the law of 1866) to a sub-settlement at all.

by multiplying the area of each soil in a village, by an appropriate number or 'factor,' could reduce each total area to a *number of units of the same practical value or productive capacity.* As a matter of fact, this has been found possible. It was observed that while people are shy about telling the true rent paid for this or that soil per acre, they will disclose (and other means are also open for discovering) how one soil is valued relatively to another. Let us suppose for example two villages in a 'circle' (p. 181) A and B. Each has 1,000 acres; but A's is made up of 300 acres 'black soil' and 700 'red soil.' B's, on the other hand, consists of 600 black and 400 red. By experimental reaping of crops, by analysis of rents and other sources of information, it is found that the productiveness of 'black' to 'red' soil is as 20 : 12. We can then reduce the area of A and B to equal area units and see whether the existing rent is equal in incidence or not.

$$\text{For A's area} = \begin{cases} 300 \times 20 = \ \ 6{,}000 \\ 700 \times 12 = \ \ \underline{8{,}400} \\ \qquad\qquad\ \ 14{,}400 \text{ units of equal value.} \end{cases}$$

$$\text{But B's} \qquad = \begin{cases} 600 \times 20 = 12{,}000 \\ 400 \times 12 = \ \ \underline{4{,}800} \\ \qquad\qquad\ \ 16{,}800 \text{ units of equal value.} \end{cases}$$

Now suppose that each village rental is at present R. 1,000. Dividing this by the number of equal soil units, the unequal incidence at once appears: A is in fact paying $\frac{1000}{14400} = 1{\cdot}11$ *anas*, while B is paying $\frac{1000}{16800} = 0{\cdot}95$ *anas*. And so if we can find out a general fair rate, we can raise one or other or both. Suppose we find (by comparison of the highest rented villages) that 2·0 *anas* is a full but proper rate, the first village would be raised to R. 1,800 and the second to R. 2,100, and yet we are sure that the general rates are equal.

Determination of 'factor' numbers.—The general factors or numbers by which each soil must be multiplied to give the equal value units, are determined for whole *tahsíls* or other convenient areas, and can be modified slightly to allow for accidental peculiarities of soils. Thus if 24 is the factor for *good 'kanhar'* rice-land: it may be taken as 22 if the situation is not as favourable for the retention of water, and as 16 if it is on a bad slope, &c. In each *tahsíl* they make out a list of the soils which it is necessary to distinguish; and under each, the varieties of position, surface, slope, &c., which represent different grades or conditions of the same soil, are noted. If land is very valuable and competition rents run high, it may be needed to make a rather extensive list of such varieties; but that is not usually the case; rents are uniformly low and not very varied—in all but the best developed districts.

Rent rates per unit.—As to the 'unit' rates of rent, they have tables of all the village areas reduced to equal units; and from these it can be seen what the maximum rates are; an analysis of them will give an experienced officer who has studied the ground, a very good idea of a suitable standard figure that may represent a fair value and yet not cause too great a rise all at once. A standard unit rate being adopted, it is easy to modify it for any particular village by a small change upwards or downwards so as to meet local peculiarities of caste or other special circumstances which affect agricultural life and can only be reached in this way. Thus, supposing the actual unit incidence of the last Settlement period is 0·65 *ana*; and with reference to increased cultivation and rise of prices, 0·80 would be a more suitable standard rate for the new Settlement; this might, in some villages, be raised to 0·82 or 0·85 and allowed to fall to 0·75 or even to 0·70 in others. Given the 'factors' and the 'unit rate of rent' it is a mere matter of arithmetic to convert the figures back into actual rate of rent for each area of soil in the village as it appears in the map and index-register (*Shajra* and *Khasra*). The rental value being thus ascertained, the Revenue rate is easily calculated and the village *jama'* made up as already described.

Applied to the Panjáb.—In the Panjáb, again, we have the same Settlement system as regards survey, records, &c.; but there was a certain difference in the method of assessment, which is, however, one of detail. Unlike the North-West Provinces, the bulk of village lands is not held by cash-paying tenants. And even where such tenants appear in the returns, it is often because they pay only at Revenue rates (which of course are cash) and not a competition rent in any shape[1]; and where there are paying tenants, their rent is in kind. Consequently it is not so easy—and at the first Settlements was not possible at all—to calculate cash rental values directly.

Standard rates derived from specimen holdings. Preliminary sanction to these required.—The Settlement officer therefore calculates direct Revenue rates per acre for each kind of soil in the village estate; and these are based on what the rental 'assets' would be if a cash rent was uniformly paid; and (as usual) the revenue is about fifty per cent. of these assets. Just as before, 'circles' (in which the conditions are approximately the same) are arranged, and broadly distinguishable classes of soil are adopted within each circle. Then certain central or standard rates are made out by *taking a sufficient number of fair specimen holdings representing each kind of soil*, and finding out what they actually pay in cash (if it is possible); and if not, what the fair cash value of the grain rental is. (Observe the same principle of basing observation on what is the actual fact). This work if well done, really furnishes a very fair standard of rental value as applying to all similar lands. But owing to their being calculated rates, they are themselves made the subject of a special preliminary report. When sanctioned, they are used, not as actual rates, but as a sort of standard around which the actual rates should hover;—they give certain limits much above or much below which a fair assessment should not go. First the average villages of the circle are dealt with—those in which, on the whole, there is no reason why rates above or below the standard should be adopted. And to them the standard-rates will be more approximately applied, but still with regard to the character of particular fields and their condition, and existing rents; the caste of the cultivators also, will often make some modification necessary[2].

[1] See p. 141, where the reason of this appears.

[2] See *L. S. B. I.* vol. ii. p. 572 for the reasons why this notice of caste has to be taken.

Second report on Assessment rates.—But in each circle there will be villages, some much above, and some much below, the average; and then the central rates will need to be raised or lowered considerably in their application. And such changes will have to be justified in a further Report on actual rates made use of.

When once rates are satisfactorily settled, the village *jama'* is calculated by the simple process of multiplying the area of each kind of soil in the village by the appropriate rate. On the total sum so obtained, some general increase or decrease may be ordered, as already explained (p. 184).

It will have been noticed that in all provinces, the rates and the final *jama'* are all the subject of careful report, so that every chance of mistake is obviated; moreover the proprietors who are being assessed have considerable opportunity, under the Revenue Procedure Law, for appealing; so that it is unlikely (in the present day at any rate) that an assessment will be unreasonable without its coming to notice and being at once revised.

Allowance for improvements.—It should also be noticed that assessments are always arranged so as to allow the co-sharer or occupant who has spent his labour or capital in making an improvement, to get the benefit of it. (See Chap. IX, at the end.)

To some extent, of course, it is unavoidable to tax improvements; for the long-continued labour and careful cultivation which have brought up what was once a desert, to its present state—perhaps of garden land paying the highest Revenue rate—is as much an 'improvement' and an expenditure of private means, as is the new well or new embankment on which a richer proprietor has just spent 500 rupees in a lump payment. But it is possible directly to encourage the expenditure of capital; and for that reason, all provinces have their rules under which a certificate of such works being executed, is granted, and then the land will be rated at a Settlement, only on its unimproved aspect—as if the work had not been done, so that the whole extra benefit goes to the maker of the improvement for the period of years which the certificate specifies. After that, the land will pay its proper rate according to its class.

Fluctuating Assessments.

Exceptional tracts subject to river action, or in a desert climate. Fluctuating systems must be self-acting to a great extent.—In many provinces there are considerable tracts of country, or even small groups of lands, where the crops are always very precarious, either owing to liability to drought or to floods, or to changes caused by the capricious action of the rivers. In such cases, no fixed assessment for a term of years, adapted to the average of ordinary conditions, can be applied. If a very low rate were fixed, even that could not be paid in the worst years; while there might occasionally be a whole series of years of fine harvests in which such rates would be quite inadequate. It is true that all assessments are strictly moderate, and *are designed expressly to meet the average conditions of harvest success.* A mere deficiency (or even a considerable failure) in any one year, ought not to affect the payment, at any rate beyond what can be adjusted by suspending the demand or making a partial remission. But the tracts we are speaking of, are subject to such violent changes, that no average considerations of this kind meet the case. Ingenuity has there been exercised to devise a system of assessment which should be, as far as possible, self-acting, and should rise and fall with the result of each harvest. without having recourse to a separate detailed Settlement for each season, with its attendant inconvenience and expense. Two points have to be considered, (1) the extent of land sown; (2) the degree of success attained on that area: for it may be that the whole area has been sown, but only a quarter-crop has been reaped: on the other hand it may be that only one half the normal area was cultivated, but the result on that limited area was very good. All systems of 'fluctuating assessment' depend on a measurement, after each harvest, of the area actually under cultivation, and on a general estimate of the crop—as full, one-half, one-quarter, or practically nil. Certain rates, already devised, are then applied.

The System designed in the Ájmer district. In Ájmer an ingenious system has been adopted, of fixing a standard area of cultivation which is recorded as reduced to units of dry (unirrigated) cultivation[1]. For this, at a certain (quite easy) rate per acre, a 'standard' Revenue-total is fixed. It is then determined that this rate *may be allowed to vary within certain limits*: e.g. if the rate is 10 *anas*, it may not rise above 11½ *anas* or fall below 8¾ *anas*. Suppose that the average area of cultivation of all kinds (when reduced to dry units) is 560 acres, and that the dry rate is 10 *anas* per acre, then the standard revenue will be 560 × 10 *anas* = R. 350. But in a good year, the cultivation will rise to (say) 670 (calculated in dry acres); applying this to the standard Revenue (of R. 350) the rate would be only 8¼ *anas* per acre: but as 8¾ is the minimum, the Revenue payable would be 670 × 8¾ = R. 366, or R. 16 more than the standard. But next year the season is bad and the cultivation falls to 460 (dry acres); here if we were to apply the standard Revenue of R. 350, it would come to 12⅓ *anas* per acre; but the maximum is 11½, so that the Collector would only take 460 × 11½ or R. 323, and remit the rest.

Further provision is also made for the case where, though the area can be measured as so much land having a crop of some kind, the crop itself was only 'one-half' or 'one-quarter' or so poor as not to be counted. The areas are first divided by these fractions before applying the rate.

Instalments.

Revenue not paid in one annual sum.—It is a matter of importance to fix the dates at which the Land Revenue is paid. This is not required in one sum, but in instalments. And these are fixed with reference chiefly to the harvests; for landlords cannot pay their Revenue till they have got in their rents, and tenants cannot discharge their rents until the harvest is reaped;—and if they are cash rents, not till they have had time to sell the grain. Again, one harvest will produce grain that is chiefly kept for food, and another the crops that are sold; a larger proportion of rent (and Revenue) can therefore be paid after the one than after the other. Moreover as the Revenue is always payable in cash, the periods of its falling due are divided, otherwise there is too great a demand, all at once, for silver

[1] This is easy, because the various irrigated rates are always multiples of the dry rate: thus the tank-rate is (say) six times the dry: the 'well' rate four times, and so on: so that every acre of tank-land counts as six dry, and of well-land as four dry.

to make the payments; and such a sudden demand causes prices to fall, while the rate of interest rises. The Central Government has enforced upon the local authorities the necessity of fixing instalments, not so much by general rules, as with reference to the needs of each portion of the district or even of individual estates.

Refusal of Settlement.

Though it was commoner in past years, it may still conceivably occur that some proprietor will refuse the Settlement; i.e. after he has appealed up to the chief Revenue authority, and has not been successful, he declines the responsibility for the Revenue assessed. In that case he is excluded from the management of his land for a term of years (fixed by the Land Revenue Act), but is allowed a certain percentage (or *málikána*, as it is called). Further details are unnecessary.

The Land Records.

Preservation of the information as to rights and as to agricultural conditions gained in the process of Settlement. —When the inquiries of the Settlement Officer have resulted in determining all the rights and interests in land that are undisputed, or at least in possession, and are not merely the subject of unsettled litigation[1]; when the assessments are ready, and rents fixed as far as the law and practice require; the varied and important details (both statistical and concerning rights) that have been got together, have to be embodied in a number of formal records, drawn up in tabular statements or otherwise, as the experience of the past has suggested or as the Revenue Circular Orders provide. The Acts prescribe the records in general terms, leaving all details as to form and contents to be regulated locally.

[1] Decrees affecting land are always communicated to the Revenue authorities, so that the necessary entries may be made when the matter is finally settled.

It will be sufficient to indicate the general nature of these records; the precise form of the chief documents, as well as the supplementary statements which different provincial rules require, can be found out in each province from the Rules and Circulars, and especially by going to a Collector's Record Office and getting some instructed Record-Keeper to show the Record of any village and explain the forms and statements contained in the volumes.

Nature of the Records.—The documents are partly *statistical*, i. e. bearing on the agricultural conditions, soil, products, and other particulars of the estate; partly having *reference to rights* in the soil and to the Revenue shares and rents payable; village customs bearing on the land revenue management are also recorded.

In general we have the following documents:—

1. The village map (*Shajra*), already alluded to (pp. 176–7).
2. The field-index (*Khasra*), which is a descriptive register showing the serial number, who owns, who cultivates, and what crop, if any, each field bears. (There may be appendices showing lists of wells and other particulars of irrigation, &c.)
3. 'Village-Statements,' showing concisely all the statistical facts, population, and other details, about the village.
4. The *Khewat*, which is a record of the shares and revenue-responsibility of each member of the proprietary body.
5. *Jamabandí*, or list of *tenants*, and their rents.
6. The *Wájib-ul-'arz*, or record of village customs [1].

Special character of the Record of Rights in the Panjáb.—In the Panjáb, owing to the position of tenants in general, the *Khewat* and *Jamabandi* (4 and 5) are combined into one detailed statement (also called *Jamabandi*), which is in itself a *complete record of all rights and interests, showing every holding, of whatever kind.* It is renewed in great detail once in four years; and in the intermediate years an abridged form is kept up. The list of shares and state of proprietary interests is there specially

[1] In the North-West Provinces and Oudh a formal acceptance of the revenue-responsibility, signed by the landlord or by the representative *lambardárs* as the case may be, is one of the Records. In the Panjáb this has been abolished as unnecessary.

shown by the *Shajra-nasb*, or genealogical tree, which gives all the family relationships in the village, and the share and holding of each.

Recording village customs in the Panjáb.—The 'Record of village customs' used to contain all sorts of customs, not merely about managing the village, about fees or dues payable by non-proprietors, and such like, but its customs of inheritance and adoption, &c. This was originally needed in the Panjáb, where the Hindu and Muhammadan laws are little, if at all, followed by the agricultural castes; but of late years such matters have been held unsuitable to be placed in formal records, as they are not always undisputed. Local customs are now collected in 'Tribal Codes,' or books called '*Riwáj-i-'ám*': these are useful for reference, but have no legal authority beyond what other works of history or general information have.

Legal presumption of correctness.—This remark reminds me to notice that the Records, when properly attested, are legally presumed to be correct till the contrary is shown—which may be either in a law-suit, or by the Record being in due course altered in consequence of change by sale, inheritance or otherwise. These changes are, however, not made in the actual documents attested at Settlement (which themselves are never altered except on one or two (limited) grounds prescribed by law). They are noted in annual papers, which are in the same form as the initial Records.

Register of mutations of rights and interests.—The registration of all changes which occur since the completion of the Settlement Record, is one of the duties of the Revenue Administration, described in a concluding chapter; but it may here receive a passing notice because it is directly connected with the prospects of future Settlement work.

Difficulty of keeping the Records in correspondence with the facts of the time.—In the old days, when the Settlements were made, the records were fairly copied and bound up in volumes; the original was placed in the Collector's Record-room, and copies were deposited at the *Tahsíl* and with the *Patwárís* in each village office. But as time went on, these Records gradually ceased to correspond with the existing state of things. Registers of mutations were indeed maintained as now; but the *Patwárís* were inefficient, inspection was unsystematic, and many changes escaped record altogether. In short, when the thirty years (or other period) of the Settlement came to an end, the maps and Records were found to be of so little use—so many changes had occurred—that the whole work of survey and record had usually to be done over again.

How overcome of late years.—The plan is now quite different. An initial set of documents is provided by the Settlement; and these represent what was the correct state of things for the date or time at which the Records were officially signed and attested. Then a set of statements, in the same form, is maintained by the *Patwárís* in a state of continual correctness, by periodically introducing all changes reported and entered in the Register of mutations as soon as they have been approved of by the Collector. In the same way, copies of the map are kept correct by entering, in red lines, all changes in the old fields and the extension of cultivation by new fields, &c. This improvement will, it is hoped, completely obviate the necessity for any future resurvey and complete compilation of records of rights. The change has been rendered possible—(1) by the establishment of the Departments of Land Records (p. 20) charged with the supervision of these documents; (2) by the organizing and training of the staff of *Patwárís* and their supervisors; (3) by enforcing, under penalty, the report of all changes by inheritance, gift, sale, possessory mortgage, &c.; (4) by organizing regular inspections by *Patwárís* and supervisors, which not only bring to light changes in the map, and in the record of rights, but also provide the requisite information as to extension of cultivation, kind of crop cultivated, harvest out-turn, and other agricultural details.

Exemplified by the Act XVII of 1887.—The Panjáb Land Revenue Act (XVII of 1887) was drafted at a time when this system had been fully developed and had already begun to bear fruit. The Act was therefore able to prescribe definitely that there is to be (1) an *initial* record and (2) a corrected 'edition' of this—namely a series of *annual* records in exactly the same form. The first is maintained untouched for reference; the others may alter year by year, showing the changes that have occurred. But this is only a legally enacted description of what the practice is, in fact, in all Northern India (including the Central Provinces).

Changes reported for sanction.—As the records have a legal prescription in their favour, it is necessary that they should only take note of changes that are real and have been acted on; hence, though the *Patwárí* notes in his diary any change that is reported (p. 29), he does not embody it in the Annual Record till it has been officially passed or approved.

The English Settlement Report.—During the progress of the Settlement there may be more than one report required—notably, under all systems, the Report on the proposed Assessment and the rent- (or revenue-) rates; these are printed. But in order to sum up, in a convenient form, not only the principal features of the assessment, but all the local, historical, land-tenure and customary lore that has been gathered together by the Settlement Officer in the course of his study of the district, an English *Settlement Report* (which is not one of the formal Records of Settlement) is prepared. These volumes are sometimes of the greatest interest and value.

In the Panjáb the latest Settlement Reports are confined to the financial aspect of the work, and the local folk-lore and land-tenure information is placed in the 'District Gazetters,' which may sometimes be capable of revision or improvement on these subjects, when a new Settlement takes place. The change is, therefore, merely one of form [1].

Records, how preserved.—The formal Records of Settlement and the Annual Records are always in the Vernacular (the local government prescribing the language). They are bound in volumes, copies being available at the Collector's Office and at the *Tahsíl*, &c. There is a formal method of attestation prescribed by the Acts.

Resumé.—It will be convenient, before proceeding to the third system (p. 149)—the *Raiyatwárí*—to give a brief resumé of the main facts about the village (or *mahál*) Settlements—which belong to the 'temporary' (or non-permanent) class (p. 149).

[1] In Madras too the Settlement Reports are fiscal: information about tenures and district history is to be found in the volumes called 'District Manuals.'

Where there happens to be a landlord over a number of villages, he may be settled with in one sum for the whole, and then there may be (in some cases) subordinate Settlements made, determining the village payments.

But when the village (or group of lands in several villages, but held by one proprietary body) is the Settlement-unit, the whole is assessed to one sum, for which the body is jointly and severally liable,—until, by 'perfect' partition, the joint liability may be dissolved. The liability of each co-sharer is, however, separately determined and recorded, and this depends on the principle of co-sharing or on the constitution of the village.

The village and all its holdings and tenures are demarcated on the ground, and recorded in appropriate records after survey.

The object of a Settlement is, briefly:

(1) To assess the Land Revenue;

(2) To furnish the Collector (and his assistants and subordinates) with a correct list of the persons by whom it is payable;

(3) To secure the right and title, not only of the proprietors, but also of sub-proprietors, or tenants, or any others that may have an interest in the village lands or be entitled to some share in the profits or to some other payment.

Absence of Title Deeds.—It will be remembered that the Settlement 'Record of Rights' does away with the necessity for all the cumbrous title deeds of European countries. There may be specific grants, and other documents for special purposes; and modern sales and mortgages are usually effected with the aid of stamped and registered documents. But these are a small fraction of the land titles; written leases for tenants are also quite the exception, at any rate in some of the provinces; the 'Record of Rights,' therefore, is the mainstay of landed titles in general.

Section IV.

Settlements without a middleman (Raiyatwárí systems).

The Madras Revenue System.—First beginnings of a Raiyatwárí system.—Interrupted by the attempt to make a Permanent (landlord) Settlement.—I have already described how the Bengal Permanent Settlement was applied to certain parts of the Madras territories (p. 166). As a matter of fact the Permanent Settlement was not introduced before a beginning had been made with another system. When that part of the present Salem (*Sélam*) district, known as the Báramahál (or 'twelve estates'), was acquired in 1792, Captain Read, and the celebrated Munro (afterwards Sir T. Munro, Governor of Madras) as his assistant, were instructed to make a Settlement, the principles of which were very much of their own devising. The plan worked out by them, though bearing but little resemblance to the modern system, still undoubtedly contained the germs of that method of dealing with separate holdings, and of laying a rate on the land rather than arranging a payment for the individual, which we call the RAIYATWÁRÍ Settlement system. The work gradually extended to the large area of other districts that were acquired in quick succession (by lapse, treaty or by conquest) between 1792 and 1801. The course of these early Settlements on original methods, was interrupted both by war and also by the general attempt to make a landlord Permanent Settlement; and when that attempt failed, the authorities were bent on trying what was called a 'village Settlement.'

Madras village Settlements.—It has been already mentioned (p. 100) that in some districts, but chiefly in Tanjore and in the country adjoining Chingleput, there were traces of bodies of village co-sharers—then distinguished by the name of *mirásidár* families. In Chingleput they were so far in survival, that Mr. Lionel Place, an able and zealous Collector at the close of the last century, had really attained considerable success by making the village co-sharers (as a body) liable for a sum total of Revenue, which they apportioned among themselves in their own way; his arrangements, in fact, bore considerable resemblance to the landlord-village Settlements of the north. But, even in the absence of such special survivals, it was thought that, as a general method, a lump sum might be fixed for each village as a whole, and that a headman or 'renter' might be found to accept the responsibility for this, on a lease for a period of years, and that the sense of the body of local cultivators could be relied on to secure—which was the essential point—that the burden should be fairly divided among the cultivating landholders. The Reports that have been written regarding these village leases hardly establish the universal failure of the experiment; nevertheless, whenever (either originally or as the result of historical conditions) the village landholders had no natural connexion or system of co-sharing, it must have been always doubtful how far the burden would have been justly apportioned, and how far the 'renter,' at the head, would abstain from making himself the virtual autocrat and proprietor of the whole [1].

Village lease system is superseded by the Raiyatwárí.—The *Raiyatwárí* system was, however, destined to gain the day. Munro always held out for dealing '*kulwár*,' as he called it—that is, treating 'each and every' (*kul*) holding individually. And as he had visited England in 1807, and had an opportunity of personally explaining his views to the Court of Directors, the end was that, in a despatch of December 16, 1812, the Raiyatwárí system was formally ordered to be adopted (on the expiry of such village leases as were still running) for all estates which were not already established as *Zamíndárís*.

Modern system begins 1855–58.—We must pass over all the early history of changes and developments, and come at once to the years 1855–58, when a general revision of the first Settlements and the appointment of a Director of Settlements were determined on.

Its features.—The Madras Settlement commences with an accurate survey, very much like that described in the last section, only that primary attention is paid to the division of the cultivated land in each village into permanent (carefully demarcated) 'survey numbers' or lots as nearly as possible representing the individual holdings. The work is carried out by a separate survey staff, which furnishes the village map. The map is (as usual) accompanied by a descriptive register of all holdings,

[1] See the matter discussed in *L. S. B. I.* vol. iii. p. 26 ff.

which serves, in fact, as an index to the map. The Settlement staff then proceeds with the grouping of villages, the classification of soils and the assessment of the revenue demand. The Raiyatwárí system does not profess to determine rights in the way that the North-West system does; dealing with the actual occupant of each field, there is no need to do more than value and assess the fields correctly. Nevertheless, as the actual occupant (or he and his relations jointly) is practically, in most cases, the owner, the Settlement records do really secure rights to a great extent; and an extract from the Settlement register is as good a working title-deed as can be wished. If there is any dispute about right, it is settled by the Civil Courts; the Settlement Officer will not take any action beyond recording the person in actual occupation of the land.

Demarcation: fixed fields a feature of the system.—Previous to survey, there is the demarcation of village boundaries, as well as those of each field or 'survey number'; and provision is made for settling disputes as to exactly where the boundary line is or should be [1].

It will be noticed (see also p. 11) that under the Madras (and Bombay) systems, the 'fields,' or 'survey numbers'—as we shall call them, for that is the correct term—are fixed things, and can never be altered except by formal proceedings as to *internal* subdivision. Every field very generally represents a holding, or not less than a holding; but there are some detailed rules which I do not go into. In Madras there is no minimum size for fields; but inconveniently small holdings of the same kind may, under certain conditions, be clubbed together [2].

It will sometimes happen that several relations jointly own a survey number, but the shares can always be demarcated on the ground by the Survey Department. In that case the shares do not make so many new 'numbers,' but are indicated by a letter attached to the general survey number: thus 21 A, 21 B, &c. Such divisions are technically called 'interstitial fields,' and there are certain conditions, e.g. that they must be compact—a share cannot consist of a little bit here and a bit there.

[1] Act XXVIII of 1860 (amended by Madras Act II of 1884) gives the necessary powers.

[2] See *L. S. B. I.* vol. iii. p. 56.

Grouping of villages under similar conditions (dry cultivation).—The next task is to arrange the villages of the tract under Settlement, into groups[1]. Cultivation is broadly distinguished into 'wet' (or irrigated) and 'dry' (which depends on rainfall supplemented by wells, &c.) The grouping is different according as one or other is prevalent. 'Dry' villages are formed into groups, in each of which the conditions are similar with regard to climate, situation, market facilities, proximity to a railway line or a town, situation on high upland or low-lying land, and the like. These groups are placed in the tables in order of excellency; and it will afterwards appear that the assessment is greatly simplified by this, since a single series of rates can be applied to the several groups by a sliding scale; e. g. what is the highest rate in the third group will be the third in the first group, the second in the second group; and so on.

Soil classification.—Practice has determined that, in general, all soils can be classified in a series of five :—

(1) Alluvial and 'permanently improved' (exceptional soils).

(2) Black cotton soil (*regar*).

(3) Red ferruginous.

(4) Calcareous (this is rare).

(5) Arenaceous—more or less pure sand in coast districts.

Each 'series' is divided into classes according as there is *more or less of the mineral constituent which characterizes* the 'series.' This constituent is technically referred to as 'clay' (whatever its actual nature). Each series may have either (1) nearly pure 'clay;' (2) half clay and half sand; (3) a preponderance of sand. They reckon fourteen classes in all to cover all the above 'series.' And, once more, each *class* may have several *sorts*—good, ordinary, inferior, &c.

Short mode of designation.—In tables of rates, however, it is not necessary to write out at length the whole description. Each kind is briefly indicated by the aid of two numbers—by a *Roman* numeral for the 'class' and an *Arabic* numeral for the 'sort.' The 'series'

[1] This is just, in fact, the formation of 'Assessment Circles,' as in Northern India (p. 181).

does not need indicating, because classes I, II always belong to the 'exceptional' series; classes III, IV and V to the 'regar'; VI, VII and VIII to the 'red'; IX, X and XI to the 'calcareous'; and XII–XIV to the 'arenaceous.' A soil described as VIII. 5 (for example) would mean red ferruginous *series*, of *class* (VIII) containing not more than half clay, and of the worst *sort* (5).

Grouping of 'wet' villages. The 'wet' villages are grouped according to the character of the *irrigation source*, whether from an anicut (i.e. a system of channels distributing water from a river confined by a weir) or from a tank which always has water, or from a more precarious source (p. 10). These distinctions are found to obliterate differences caused by situation. In the 'wet' groups, the 'series' and 'class' of soil remain as before; but the 'sort' gradation is replaced by three or four distinctions based on the greater or less advantage of level, drainage, &c. for irrigation purposes.

Assessment.—The basis of the assessment is, in theory at any rate, that it is not to exceed 50 per cent. of the *net* produce. To find out this, the gross produce is first ascertained and valued at average prices[1]; the costs of cultivation, &c. are then deducted, and half the balance is taken as the Revenue (omitting fractions). In many cases this calculation had to be laboriously worked out. The first question was what 'produce' should be taken into consideration? for different fields bear different crops. A sort of average or standard produce was taken as fairly representing the cultivation of a whole *taluk*; the guide being the recorded statistics, which showed what percentage of the whole *taluk* was under cultivation for each kind of grain. *Food* grains were dealt with always; other crops could be allowed for on the basis of a comparison of their value with that of food grains.

Taking the statistics of a *taluk*, for example, it might be that (for dry crops) the largest percentage of the area was cultivated with *Rági* (a millet) and another grain called *Varagu*, and that other crops so approximated to them in value, that, speaking broadly, we might treat the whole cultivation as consisting of or

[1] Tables of prices for the twenty (non-famine) years preceding Settlement are compiled. Certain percentage deductions are also allowed for the fact that raiyats get less for their grain than merchants; and to cover costs of carriage or to allow for difference between local and market rates.

being equivalent to, half *Rági* and half *Varagu.* By the result of experiments, on a given soil, we find that an acre of *Rági* gives (say) 320 Madras measures, and *Varagu* 440 measures; then as each acre is treated as bearing, half of it one, and half of it the other, its produce is 160 + 220 measures. Now the money values of these are[1] *Res.* 7-1-7 and *Res.* 6-1-11 respectively. The total gross produce value is thus *Res.* 13-3-6. It is also known (as the result of inquiry and calculation) that the cost of production may be taken to be, per acre (say) *Res.* 9-3-6; then the net result is *Res.* 4-0-0, and the Land Revenue is *Res.* 2-0-0.

Such calculations not repeated for all cases.—As a matter of fact such calculations are never of themselves uniform enough in their results, to be the real basis of working rates. At best they give some sort of *standard*, which is referred to as a check or as a limit beyond which the actual rates should not go. Attention is always paid to the existing rates, especially to those employed in neighbouring localities, and also to general considerations on which the existing rates (of the last or now expiring Settlement) may be raised (or possibly lowered).

In any case the calculation of rates has not to be separately made for each of the 'sorts' of each 'class' of soil—for many of them are of nearly equal value; and in practice a limited number of rates will answer all purposes[2].

'Taram' lists.—The general rates so arranged are called *Taram*; while the different village-*groups* are provided for, not by making separate rates, but by a sliding scale; the second *Taram* of the first group becomes the first of the second group, and so on; one or two lower rates may be added on to the inferior groups for soils that do not appear in the superior group at all.

To a large extent, therefore, the maximum or initial rates are empirical ones, only nicely adjusted to each variety of soil and circumstance. The rates, it will be observed, simply regard the land, and take no notice of such personal considerations as

[1] As found from the tables of prices mentioned in the preceding note.

[2] It hardly needs explanation, that e.g. inferior clay *regar*, fair loam *regar*, and best sandy ferruginous, though distinct in character, may yet be about equally valuable, and so bear the same rate. At one time it was attempted to draw up a general scale of rates for the whole country (*L. S. B. I.* vol. iii. p. 69), but this was going too far in the direction of generalization. Each Settlement has its own scale for the *taluk*, or district perhaps.

the ability of one agricultural caste as compared with another, and the like.

Single and double crop assessment.—'Dry' land is assessed on the supposition that it yields one crop; if it yields a second dry crop, no extra charge is made. Wells on dry land do not alter the classification, unless the well is in one or other of the exceptional positions indicated in the rules; (in those cases the well really takes the water from an irrigation source, and the land is virtually 'wet.') Wet land in general is assessed as two-crop land[1]; but in the case of the source of irrigation being precarious, and when the water has failed, a deduction is allowed at the annual settlement of accounts or *jamabandí* (of which we shall speak hereafter).

As the distinction of 'wet' and 'dry' land is important, the Settlement operations include a careful scrutiny of the actual holdings in each *ayacut*, or area commanded by a tank, or which are reached by the *anicut* system from a river weir. There are also various rules about alteration of fields from wet to dry and *vice versâ*.

Distinctive features of the system.—It will be borne in mind that it is the distinguishing feature of the regular Raiyatwárí system of Madras (and Bombay) that there is no joint responsibility under which the cultivators in a village may be called on to make good the default of one of their number. Each raiyat is free to *relinquish* his holding or any separately demarcated and registered part of it on giving notice in due time according to rule (see p. 126).

Records of Settlement.—The records prepared at Settlement may now be briefly described. (1) The main document (answering very much to the *Khasra* of the last section) is called the 'Settlement Register.'

[1] The assessment for the second crop being half that of the first; but in all cases, if one of two crops (whether first or second) is raised by the aid of irrigation (from a public source), a full single crop, wet, assessment is levied. In cases where there is a liability each year to have the recorded single-crop assessment raised by reason of a second crop being obtained, there are rules for *compounding* for the whole in one fixed sum; and then, if the irrigation for one crop fails, there is a special rule about the rate to be paid for the year.

'It forms,' says the *Madras Settlement Manual*, 'a complete doomsday book, recording accurate information regarding every separate holding, whether large or small. The area is given in *acres* and *cents* (hundredths of an acre) and the assessment thereon stands in parallel columns. A single field on the survey map may be actually divided amongst twenty raiyats. In such a case there will be twenty subletters (p. 201), and each raiyat will have a separate line in the register, giving full particulars of his holding, even though the extent of it (as sometimes happens) is no more than the one-hundredth part of an acre.

'From the Register is prepared a ledger known as the *chittá*, which gives each raiyat's personal account with the Government. Every field or fraction of a field held by the same raiyat is picked out from the Settlement Register and entered in his ledger, under his name, with particulars of area, assessment, and other details. The total of the area shows the extent of his different holdings in the village, and the total of the assessment is the amount due thereon by him to Government. A copy of this, his personal account, is given to each raiyat, with a note as to the date on which each instalment falls due, and is known as his *pattá*.'

(2) An English descriptive memoir, giving full details touching each village and its Settlement, and an account of all lands held revenue-free, or on favourable tenure, is also printed. A sketch map of the village, showing the tanks and channels and all similarly assessed fields laid out into blocks, is attached to it. A scroll map in two or three sections, showing the classification of a whole *taluk*, is also prepared and lithographed at Madras.

The descriptive memoirs of all the villages in each *taluk*, consecutively numbered, are bound into a single volume, with their respective eye-sketches, which thus supply complete information regarding each village.

It may be noted that the various annual and other statements which the village Patwárís (*Karnams*) have to prepare, are designed to keep the information gained at Settlement continually correct by noting all changes that occur.

Duration of Settlement.—The Settlement is for thirty years, but the remarks made (p. 152) apply here also.

Bombay System.—The second great Raiyatwárí system of India is that of BOMBAY. Unlike Madras, Bombay possesses a complete Revenue Code (Bombay Act V of 1879), which includes all powers for survey, assessment, and other matters connected with Settlement. As some of the Bombay districts contain special classes of estates, e. g. in the Gujarát districts and on the west coast, provision has been made for the necessary exceptional measures of Settlement and the acknowledgement of inferior rights, by Acts expressly relating to the *Khot* estates, the Ahmadábád *Taluqdárs* (pp. 110, 113), and the few *joint-villages* of the Kherá and Bharoch districts (pp. 75 note, 15).

The bulk of the villages being in the Raiyatwárí form [1], the Settlement in general has the same leading features as that just described. There is an elaborate demarcation of boundaries, followed by a scientific survey, a fixing of permanent areas to be fields or 'survey numbers,' and a classification of soils. The mode of assessment is, however, special to Bombay. The Records of Settlement, as in Madras, have no direct concern with rights, but do really protect the holders, and serve instead of title-deeds. The landholder, however, in Bombay has his title defined by law as 'occupant' (see p. 126).

We will therefore confine our attention chiefly to the 'survey numbers' of the ordinary occupancy or survey tenure—to the mode of their classification and assessment and to the Records prepared at Settlement.

Size of the survey fields.—The rules as to the size of the field taken as the unit of survey have altered. As first it was enough to fix a convenient but arbitrary area, which was large. The code now directs that no field is to be below a *minimum* size, fixed in each district, and for each class of land, by the Commissioner; but existing numbers below the minimum, if already recognized by the Records, are saved; and practically, every independent holding is separately measured and assessed on its own merits. Should a holding be too small, it may be

[1] **Question in Bombay as to the possibility of village-Settlements.**—The question was at first raised whether joint-village Settlements could not be made; the decision was, however, in favour of the separate dealing with holdings. For a long time no very satisfactory results were obtained; but at last, in 1835, a new start was made. The developement of the system is chiefly due to the exertions of Mr. Goldsmid Lieut. (afterwards Sir G.) Wingate, and Lieut. Nash. The results of their experience appeared in the compilation called the 'Joint Report' (1847).

clubbed together with others; but each will constitute a sub-number (or *pót* number, as the phrase is). In all cases a field, part of which is revenue free and part not, will be separated; and the larger 'numbers' of former surveys have been divided. Generally speaking, the survey numbers of 'garden land' are the smallest, of 'rice land' the next in size, and of 'dry' the largest.

Forms of cultivation.—This enables me to mention that these three classes of land are always recognized. Rice land is, of course, always irrigated or flooded. 'Dry' land (*jiráyat*) may have a well or some irrigation source on it; it is not necessarily absolutely dependent on rain. When it is irrigated and manured, and has thus been changed in character, it may become *bágháyat*, or 'garden land.' The area under irrigation of any sort is always measured at survey, because there may be a different rate for the irrigated part.

Classification of soils for assessment purposes.—The assessment here fully exemplifies the principle noted at p. 48. The actual rates selected for each class of soil recognized in each group or circle, are empirical rates; they do not pretend to represent rental values or a share in the produce; but the soils are so classified and so accurately valued *relatively*, that the rates, assumed to be fair as *maxima*, can be graduated to suit each degree of relative value in the individual field.

Hence we must take notice of the classification. Dry land is taken as the standard, because there are more varieties; rice land has rates of its own; and so with garden land, which has artificially acquired a special character.

In the Dakhan districts, the soils, though they vary much, are all found to belong to one or other of three 'orders'—fine black soil, red soil (coarser), and light soil (*barad*). The depth of soil is found to be the important consideration; and 1¾ cubits is the maximum of value in this respect; while with less than a quarter cubit, soil is uncultivable. Each diminishing degree of depth gives a lower grade in value; so reckoning (in the usual Indian fashion) by *anas*, we take 16 *anas* (one rupee) as the full or maximum value, and other values will be 14 *anas*, 12 *anas*, and so on. It is found, in practice, that nine classes suffice in ordinary cases, and a tenth is added for very poor soil. The first class only occurs in the first order;—no other 'dry' soil reckons as 16 *anas*; the 14 *ana* value is the highest of the second order, as it is the second of the first, and so on; thus:—

Class.	Relative value.	1st order, 'Black.'	2nd order, 'Red.'	3rd order, 'Light.'
	Anas.	Depth in cubits.	Depth.	Depth.
1	16	$1\frac{3}{4}$		
2	14	$1\frac{1}{2}$	$1\frac{3}{4}$	
3	12	$1\frac{1}{4}$	$1\frac{1}{2}$	
4	10	1	$1\frac{1}{4}$	
5	8	$\frac{3}{4}$	1	
6	6	$\frac{1}{2}$	$\frac{3}{4}$	1
7	$4\frac{1}{2}$	$\frac{1}{4}$	$\frac{1}{2}$	$\frac{3}{4}$
8	3		$\frac{1}{4}$	$\frac{1}{2}$
9	2			$\frac{1}{4}$
10	1			$\frac{1}{4}$ (very poor).

Observe that these are only *relative* values; whatever the full rate, only class 1 will pay it; class 3 would pay three quarters (or 12 *anas*) of the full rate; the 5th class one half (8 *anas*), and so on.

Accidental defects in soils.—But they also recognize seven accidental (chiefly surface) defects which may occur in any soil; and the occurrence of one of these, lowers the 'class' one degree, or if it is bad, two degrees. The accidents are indicated by conventional signs, and a 'bad' case is shown by writing the mark twice.

Field diagrams.—It, however, rarely happens that a survey number is uniform throughout; so a kind of diagram of each is drawn. No attempt actually to measure the limit of each variation of soil is made, but by the eye a sufficient division of the diagram is made. Let us suppose a case where the field includes four kinds of soil. The classifier will divide his diagram into four parts; on each he will mark, by means of one or more *dots*, that it belongs to first, second or third 'order'; the depth (ascertained by actual digging) he will also enter in figures; if there is any accidental defect he will mark its conventional sign. Suppose that the first compartment has one dot (first order), and is one and three-quarter cubits deep; that would be in the first class; *but* it has also two defects, and one so badly as to be marked twice; here the class comes down from one to four. Then the number '4' is written in the upper left-hand corner. Let us suppose that by a similar process the other three divisions are marked fifth class, third class, and eighth class; then we have a field composed of the four values 10 *as* + 8 + 12 + 3, and the average value is $\frac{33}{4}$ or 8 *as* nearly; the whole field will then pay half the full rate, whatever it is.

This classification, in the hands of an experienced staff, is performed very rapidly, and with such accuracy that the test classifications applied by way of check, rarely differ appreciably.

These are Dakhan soils; but all other dry soils are treated in the same way, though the scale may be somewhat different. When there is part of the land 'irrigated,' an additional rate may be put on for this: but private wells (sunk with private capital) do not increase the assessment[1].

'Rice land' and 'garden land' have rates of their own.

Calculation of the maximum rate to head the sliding scale.—The *relative* value being thus accurately graded, we have only to find out the full or '16 *ana*' rate; and this will be applied to each field according to its fractional value by simple division;—the '12 *ana*' fields paying three-quarters of the rate, and so on, down to the '1 *ana*' field which pays only one-sixteenth.

The actual full or maximum rates required for 'dry,' 'garden' and 'irrigated,' are found out with reference to previously paid rates and to general considerations of present prosperity, increase in cultivation, &c. The late Mr. Pedder, than whom no better authority can be quoted, says:—

'The Bombay method is avowedly an empirical one. When a tract (usually a *táluka*) comes under Settlement . . . . its revenue history for the preceding thirty or more years is carefully ascertained and tabulated in figured statements or diagrams[2]. These show, in juxtaposition for each year of the series, the amount and incidence of the assessment; the remissions or arrears; the ease or difficulty with which the revenue was realized; the rainfall and nature of the seasons; the harvest prices; the extension or decrease of cultivation; and how these particulars are influenced by each other;

[1] The nearness of water to the surface, which is a natural feature, may be taken into account in fixing the rates, but not the (private) well itself.

[2] They make great use of diagrams showing the rise and fall of prices and quantities by means of curves, or points on a scale connected by lines.

the effect of any public improvements, such as roads, railways, or canals and markets, on the tract or on parts of it, is estimated; the prices for which land is sold, and the rents for which it is let, are ascertained. Upon a consideration of all these data, the *total* Settlement assessment (of the tract) is ascertained.

That amount is then apportioned, pretty much in the same way, on the different villages; and the total assessment of each village is distributed over the assessable fields in accordance with the classification which has determined their relative value....'

Limit to increase in rates at revision.—It will be remembered that at all revision-Settlements, it is a rule never to let the increase be too great all at once. A suddenly raised revenue, even if justifiable in itself, could not be paid without great inconvenience. It is therefore a rule in Bombay, to limit the increase taken, to thirty-three per cent. on the whole *táluka*, or sixty-six per cent. on the village total, or one hundred per cent. on the single holding, above the last assessment. This is not exceeded without special reasons and due sanction. Sec. 107 of the Revenue Code also expressly prohibits the increase of assessment in consequence of any private improvements effected during the currency of the previous Settlement.

Survey now complete in Bombay.—The field-to-field survey and the classification and relative valuation of soils is probably, by this time, nearly or quite complete throughout Bombay; and as the work has been all thoroughly revised during the past decade, it is final and will never have to be done again. All that will be necessary at future revisions will be to adjust the revenue-rates to the increased value of produce or land, within the proper percentage limits.

Period of Settlement.—The Settlements are made for thirty years, as a rule (p. 152).

Sindh Settlements.—In Sindh, a shorter period has been made use of. I may here add that in this Division, the assessment rates depend on the kind of irrigation made use of. Cultivation depends wholly on water, either percolating from the river (Indus), or obtained from wells near it, or raised by wheel or lift from irrigation channels. And as land so treated, has to be subjected to continual periods of rest, a special arrangement is made. A holder can register himself as occupant of a number of 'fields'; and under certain rules he is allowed to pay only for the ones actually tilled, retaining a lien on the others that are fallow [1].

The Records of Settlements.—The records prepared at the Settlement-Survey are in fact almost exactly the same as those mentioned as in use in Madras, only that the names, and the precise forms, are different.

1. There are the large-scale village maps.
2. The general Land Register.
3. The *Botkhat* (*chittá* of Madras, p. 206), which is a personal ledger grouping together all the fields or recognized shares in fields held by the same occupant.

The Register shows the actual occupant; should a person be cultivating, say, as a tenant, and not claiming to be 'occupant,' the record would give the real occupant's name. It will show all such shares as are allowed to be separately demarcated on the ground, and also any shares that are recognized officially but not demarcated.

The original Records are attested and kept unaltered (except to remove clerical errors or mistakes admitted by all parties concerned). The changes in occupancy and other features that *can* change, are noted in the various registers and returns which the *Kulkarní* of the village has to keep up (p. 30).

Berár.—It is only necessary to add that *Berár* is settled under the Bombay system, and there is little or no difference, in principle at any rate, such as need here be noted. The Berár authorities have recently been drafting a Code of Revenue Rules of their own.

Resumé.—Let us now, as in the last section, give a brief

[1] *L. S. B. I.* vol. iii. p. 321. The whole history of land in Sindh is very curious; the fact is that land, as land, has no value whatever; right in land therefore, as established by conquest, meant a right of taking certain fees or dues on cultivation established by irrigation, within a certain territorial area. This led to difficulties, because persons claimed the ownership of large areas only part of which could be cultivated—now here, now there. Such persons could only be put down in the Register as in 'occupation' of all the numbers comprised in the claim, on the understanding that they would annually pay the Revenue of the whole. This would be hard; so the system was modified, and gradually the rule stated in the text has been arrived at.

resumé of the features of a Raiyatwárí Settlement. In the matter of duration for a *term of years*, in requiring a *demarcation of boundaries* and a *survey*, the raiyatwárí systems are like the others. But the survey numbers are never allowed to be altered as they represent fixed units of assessment. In the other Settlements (except as a matter of private right for the time being) the fields are of no particular consequence. Each holding is assessed separately, on a principle which starts with maximum rates more or less empirical, but which are accurately adjusted to every degree of relative value in the kinds of soil. There is *no joint responsibility*, except among joint holders of the same survey-number. The landholder is not bound to the holding for the term of Settlement; any holder can *relinquish* his holding (or a defined part of it) provided he does so at a certain date. The Revenue payable is ascertained by making out an annual account of the lands actually held by each *raiyat* for the year.

There are maps and Registers and Statistical records; but the Settlement does not profess to record or to define varieties of right, so the papers do not (formally) include any *Records of rights*. Practically, of course, in all simple occupant-holdings, the Field-Register does give perfect security of title.

Section V. Settlements that are in principle, but not formally, raiyatwárí.

The Provinces of Burma, Assam and Coorg are all managed under simple systems which are in fact *raiyatwárí*,—because there has been no trace found of groups of cultivators who have a joint-tenure[1]. The system has in each case simply followed

[1] In Assam we have one curious instance (Káchár district) of a sort of joint-tenure which is special, and may really afford a clue to some of the (much older) joint-settlements of colonists in other parts. The cultivators voluntarily formed close groups with a joint responsibility for their revenue, on purpose to keep out strangers, and prevent the intrusion of Revenue-farmers and officials to look after the collections in detail. See *L. S. B. I.* vol. iii. There may be anywhere a single holding which is enjoyed by a number of members of a family together,—in a 'house community' as in Coorg; but that does not give rise to any of the complicated features of the joint-village of Upper India.

the facts, and created no artificial middlemen; nor has there been much occasion for rescuing, and providing for, rights in danger of being trodden down under superior interests which have arisen out of conquest or State grant.

The simplicity of the Revenue system enables us therefore to deal with these provinces in a few paragraphs; but it should be said at once, that this is not due to any tendency on my part to undervalue these systems, or to imagine that because these provinces are in the outer corners of the Empire, therefore they are unknown or of little consequence. Assam and Burma are both provinces which have a great future before them: they are still undeveloped as to their resources, and rapid progress cannot be expected without a larger population (which is one of their greatest needs) and easier communication. These needs, it is true, are being gradually supplied, as the last census returns show; the former might be easily met by emigration from some of the densely stocked districts of Upper India, if only the popular feeling was not so strongly against moving away from home. Even this feeling however is shown, by statistics, to be gradually giving way. Burma has already seen its coast towns undergo the most wonderful expansion [1], and it can hardly be doubted that the same prosperity will gradually overtake the country districts. Already Burma is one of the best paying provinces, and it has magnificent forest resources. But owing to these very considerations, the Land Revenue Systems themselves are in a more or less elementary stage. They will almost certainly undergo some change in the future; and therefore it is not possible to commend them to notice in the same way as we can those systems which have reached their final development.

Assam.

Constituents of the Assam province.—The Assam Government, formed in 1874, received as its charge some of the old Bengal territory which had been permanently settled (Goálpára,

[1] See Sir W. Hunter's *Brief History of the Indian people*, p. 216.

and part of Sylhet), and Cachar was also a Bengal district, though, as it was only acquired in 1830, it came under the Temporary Settlement. For the rest, the Assam province has to deal with the districts in the valley of the Bráhmaputra, which were never under the Regulation law, and with the Hill districts which are still under a distinct and administrative system adapted to the more primitive condition of their tribes.

The Assam valley districts.—The Assam valley as a whole was acquired when the Burman invaders were driven out (1824-1826). For some years it was left to the management of local chiefs under the supervision of British officers. This system broke down, and Act II of 1835 was passed to provide for a suitable administration. The Revenue System remained an informal one,—yearly assessments, levied at certain known customary rates for each class of land, according to annual measurement of cultivation.

Early condition of Assam.—The Aham Rulers (a Hinduized dynasty of Tibeto-Burman (Shán) origin, which had ruled from the thirteenth century down to our own times) had organized the entire population *into groups for service of all kinds*. Each *páik* or individual in the groups was allowed a certain area of land for his support. There was no regular land-revenue; the State income was derived from a poll-tax, and the profits of the service exacted, which was of all kinds,—military service in the ranks, labour on works, contributions of gains in trade, and even a portion of the products of handicraft. Any one, it seems, might cultivate land over and above his stated allowance, and then he paid a fixed rate for it. Proprietary right in land was apparently not thought of; and the lordship, by grant, or by official position, over an area which the serfs or subjects tilled, and from which the requirements of the lord's household were supplied, was the only form of 'estate,' other than that implied by the ordinary peasant holding.

Land Regulation I of 1886.—When, in modern times, it became desirable to formulate the conditions of landed right in a Regulation (and this was first done in 1886), the only 'proprietors' in the province were the Permanent Settlement land-

[1] The ruler of this line became a Hindu in A. D. 1655; the kingdom was able to bear up against Muhammadan invasion, but eventually fell under feeble princes, whose dissensions at last resulted in one of the rulers calling in Burmese aid. This proved fatal.

holders of the older Bengal districts, and a few other permanent grantees, such as large Revenue-freeholders, and grantees of proprietary right in Waste-land (under the earlier Rules). For the bulk of ordinary cultivators, it was thought best to recognize a practical title which was not in name proprietary, but is defined as that of a 'landholder,' in section 8 of the Regulation (I of 1886). As usual in raiyatwárí systems, the land held on such a title may be relinquished by notice at a certain date.

Old Permanent Settlement Estates.—The Regulation of course preserves the privileges of the old Permanent Settlement estates in Goálpára and Sylhet.

Revenue free estates. Nisfkhiráj.—As usual, some of the tenures recognized have arisen out of Revenue-free estates; and these gave some trouble. On the conversion of the Assam princes to Hinduism, they began, with all the zeal of converts, to make grants for religious purposes and to Brahmans; and there were certain lands held on a free tenure by the old Court officials and Chiefs (of many titles) or their descendants. The British Government declared that all those grants were formally cancelled (as they were only held at the pleasure of the former Government). But it was not intended actually to deprive old established holders of real grants. In some cases local chiefs were allowed to retain their lands Revenue-free; others were subject to assessment. A number of other cases were dealt with by the officer in charge of the inquiries, who allowed the holders to pay revenue at half rates; by some mistake this was not reported as it ought to have been; and when some years had elapsed, the Government thought it impolitic not to recognize what had been done, and it condoned the irregularity. These holders are therefore recognized by a name that came into use about twenty years ago, '*nisfkhiráj-dár*' (= half-revenue holders). They are not reckoned as 'proprietors' under the Regulation, only as 'landholders;' and they will have to pay half whatever revenue is ordinarily payable for the term of Settlement.

'Landholders.'—The ordinary 'landholder's' title is not acquired by merely temporarily cultivating: the land must have been held for ten years *before* the Regulation (on whatever title, or even with no title). *After* the date of the Regulation, as no one is at liberty simply to 'occupy' waste-land, the land-holder's title is only acquired by a lease, or by grant of a Settlement for ten years.

Wasteland grants.—As in Assam there is as yet no district with more than 25–30 per cent. of its area under cultivation, titles under *grants of waste* must always have considerable importance. A great deal of land will be simply brought gradually under cultivation as an extension of existing villages, by means of the ordinary application to the Collector. But for larger grants, especially for tea-planting, there have always been special rules.

A few grants under the first rules of 1838 (proprictary estates with reduced revenue terms) still survive. A much larger number are under 'the Old Assam Rules' (1854) which began as long leaseholds, held under condition of bringing a stated portion of the area under cultivation within a fixed time. These have now become proprietary estates, and many of them were allowed to *redeem* the Land Revenue. There are also estates under the 'fee simple' rules (as they were called) of 1862–1876, under which the land was sold outright and revenue-free, but by auction, and at an upset or minimum price per acre which was gradually raised.

Since then, the more reasonable modern policy (p. 60) of granting land only on lease, has been followed. The lease is for thirty years; the land is put up to auction at an upset 'entrance fee' of one shilling an acre. It pays no revenue for two years, and then small rates per acre (only reaching a rate of one shilling per acre in the last ten years of the thirty). There is no condition about any proportion of the area to be brought under cultivation. At the conclusion of the thirty years, the holder remains in possession on certain conditions as to punctual payment of the assessment [1], of devoting the land to the purpose for which it was granted, of residing personally, or

[1] Which is limited to the highest rate paid in the district for ordinary agricultural land.

keeping an agent, on the estate; of maintaining the boundary marks, and of not alienating the estate piecemeal (it may be sold *as a whole* with due notice to the Collector). If the conditions are broken, the favourable rates of assessment may be withdrawn.

Ordinary land and its Settlement.—Apart from the special 'proprietary' holdings, and those held on lease, or by 'landholders,' a great deal of land is still held on an annually renewed permit or '*pattá*'; at any rate on a lease for less than ten years.

In backward tracts, or where, from the nature of the soil or otherwise, the cultivation is not permanent, no regular Settlement operations have been introduced; the extent of cultivation is annually measured, and a simple record of it made out, from which a written form giving particulars (and called a *pattá*) is copied out and given to the cultivator. Where the cultivation is by 'landholders,' and is permanent, a ten years' Settlement is made under the Rules.

There has been an old standing classification of land in Assam, into 'homestead and garden' (*bárí* or *bastí*), 'rice-land' (*rúpít*), and a residuary class for all kinds of land that is not *bárí* or *rúpít*, named *faringatí*.

At present there are established rates for each kind[1]. The rates were revised in 1861, but I have not heard of any subsequent rise. Apparently, at present, the cultivation is so little developed, that the increase of land-revenue is sufficiently secured by the assessment of newly formed fields at the old rates. But the rates are of course liable to revision.

The mauzadár system.—As to the nature of the Settlement, and the records which accompany it, it is necessary first to remark, that though *local* village boundaries are known, they are not of much importance; they are superseded by an official aggregation of land into *mauza* areas, each in charge of an official called *mauzadár*. The term *mauza*, as used in Assam, bears this meaning only. The *mauzadár* was formerly charged with making *all* measurements (having the aid of a sort

[1] These rates are not applied to land which has become more valuable as being within a radius of five miles from a civil or military station.

of '*patwárí*' locally called *mandal*); at present he is only concerned with measuring *unsettled* lands. He collects the revenue of all holdings in his charge, and is held primarily responsible for it: he has, however, no concern with the revenue of any 'proprietary' estates that happen to be within his *mauza*. He nevertheless maintains registers giving an account of all the kinds of land or estate (Revenue-free, Government Forest, unappropriated waste, &c.) within his circle or charge.

Where permanent cultivation is more extended, and Settlement operations have been carried out, the *mauzadár* system is giving place to a regular *Tahsíl* agency (p. 24).

Surveyed tracts.—Having mentioned that operations for a Settlement (for ten years) have been introduced in the better cultivated districts, it has to be noted that this Settlement includes a regular survey giving correct maps (instead of the old rough recorded measurements); land Registers in an improved and more detailed form are also being introduced. The 'survey-numbers' are arranged on certain simple principles, which, as usual, are designed to secure that separate holdings should, as far as possible, be separate 'numbers,' and that very large fields should be subdivided [1]. Wherever there is a landholder's estate, or a proprietary estate exceeding fifty *bighás* in extent, separate registers are made out for it, and a separate report is made of its Settlement.

The Hill districts. The Regulations of 1873 and 1880.—These remarks apply to the Assam valley. But a glance at the map will show how great a proportion of the province consists of hill-country. This not only extends along the northern and north-eastern frontier, but also occupies the centre of the province, in fact separating the Assam valley from Sylhet and Cachar. The hill districts (when they are British territory) are managed under Regulation II of 1880 (as extended by III of 1884), which enables simple local rules to be substituted for the ordinary (more complicated) statute-law. When the hills are not wholly within British territory, Regulation V of

[1] *L. S. B. I.*, vol. iii. p. 424, gives some further details about the rules of Survey.

1873 is made use of to establish an 'inner line,' which means a boundary beyond which British subjects cannot ordinarily proceed, except under certain restraints and precautions. For there is a not inconsiderable trade in ivory, caoutchouc, and other wild produce, which invites the presence of merchants and their agents. The traffic is accordingly regulated, and the acquisition of land is prohibited, so as to prevent the occurrence of any disputes that might lead to raids and disorders.

No Land Revenue System applies to the hill districts, but there is a 'house-tax' and other dues also, locally. Cultivation is in some parts permanent on terraced fields along the hill sides. The forest-clad slopes however are still cultivated largely by the temporary or shifting method, called '*júm*' (p. 12).

The old Bengal districts. Goálpára.—Of the older districts now attached to Assam, it may be sufficient to note that Goálpára consists of a portion of the old Rangpur Collectorate, in which certain *Chaudharís* and other local magnates were recognized as landlords under the Permanent Settlement. There are in fact some nineteen such estates in the plain country above and below the Gáro hills district (which was from an early date removed entirely from the control of the Zamíndárs). In 1866, the Eastern Dwár districts were acquired from Bhután, and were added to Goálpára: these were not permanently settled; and with the exception of two tracts in which local Rájás have been recognized as landlords, they are under the ordinary 'landholders' tenure of Assam. A special Act (XVI of 1869) still applies to the Dwárs.

For the two remaining districts, we have to look below the central range of hills, to what is in fact the plain or valley of the Surmá river.

Cachar.—Cachar (*Káchár*) is part hill country and part plain. The hills beyond the lofty limestone cliffs of the *Baráil* range are under a separate jurisdiction. On the lapse of the district (owing to the death of the *Rájá* without heirs, in 1830) it was placed under a special administration formulated by Act VI of 1835. An 'inner line' (Regulation V of 1873) separates the district from the hills to the south (occupied by independent tribes). Cachar, having been acquired only in 1830, came under the 'temporary' Settlement law. I have already alluded to the joint-tenure of the colonist bodies who established most of the ordinary agricultural holdings in the district [1]. Apparently this method of colonization only began under native rule and was mostly developed under our own. There is no (legal) right in the land other than that of 'landholder' under Regulation I of 1886, but the joint responsibility for the revenue is continued. In this district there are many grants under the 'Waste Land Rules,' especially for tea estates.

Sylhet.—Sylhet (*Sílhat*, a corruption of *Srihattá*) was one of the old Bengal districts of 1765, and had come under Rájá Todar Mal's Settlement (and consequent land-measurement) in the sixteenth century. The Bengal Permanent Settlement was extended to the district in 1790, but was not made with Zamindárs or local land officers, but with actual occupant settlers of measured holdings, who were called *mirásdár*. Practically these holdings are raiyat-holdings; only that as they are under the old Regulation VIII of 1793, they possess a full proprietary right and a permanent assessment [2]. The Permanent Settlement, however, extended only to land held in 1790; consequently a large portion of the district then uncultivated, is not subject to the old Settlement law, and is now under Temporary Settlement (see p. 162).

I cannot attempt here to give any account of the curious proceedings and complications that have arisen out of this division of land in Sylhet. I can only say that early in 1804, the Collector issued a proclamation inviting people to take leases of the then unoccupied lands: very few responded to the invitation; but as gradually different grants were made, a number of different holdings became distinguished (by the most heartrending terminology according to their origin), as under the 'proclamation' (*ílám* land), as newly-cultivated (*hálábádí*), &c., &c.[3]

[1] Page 213, note; and see *L. S. B. I.* vol. iii. p. 434.

[2] An immense number of these are very petty, paying no more than one rupee revenue! *L. S. B. I.* vol. iii. p. 444.

[3] Why all these distinctions are not abolished, and all lands brought on one simple *raiyatwárí* form of register,—merely noting against certain

The revenue is collected by a peculiar arrangement at the Tahsíl[1], designed to facilitate correct account-keeping with a multitude of petty holdings. In all estates, large or small, that have a Permanent Settlement, the rule of sale for default applies; but as there might be considerable injustice done by selling a small holding, the absent owner not being aware that it was in arrear, special rules have been legalized for securing service of a notice of demand on the owner, before proceeding to notify the land for sale.

Burma.

Upper Burma not described in this work.—The following brief note on the province will only apply to Lower Burma. The districts of Upper Burma, annexed in 1886, are passed over because their management under Regulation III of 1889 is admittedly a provisional one. The land-revenue is still largely replaced by an old native tax, the 'tithe' or *thathámedá*; and a large proportion of the land is claimed as 'Royal land,' the holders of which are only tenants-at-will of the State. It is certain that, in time, a regular Land Revenue system will be introduced; and at present it is not possible to say how the administration will ultimately be arranged.

Lower Burma Official charges.—As regards Lower Burma, it may be convenient first to mention, that though the organization of districts under Deputy Commissioners (Collectors) is just the same as in other provinces, inside the district, the local sub-division is different in detail, though very much the same in principle. Each district consists of a number of 'townships' (so called, I suppose, because the officer in charge is styled *Myó-ók* (*myó* = town or city). The 'township' is very like a *Tahsíl* elsewhere; and the officer in charge is like the *Tahsíldár*, though of somewhat higher rank and with somewhat

numbers that they are 'permanently settled,'—passes the comprehension of any one outside the mysteries of local revenue management.

[1] For further details I must refer to *L. S. B. I.* vol. iii. p. 449.

larger powers. Each township contains a number of 'circles' containing several *kwins* or villages; the officer of the circle who collects the revenue (and is paid by a commission thereon) is called *thúgyí*; and he may have one or more assistants: he is like the Indian *patwárí*, inasmuch as all the survey work (subsequent to Settlement) is done by him, and the land records are in his charge: he is unlike the *patwárí* because in India the *patwárí* has nothing to do with the actual collection of revenue: on the whole the *thúgyí* is more like the *mauzadár* of Assam (p. 218).

Revenue under the Burmese kings.—In Lower Burma, land was apparently recognized, in quite ancient times, as belonging to the 'first clearer'; the king also received a share in the produce[1]. But the tithe-tax, a capitation-tax, and the produce of 'royal lands' were more relied on by Burmese kings; and where a 'rice-land tax' was levied, it was mostly assessed by a rude calculation of the *number of cattle employed in the cultivation* of a certain area.

Under the British rule, a survey and general adoption of a regular Land-Revenue have been introduced.

'Villages' in Burma.—There are no 'villages' exactly in the Indian sense; that is to say there is no body of joint-owners claiming a whole area; nor is there the regular *raiyatwárí* village, i.e. a body held together under a common hereditary staff of village officers; but there are local groups of families, and a State headman is appointed[2]. The cultivated area is held by families who are separate; but the joint-succession is recognized by Burmese law, and a holding may be held for some time jointly by the heirs (wife and daughters included) of

[1] In ancient times there is no doubt that princes whose blood was to some extent that of the Aryan military caste, entered Burma from Arrakan and through Manipur, and founded kingdoms; thus it may have been that Indian notions of the State organization became prevalent. There were however, formerly, 'royal lands' in Lower Burma as in the Upper province. The British Government did not retain a special right (under the law of 1876), in Lower Burma, to royal lands.

[2] Act III of 1889 was passed to improve and consolidate village government, regulating the appointment, status and duties, of headmen; this Act only operates in districts to which it is specially extended.

a deceased landholder. Hence the local groups, though not forming in the Indian sense a joint body, are still often connected together by natural ties. It has thus been found possible, for survey purposes, to recognize areas which are practically villages, under the name of *queng* or *kwin*. Any area of land held on separate grant or lease, is also treated as a *kwin*.

Title to land.—All titles to land are comparatively recent, and depend either on express grant or lease or on long possession following on occupation and 'first clearing.' Act II of 1876 has (rather technically and with too much refinement) explained what gives the title of 'landholder.'

Land assessment under the first form.—At first, especially when land was very largely in excess of the population, temporary cultivation was undertaken for a year or two, and then shifted elsewhere. Settlements for a term of years were not thought of. The law permitted the chief Revenue Authority to declare certain rates for revenue purposes, which rates were to hold good (usually) for a term of years; and these were applied, by an annual measurement, to whatever land was liable to assessment. All land in Lower Burma is either rice-land, or garden and orchard, or (occasionally) miscellaneous cultivation called *Kaing*. Rice-land occupies the easily flooded, deep-soiled, alluvial plains; it furnishes the principal harvest. Small patches near the homestead are cultivated with vegetables or garden produce. *Kaing* cultivation on ridges or on laterite slopes on the edge of the alluvial plain, is more precarious and the soil adapted to it is more easily exhausted.

Orchards and palm groves are not taxed by a rate on land, but on the trees.

Settlements.—Settlements, when made for the more advanced portions of the country, exhibit many of the features of a *raiyatwárí* system. The land may be relinquished piecemeal, or the Settlement on the entire holding can be given up, and the holder will then revert to annual measurement and payment at the rates published for the circle.

Demarcation.—Where a district is notified for Settlement, *demarcation* of such boundaries as are permanent, and the erection of temporary marks required for survey purposes, are the first requisites. This is in Lower Burma provided for by a special Act (V of 1880).

Survey.—The survey work is done by a professional staff under the direction of the Imperial Survey Department. It results, as usual in all modern Settlements of whatever class, in very complete, large scale, village (*kwin*) maps, showing every field and holding by a separate number. And a descriptive field Register, which is an index to the map, is prepared.

Records of rights.—The Settlement staff makes out all the Records of rights. These rights may be of 'landholders,' or of 'grantees'; or there may occupation on a terminable 'lease.'

The important registers are:—

(1) Description of holdings in each *kwin*:—holder's name; on what sort of tenure; what sort of cultivation; and if there are fruit trees on the land.

(2) Gives an abstract account of such land in the *kwin* as is still unoccupied; or is excluded from assessment as village site, sacred place, jungle, grazing-ground; and often, 'parts under water' are mentioned.

(3) Is an abstract of decisions about 'landholders'' rights, in cases in which there has been a dispute.

(4) Is a list of the 'grants,' mentioning the part of the grant still uncultivated and the number of years' exemption from revenue—an allowance always made to encourage settlers; for during the first year or two there is much outlay and little return.

(5) Refers to 'leases' as (4) does to 'grants.'

(6) Is a register of tenants; and it may be mentioned that no tenants exist but under agreement; and there are no artificial (or other) occupancy rights.

(7) & (8) Show the grazing-grounds, which under the Rules can be allotted to village use[1]; also the gardens and the 'miscellaneous' cultivation.

[1] See also Act II of 1876, sec. 20.

(9) Shows the classification of soils in each village, which will be explained directly.

These registers are kept in Burmese.

'Supplementary Survey.'—Though the *thúgyís* take no part in the original survey, they have to conduct what is called in Burma the 'supplementary survey,' the object of which is to keep the maps correct by annually noting all new cultivation and changes that occur. They have also registers of mutations, so that all changes in landholding, or by sale or inheritance, may be at once recorded. Just as in Northern India, the Rules prescribe a set of forms or schedules exactly the same as those of Settlement, which have to be periodically filled up according to the true facts for the year. There are Revenue-Inspectors who look after this work, under the Director of Land Records and Agriculture.

Soil classification.—As in other Settlements, uniform tracts or 'Circles' are distinguished for assessment purposes, so as to bring together the different villages that have the same general advantages and are similarly circumstanced: in these the same rates will generally apply.

In each circle or tract, a certain number of soils (which are natural and easily recognized—not fanciful or uncertain) are distinguished. There may be deep clay that is not exhausted by continuous cropping, or a poorer clay that needs fallow; there may be laterite and sandy soil (usually on the edges of the alluvial plain); whatever the distinctions, they are purely natural, and no more in number than are necessary, as bearing different values.

Assessment.—The principles of assessment (1) of land, (2) of orchards and palm groves, depend on the provisions of secs. 23, 24, Act II of 1876. Land is assessed at an annual money-rate per *acre*. The chief Commissioner is empowered to make Rules as to fixing the rates, which may be altered 'from time to time as the chief Commissioner may direct.'

That of course applies to rates in general; when in the case of permanently established cultivation, the holder gets a Settlement, the rates are not changed during the term of the Settlement, which at present is fixed at not less than ten or more than fifteen years. The old standard was, one-fifth the *gross* produce; the modern standard is (nominally or theoretically) fifty per cent of the value of the *net* produce. Detailed instructions for assessment are given in the Rules under the Act, and in a little volume entitled 'Directions to Settlement Officers' (chap. iii).

Nature of the assessment adopted in practice.—Miscellaneous cultivation is not assessed at these rates, nor are gardens or orchard land. For these, empirical rates are made use of, calculated on the best data available. In rice-land, a 'normal' produce is first ascertained;—that is, the average out-turn for each class or kind of soil, under different conditions of agriculture. The money value of this out-turn is ascertained on the average of the prices ruling during the three months after harvest, in a series of years, and making allowance for the cost of carriage, so as to obtain a local, not a market, value. The costs of cultivation, and of living, are then worked out; and deducting these from the *gross* value, we have a *net* value, fifty per cent of which is the Land Revenue. These calculations are usually made and explained in the Settlement Reports; but I have never seen the rates so obtained, actually applied without alteration, to lands of any class. It seems to be rather a matter of form; or perhaps I should say that such rates afford a kind of standard—actual rates being kept below and not above them. *Really*, the rates used are empirically calculated, but carefully considered with reference to existing rates, and to statistics of increase in prosperity, and rise of prices, since the last assessment. There are many different considerations present to the mind of an officer who has carefully studied the people and the locality, which guide him to a right conclusion as to rates; but he has to justify these in his report, and so requires standards with which to compare his actual figures. No *actual* rates ever are ascertained wholly by any arithmetical process or mechanical rule; but certain standards, marking upper or lower limits, can be arrived at by rule, and then the real rates can be judged of by comparison with such standards.

Cesses.—There is, as usual, a local cess or rate levied (under Act II of 1880 or III of 1889 if applicable) for district roads, sanitation, education, and local postal service. (In Burma it is ten per cent. on the Revenue). Sec. 34 of Act II of 1876 also provides that 'a capitation-tax' is payable by all males between eighteen and sixty years of age. In some cases this tax may be commuted to a rate on land.

Shifting cultivation called taungyá.—A great deal of cultivation in the low hills of the Yoma, &c., is still carried on by the method of burning the forest and dibbling in seed with the ashes just before the rains (p. 13). The Land Act expressly declares that no right in the soil is acquired by this process, for there is no permanent occupation; and it may be added further that this destructive practice (see sec. 11 of the Forest Act XIX of 1881) is not allowed (on obvious general principles of law) to become a right of user or easement. At the same time it would be neither possible nor desirable to put a stop to it all at once. There are places where it does little harm, as there is no prospect of utilizing the forest material; and the Karen and other tribes could not (at present) live without it. But it is quite right that such a method of cultivation should be subject to regulation, and allowed only as a matter of concession. Where land is taken up as State Forest, and provision for the practice is desirable, a large area is set apart, and carefully surrounded with a cleared belt so that fire may not spread to the forest that is being conserved. Gradually, as population increases, and as the wood in the forest becomes valuable and marketable, this form of cultivation will be brought to an end; people will be induced to settle (by the encouragement of favourable terms) in the plains, or will perhaps permanently occupy the hill-sides by terraced fields[1].

Taungyá cultivation is assessed merely by means of a small money-rate (Act II of 1876, sec. 33) levied on each

[1] See *L. S. B. I.* vol. iii. p. 504, and a very curious account of a sort of advanced or organized *taungyá* system on the Salwín River, p. 506.

male member of a family able to wield the *dah* or heavy knife with which the jungle is cut for burning. The family is jointly responsible for this annual tax.

Waste Land Rules.—In conclusion it may be mentioned, that (1) land may be given out by local orders for temporary cultivation on annually renewable lease or other short terms; (2) it may be regularly leased for terms not exceeding thirty years—either for ordinary cultivation or on special terms for tea, coffee, cinchona, &c.; (3) it may be applied for with the design of acquiring permanently the 'landholder's' title.

Grants and Leases require the sanction of different authorities according to their size. Grants or leases of over fifty acres, require the approval of the Financial Commissioner (Chief Revenue Authority).

CHAPTER IX.

The Revenue Administration and Public Business connected with Land Management.

Special jurisdiction of Land Revenue Officers.—The permanent Settlement of Bengal having certain peculiarities which were noticed in the last chapter, it has followed that the course of Revenue Administration and the modes of realizing the Land Revenue, are somewhat different in Bengal, from what they are elsewhere.

In Bengal, the Revenue being fixed in perpetuity, and therefore likely to become easier and easier as the estate progressed and land rose in value, it was, from the first, understood that punctual payment (without remission or drawback in bad years) would be insisted on; and the estate was declared liable to sale at once, in default of payment. Again, the desire being to leave the landlords in as much independence as possible, there has been no room for that 'paternal' care of the estates and their condition and prospects, which has been extended in the districts where smaller village-estates are the Revenue payers.

'Revenue Courts' objected to in Bengal. The feeling counteracted by other considerations, in other Provinces.—Among the first Bengal Regulations codified in 1793, was one which rather ostentatiously abolished the '*Mal-Adawlut*' or Revenue Courts in which the Collector and his Deputies formerly decided a variety of matters directly relating to land, and more especially to rent payments (and dealings generally) between the landlord and tenant. Everything was made over to the Civil Courts. In 1859, rent-suits (for enhancement, arrears, &c.) were once more restored to the jurisdiction of the Collector; but the feeling in Bengal had become fixed; and ten years later, the jurisdiction was altered back to that of the Civil Courts, where it still remains under the existing law [1]. This feeling that the Collector is to have no jurisdiction as a Court, is perhaps an exaggerated one; for it cannot really be said that he is in any sense a judge in his own cause. However that may be, the feeling has never taken such hold in other provinces, because there was a strong countervailing reason. In the first place, these provinces were not managed by great estate-holders anxious to avoid all scrutiny and control; but much more than that, the whole method of Settlement required a special staff of officers whose duty kept them constantly out in camp and dealing with the villages on the spot; they thus acquired special experience and special knowledge of land affairs; and the Settlement Officer was, in fact, more 'the friend of the people' than the Civil Courts at head-quarters with their pleaders and formal procedure. It became a principle of the Revenue administration of Upper India generally, that questions of land-value, of rents and agricultural interests, had much better be entrusted to the decision of Officers accustomed to Settlement and Revenue work.

This reason less applicable to Bengal. Consequent differences in the law relating to Revenue Courts and jurisdiction.—That such a view did not become prominent in Bengal is not remarkable; because when the Permanent Settlement was once made (without any reference to actual land valuation) there was no further question about the assessment; and there was no need for a staff of Settlement Officers familiar with land-customs, and able to make use effectually, of evidential indications of landed-right and of the fairness of rentals, which would be unintelligible to the Civil Judges. To this day, knowledge of land-details is only obtainable in Bengal, indirectly and by means of the Temporarily Settled districts and estates, as well as from the Government estates (p. 103) which are kept under direct District

[1] Except in a few districts.

management. It will therefore not surprise the student when he finds that the different Revenue Procedure Laws vary as to their recognition of 'Revenue Courts'—meaning that the Land Revenue Officers have definite (judicial) powers of deciding questions connected with land management, often hearing suits between landlord and tenant as well, and subject (ordinarily) to an appeal in the Revenue Department only. In BENGAL, no such Courts are recognized; but the latest Tenant Act (of 1885) has once more found it desirable to make provision that rent and tenant-questions may be settled on the spot by a Revenue Officer accustomed to such inquiries; this is, however, only in certain cases and under special conditions. In MADRAS, Revenue Courts are not mentioned; but the Collector has a recognized jurisdiction in 'summary suits' and other matters, under Madras Act VIII of 1865 (e. g.); and, when so acting, he has the same powers as a Civil judge for the purpose of securing the attendance of parties and witnesses, and the production of documents, &c.

Bombay.—In BOMBAY, the code (chap. xii) speaks only of Revenue officers, their powers and procedure; but it mentions their holding a 'summary' or a 'formal' inquiry; and provides that these are to be deemed 'judicial' proceedings. An earlier Act (XVI of 1838), still in force, mentions directly, Revenue Courts (Courts of Collectors) and declares that they are not to have jurisdiction 'in regard to tenures' or the interests in land which arise out of a tenure claim, nor in claims to possession of land.

The North-West Provinces law as to Revenue Jurisdiction.—In the NORTH-WEST PROVINCES, on the other hand, the Revenue Courts are fully recognized as such; and the Land Revenue Act (IX of 1873) expressly mentions a number of matters (sec. 24) in which the Civil Court has no jurisdiction. So all rent suits and other disputes between landlord and tenant are heard by the Revenue Courts (Act XII of 1881, sec. 95 ff.). But in rent suits there is an appeal, in certain cases, to the Civil Courts (i. e. to the District Civil Court), or in large and important cases, direct to the High Court.

The Central Provinces.—The CENTRAL PROVINCES (Land

Revenue Act) does not refer to Revenue Courts generally; but there are a number of matters in which Revenue Officers have to pass orders, and a Civil suit cannot be brought to question the decision (see sec. 152, Act XVIII of 1881).

In the Tenancy Act (IX of 1883) also, certain matters (including the *fixing of rents*) are reserved to Revenue Officers; but other suits between landlord and tenant (as such) are left to the Civil Courts, provided that the Court must be presided over by an official who is also a Revenue or a Settlement Officer, and so has the experience of land matters which such an appointment gives.

The Panjáb.—In the PANJÁB Acts, no mention is made of Revenue Courts under that name; but the Land Revenue Act reserves certain matters from the jurisdiction of the Civil Courts (Act XVII of 1887, sec. 158). In this province, Settlement Officers can be invested with powers to hear land-cases, and there are special provisions in secs. 136, 137 of the Act. The Tenancy Law (Act XVI of 1887) goes into more detail (sec. 75 ff.). Revenue Officers alone have jurisdiction in suits between landlord and tenant (shown in the Act in groups) and in various 'applications and proceedings' (also exhibited in groups). Provision is further made for the determination of any question of doubtful jurisdiction; and also for the validity of decisions which are fair and proper, only that there has been a technical defect of jurisdiction; and for the reference of certain points to the decision of a Civil Court (sec. 98).

Burma and Assam.—In the province of BURMA there is no need of a tenancy law; and the Land Act (II of 1876) deals with the special jurisdiction of Revenue Officers in sec. 56. The Land Regulation (I of 1886) of ASSAM is similar.

Law of Revenue jurisdiction and procedure to be referred to in each Province.—For all provinces *except* Bengal and Madras, the powers and jurisdiction of Revenue Officers, their procedure in summoning parties and procuring evidence, the course of appeal, and the revision of orders, are provided in the 'Land Revenue Act' and perhaps in the 'Tenancy Act' also. In Bombay everything is to be found in the Revenue Code.

In Madras there are several of the earlier Regulations giving certain powers to Revenue officers; such are Madras Reg. II of 1803, and Reg. VII of 1828; but the principal provisions regarding powers and procedure are contained in two Acts—Madras Act VIII of 1865, called the 'Rent Recovery Act,' and Madras Act II of 1864 for the 'Recovery of arrears of Revenue.'

In Bengal, there is a longer list of Acts and Regulations which indicate the powers and procedure of Revenue officers; but there is no occasion to give any details, because there are 'Collectorate-Law Manuals' (e. g. that by Mr. H. A. D. Phillips) which give all the Acts, Regulations, &c. collected in one volume.

Nature of the procedure adopted for Revenue cases.—The Revenue Court procedure is simple and untechnical. Where the law provides a special jurisdiction for the hearing of 'applications,' or of contentious cases between parties, which are in the nature of 'suits,' either the Civil jurisdiction is adopted (with such modifications as may be needed) or the entire procedure is laid down specially. It may be said broadly, that the object of Revenue procedure is to make the hearing of cases as easy and expeditious, and free from technical difficulties, as possible.

In some cases the law insists on the personal attendance of the parties, and discourages the expense and waste of time that too often follow on the employment of legal practitioners. Permission can of course always be had to appear by agent or to employ legal aid where it is really needed; but in the vast majority of cases that come before the Revenue officers, there is nothing but a simple question of fact to be gone into.

Heads of Revenue duty.—I have already (p. 23 ff.) indicated the grades of Land Revenue Officers—how the Collector is the District head; and how he is always Magistrate as well, and has the general supervision of all administrative work in his district: how he has Deputies and Assistants; how an appeal ordinarily lies from the decision of the lower grades to the Collector, and in other cases (including the orders of the Collector himself when these are appealable) to the Commissioner, with a final appeal to the Board of Revenue or

Financial Commissioner. We have here, therefore, to turn our attention to the everyday matters of land management and Land Revenue business which the Collectors have to dispose of. The heads of Land Revenue business naturally vary somewhat with the Province; but there is sufficient similarity to warrant a general description being included in the same chapter.

In Bengal, though the Collector has no concern with the internal affairs of ordinary landlord-estates, he still has to keep a watchful eye on the country in case of the approach of famine; and he may have the actual care of estates (with or without the aid of a paid Manager) in case they come under the Court of Wards, while the owner is a minor or incapable. He has the charge of Government Estates when they are either farmed, or managed direct,—the tenants paying their rent to Government. When these estates consist of large tracts (exceeding 5,000 acres) they are technically called 'raiyatwárí tracts,' the direct holders of land (raiyats) being the tenants of Government though not necessarily tenants at will. The Settlement of rents in these tracts, as well as of the Revenue in temporarily settled estates and districts, is the duty of the Collector (with the aid, if need be, of Settlement Officers specially appointed). I have already alluded to the special procedure of Act VIII of 1885 (Bengal Tenancy) under which Rent Settlements may have to be made under certain circumstances even in Permanently Settled estates. There are also duties under the general Survey law, including orders regarding the erection and maintenance of boundary marks (Bengal Act V of 1875, sec. 20). The Collector is also concerned with the Registration of landed estates and with 'mutations,' i.e. the record of changes in the proprietorship by sale, &c. He also has the duty of registering 'tenures' (p. 130) for the purpose of their protection from being voided if the estate comes to sale for arrears of Revenue. When partitions of jointly owned estates are applied for, the Collector alone has jurisdiction to make the division and to determine how the Land Revenue liability is to be distributed over the shares: and even if there is no formal partition to make, there may be the right of co-sharers to have their Revenue apportioned, and a 'separate account' opened with each, so that the default of one may not imperil the others—except under such circumstances as the law provides (Act XI of 1859, secs. 10–14). I need hardly say much on the Collector's duty in respect of Drainage works and Embankments, the maintenance of which may be of first-rate importance to agriculture in certain districts (Bengal Acts VI of 1880, and II of 1882). So too I only just allude to the assessment of estates and tenures to the 'District Cess' (p. 153) (Bengal Act IX of 1880). Lastly, there are the important duties of the collection of the Land Revenue, and the realization of arrears.

In other Provinces.—Though some of the duties thus stated are peculiar to the locality, others are common to all provinces. It will be possible, therefore, at once to give a brief comment on a series (selected) of the subjects of general Land Revenue administration most likely to be useful [1].

Tenancy procedure not included, but the jurisdiction noted.—As regards those provinces which entrust rent and other Tenant cases to Revenue Courts, I may say at once that it is not my intention to give any details as to the procedure in Tenancy cases. I have sufficiently alluded to the Tenancy law in general (p. 133 ff.), and I will only further remind students that, in each province, they will have to see:—

1. Whether suits between landlord and tenant are heard by the Revenue officers or by the Civil Courts.
2. Or whether being heard by Revenue Courts, the course of appeal is wholly in the Revenue Department, i.e. to the Commissioner, Board, &c., or wholly or partly to the Civil Court.
3. In the Central Provinces only, is there a special provision, dividing, so to speak, the landlord and tenant (original) jurisdiction between the Revenue and the Civil Courts: but then there is an express provision that most rents must be, and all may be, determined for the term of Settlement, by the Settlement Officer. Hence the class of suits likely to come before the courts is special in kind, and limited.

[1] When I speak of the 'Collector' it is hardly necesssary to explain that I include the Deputy and Assistant Collectors who act according to their grade in the manner provided by the Acts.

Heads of Land Revenue duty enumerated.—Confining our attention then to the Land Revenue business, we shall find that the main heads of official duty calling for our notice are the following :—

1. The collection of the Land Revenue.
2. The care of estates in general—including the preservation of boundaries, the maintenance of the records, especially with reference to the due registration of all changes in ownership.
3. Partition of joint estates.
4. Appointment and control of village officers.
5. Minor assessments—i. e. special cases where the Land Revenue has to be fixed subsequently to, or apart from, the general Settlement of the district.
6. Agricultural advances (*Taqáví*).

It will not be necessary for our further remarks, to separate the provinces and repeat a notice of Revenue duties for each : there are some distinct features in the Permanently settled districts and estates of Bengal and Madras, in the Raiyatwárí provinces, and in the village-estate Provinces (North-West Provinces and Oudh, Panjáb, Central Provinces and Ájmer), but they can be sufficiently indicated in briefly describing the action taken in general, under the above six heads.

1. Collection of the Revenue.

Difference between permanent and temporary Settlements as regards Revenue in arrear.—Naturally we consider that the first duty of a Collector being to 'collect'—the ingathering of the Revenue, and the enforcement of payment in case of default, is the first subject to be considered.

We have here to take notice of the different procedure under each of the three great systems. In Bengal and in the Permanently Settled estates of Madras, the gift of the landlord-right was accompanied with the condition that the Revenue must be paid punctually under threat of the immediate sale of the estate. It was thought that this was better than subjecting a great landlord to the indignity of personal imprisonment or attachment and distraint of moveable property [1].

Sale law and Public demands recovery law in Bengal.—The existing Act (XI of 1859) regulating the Sale law of Bengal is I believe under discussion, but no change has yet taken place, nor is it likely that any principles will be altered. As, however, Land Revenue is not confined to Permanently settled estates, and moreover various other items of public money are provided to be recovered 'as if they were arrears of Land Revenue,' there is a double procedure. The whole law of (1) sale of estates and (2) the 'certificate procedure' for the 'recovery of public demands' is read together, being contained in Act XI of 1859, Bengal Act VII of 1868, and Bengal Act VII of 1880.

Where there is some kind of 'estate,' with a landlord over it, the estate is liable to sale, as the first and direct mode of recovery; certain fixed 'tenures' (p. 130) are also treated as estates. Where it is a case of recovery from a Revenue-farmer (still occasionally employed on certain lands) or from a Government raiyat, or from some other person, where there is no 'estate' to sell, a *certificate of the arrear* is issued by the Collector, and this operates *like a decree of Civil Court*, and is executed under the Civil procedure Code.

1. **Sale law.**—In the case of estates, the old custom was that the Land Revenue fell due in monthly instalments, and the failure of any one month's payment was held to authorize the sale; but this was found to be too harsh; and now, a certain date (or last day for payment) is fixed under the authority of the law, by which (up till sunset) all dues for the preceding year must be made good.

The 'sunset law.'—Directly the sun has set, the time is past, and the estate *must* be notified for sale,—the sale to take place

[1] In Madras there is some difference: the Act (II of 1864) says the recovery shall be according to the terms of the title deed; and Reg. XXV of 1802, sec. 7, provides that personal property shall in the first instance be attached.

thirty days later. It will be understood, however, that in practice, a very small percentage of estates is ever actually sold. The Collector may accept a payment after date, if it is desirable to do so. A reference to section 18 of the Sale Act will show that the Collector has absolute discretion (provided he makes a written order and states his reasons) to forego a sale, or even to refuse to allow one. And this latter power may be specially required in order to obviate the necessary evil of a sale law, viz. that a landlord may be tempted to raise all the money he can by creating encumbrances on his estate (which will be all voided when the estate is sold) and then may purposely let his Revenue fall into arrear. If it were compulsory to put up the estate to auction, the fraudulent owner might virtually get the price twice over [1].

Sale of Estate with a clear title.—The auction purchaser gets a clear title and can void all encumbrances and contracts entered into by the defaulting landlord, and all tenures created by him; certain old standing tenures are, however, protected (by law) and so are others if duly registered; but registration only applies to the tenures mentioned in the Act, and then prevails only against private purchasers, not against Government. So that if an estate were heavily burdened with tenures which a private purchaser could not void, there would be no sufficient bid for the estate at the auction, and Government would buy it in. It is true that there is a 'special registration' of tenures which will protect them even against being voided by Government; but such registration can only be had on condition that the tenures are such as leave a sufficient security (in an unburdened proportion of the estate) for the Land Revenue of the whole.

2. **Certificate Procedure.**—The 'certificate procedure' classifies the demands into two series: in the one—to put it shortly—the certificate is more absolute and difficult to contest than in the other. A separate form of certificate for each class is provided: in either case, if there is any objection, a petition must first be lodged with the Collector within a certain time.

[1] The encumbrances in all probability would be such as could not be registered to secure them (e. g. mortgages), and so purchasers would bid the price of the estate as free from encumbrances. Should, then, the sale-price exceed the value of the arrears, the Collector would be bound to hand over the whole surplus to the original owner.

In the first class of cases, the money must be paid up (in deposit), and then a civil suit may be filed (against Government) to contest the certificate. In the second class of cases it is not necessary to deposit the money, but a suit may be filed to contest the liability; provided that the plaint must set forth that the grounds of objection sued on have been duly enumerated in a petition (as above) to the Collector: the suit can only proceed on one or other of the grounds permitted (sec. 8, Bengal Act. VII of 1880).

Land Revenue recovery in Northern India.—The Land Revenue Acts of the provinces where village-estate Settlements prevail, have a different procedure for the recovery of arrears of Land Revenue and other public dues that are provided by law to be recoverable as if they were arrears of Land Revenue. Briefly, instead of sale being the first and ordinary procedure, *it is only adopted as the last resort.* There are a series of measures, beginning with a simple notice of demand; and only if the others fail can the sale of the estate be ordered. All the Acts are similar in principle.

The Revenue is, I have explained (p. 192), made payable by certain instalments; and if these are not paid up in full at due date, the responsible party becomes 'a defaulter.'

Responsibility of village headman or lambardár.—In the North-West Provinces and Central Provinces, the headmen are primarily and personally liable as defaulters for the Land Revenue arrears of their village or section (*patti*) of a village. In the Panjáb this rule is modified; the headman is only responsible if he neglects the duty of collecting—has not taken the proper steps to get in the Revenue from the co-sharers who are liable.

If it is necessary to adopt legal measures to realize the arrear, a certificate of the amount due is prepared and signed by the Revenue Officer—usually by the *Tahsíldár.* This certificate is absolute proof of the arrear: it can only be contested by a civil suit, which again must be preceded by a deposit of the whole amount due. The processes of recovery are (in order of severity):—

1. Serving a writ (*dastak*) of demand.

2. Arrest and detention of the person[1].
3. Distress and sale of moveable property including crops —but tools, seed grain, and agricultural cattle are exempt, and the Panjáb Act expressly exempts a portion of the crop necessary for subsistence.
4. Attachment of the whole estate (*mahál*) or the defaulting share only. The effect of this is to place the land under a Government manager, who receives all rents and profits: (payment to any one else will not avail against the demand of the manager). This is popularly called *khám-tahsíl*).
5. Is a similar process; only that instead of making over the estate (or share) to a manager, it is made over *to a solvent co-sharer* who undertakes to pay up the arrears and holds the share till he has recovered all.
6. Annulling the Settlement of the whole estate, or of the share; in which case a new Settlement will be made; and the proprietor may find himself excluded for its term which will not exceed fifteen years.
7. Sale of the estate or share (*pattí*).
8. Sale of other immoveable property of the defaulter.

There are small variations in detail in the Acts; but the foregoing list will give a sufficient general idea of the procedure. It may be mentioned that in Oudh, the Taluqdár's estates are (unlike the landlord estates of Bengal) treated by the same process as the village estates; they are not sold in the first instance; the only difference is that the Taluqdár is not liable to personal arrest and detention.

No interest charged.—Interest is not charged on arrears of Land Revenue; but the costs of process, &c. are included in the arrear to be recovered.

Cases of real inability to pay.—It will be borne in mind that while, in the Permanently settled estates of Bengal, and Madras, no remissions or suspensions are contemplated, in the village-estates, the Collector is ever watchful to distinguish whether the default is due to neglect, or fraud, or (as it often may be)

[1] This is usually a brief detention in a suitable place at the Tahsíl office: the Central Provinces Act directs detention at the Civil Jail.

to real inability to pay, owing to loss of crops, bad seasons, &c. In the latter case, he will apply his power of *suspending* the demand (p. 244), and ultimately perhaps, recommending the whole (or a part) of the arrear for *remission*.

It may also be mentioned that where there is a Revenue-assignee, *jágirdár*, &c., there may be local rules as to whether he must receive his Revenue through the Treasury, or be permitted to collect it himself in cash (or sometimes in kind).

Collection in the Raiyatwárí provinces—the jamabandí.—In the Raiyatwárí provinces of MADRAS and BOMBAY, the really essential point to notice is, that each year, before the collections are closed, an account is prepared, village by village, by the village officers, and under supervision of the Assistant Collector (and occasionally of the Collector himself, as the rules may provide) of the lands actually held, and the correct total dues, for the year. This is necessitated by the fact that the raiyat may have relinquished (whether absolutely or by transfer) some of his land, or taken up new fields on application. In Madras, also, there are various items of Revenue account to be gone into; certain remissions which are always allowed for spoiled crops, and certain adjustments with reference to water rate, as e.g. where a full supply has not been received, or where the assessment is for a double crop, and water for only one has been received; or where a second crop has to be charged, the assessment being for one only (p. 205). This process, characteristic of the *raiyatwárí* provinces of Madras, Bombay, and Berár, is called the *jamabandí*. The details of practice must be learned from the local Manuals and Circulars [1].

Process of recovering arrears. Madras law.—As regards the actual process of recovery of Revenue in arrears, in MADRAS, the law provides for the attachment and sale of moveable and immoveable property, and the imprisonment of the defaulter (which latter process does not extinguish the arrear. Madras Act II of 1864, sec. 8 ff.). Immoveable property is not sold without first issuing a writ of demand and seeing whether the defaulter

[1] Some further particulars may also be seen in *L. S. B. I.* vol. iii. pp. 95, 312.

can make some arrangement for payment (sec. 26). The property, moreover, need not be sold outright, but may be taken under management. As to the conditions under which personal arrest and imprisonment are allowed, see sec. 48.

The Bombay law.—The BOMBAY Code is so clear (chap. xi. secs. 136–187) that it is only necessary to refer to it. It will be remembered that there are other tenures besides *raiyatwárí* to be considered in Bombay; hence the legal provisions require some variety. I will only notice that in principle, if the *registered* occupant of land fails to pay, the amount may be recovered from any *actual* occupant; and he, having paid, is protected by certain provisions (sec. 136). Power is also given to attach crops before the Revenue falls due, in certain cases where such a precaution is judged necessary.

When default occurs there may be:—

1. A written notice of demand.
2. Forfeiture of the occupancy.
3. Distraint and sale of moveable property.
4. Sale of the defaulter's immoveable property.
5. Arrest and imprisonment.

When, in alienated lands (pp. 52, 118), the estate consists of a whole village or a share of one, the whole (or the share) may be taken under direct management by the Collector: and if at the end of twelve years, the owners have not 'redeemed' the land, it will finally pass to the Government (sec. 163).

Interest chargeable.—In Bombay and Madras, interest is (or may be) chargeable on arrears of Land Revenue (Madras Act II of 1864, sec. 7, which fixes six per cent.; Bombay Act V of 1879, sec. 148).

Other Provinces. Burma.—I do not propose to go into the details of the laws of other provinces; it may be noticed, however, that in BURMA a convenient practice is provided by Act II of 1876 (Land Act) for the issue of *demand tickets* before any process to enforce payment is adopted. In general, the arrear of Revenue is recovered as if it were a sum due on a decree of a Civil Court, and by the Civil procedure; or if there is a saleable interest in the land, the land may be sold; or Government may eject the landholder and take possession (Act II of 1876, secs. 47, 49).

Assam.—In Assam, the Land Regulation has to make provision for the ordinary landholdings of the province, as well as for the old Permanently settled estates and holdings, some of which are subject to the Bengal Sale law (as also provided in the Assam Regulation). And the small (Permanently settled) holdings of Sylhet and the Temporarily settled lands of Káchár have always had certain peculiar features connected with the Revenue collection [1].

In concluding this notice of the Collection of Revenue, it is only necessary to say that, in general, resort to the severer forms of process for recovery is now rarely necessary. As a rule the Revenue is punctually, and in ordinary seasons easily, paid.

Suspension and remission of the Land Revenue demand.—One important matter remains to be noticed. There are, owing to the climatic conditions of most Indian districts or Provinces, times when the land could not be sown, or the crops have suffered or been destroyed outright, owing to failure of the usual rainy season, or to failure of river, tank or canal irrigation, (pp. 7, 10), or owing to some disaster—flood, blight, locusts and the like. The calamity may be (1) in the nature of a famine or some evil that affects the crops *over a wide area*; or (2) some *purely local* misfortune affecting perhaps only a single village, or a small group of fields. The Collector needs then to be armed with a power to afford immediate relief by suspending the usual demand for the Land Revenue, when the instalments fall due. For though the Assessment is moderate and adapted to *average* seasons and conditions generally, these climatic disasters upset all calculations. I do not speak here of those special relief measures to be taken when widespread famine threatens the population. The suspension of the Revenue demand is not only needed in times of actual famine, but on other occasions also. As a rule, however, it will be most needed—and that without delay—in widespread calamities; and will be more cautiously resorted to in local and partial cases. It may only be rarely

[1] See *L. S. B. I.* vol. iii. pp. 448, 449.

required in estates and districts classified as 'secure.' Suspension is usually ordered on the Collector's own authority, for six months[1]—i. e. till the results of the next harvest appear, and it is seen whether the amount can then be paid. Sometimes a longer period of observation is needed, and then a report will have to be made and the sanction of the Commissioner obtained. Usually, if the succeeding harvests are fair, and the loss has not permanently crippled the estate (as it does if the greater part of the cattle have perished), the recovery of the amount suspended will be ordered;—usually in part payments, added to the current demand. Where the circumstances are such that *remission* is called for, sanction of superior authority, on a full report of the facts, is necessary. The local Government itself will have to sanction any widespread remission affecting a considerable percentage of the local Revenue; and in cases sensibly affecting the Revenue of an entire province, the remission has to be approved by the Government of India. It is often (in landlord estates where there are tenants) made a condition of remission or suspension, that favour shown to the landlord shall be passed on to the tenants; and the Rent Act of the North-West Provinces as well as that of Oudh, contain special provisions on the subject[2].

These remarks apply to the country generally, and not to those exceptional tracts for which a 'fluctuating assessment' (p. 191) is already provided.

The permanently settled estates are not, as a rule, allowed to claim any remission or suspension—because their Revenue, fixed many years ago, is now excessively light: but I do not apprehend that relief would be refused (as a matter of favour) in case of any serious famine or unusually severe calamity.

Revenue accounts.—It hardly comes within my scope to say anything of the Revenue-rolls, registers and accounts kept both at the local (*tahsil*) treasuries and at head-quarters, by aid of which it is at once known what is the correct demand for every

[1] The object is to give relief so that the Revenue payer may not be forced to get into serious debt to meet the instalment.

[2] See Act XII of 1881, sec. 23; and Act XXII of 1886, sec. 19.

estate and holding, both for Revenue and cesses; what is in arrear, and what has been duly paid. In Bengal, the Collector's office has a regular department for this work, known as the 'Taujih Department'—so called from the Revenue (Arabic) term *taujíh* (*tauji* in Hindí dialects), meaning a statement showing the Revenue demand,—the part paid and the balance still due[1].

2. Care of Estates. Boundaries. Records and their maintenance.

Duty of inspection and free intercourse with the people on the spot.—In provinces where the Settlements deal with village-estates and separate holdings, a great deal of care is taken to watch over the condition of the villages and the welfare of the peasant holders, which is not a matter of law or legal provision. I have frequently alluded to the repeated inspection which is given, on the part of village *patwárís*, Revenue Inspectors, and District Officers. Great stress is laid on the duty of the District Officers to spend as much time as possible in camp. When in the village itself, they can freely talk with the people without the constraints of a public office, and the presence of subordinate officials which checks confidence. It is notorious that by this means, Revenue Officers can learn more regarding popular wants and difficulties, and of the condition of the district generally, than they could in any other way.

Care of Estates.—Besides this, there is a regular system of reporting any unusual occurrence—such as locusts, destructive storms, cattle disease, and every other accident, that may tend to place the villages in difficulty. When the condition of an estate is known to be precarious, and the time comes for Revenue payment, the Collector has (as above noted) the power of suspending the demand at once; and to facilitate the efforts of the Collector in this direction, and to bring statistical knowledge to a *focus*, as it were, the Government of India within the last few years, has directed a detailed record to be prepared—either in the form of notes, or maps coloured for the purpose—of

[1] Whence the term *taujíh-navís* for the clerks employed to keep these statements.

the character of each part of the district and (if need be) of separate estates and parts of estates, as regards their position of greater or less security.

Some villages will be protected by a permanently flowing canal: others will be in the low lands where water in wells rarely or never fails, and is reached at a depth of a few feet; others again are so situated that the river moisture on which the fields depend, may be extremely precarious owing to the changes in the course of the river and its subsidiary channels: some places are climatically precarious —the rainfall very uncertain, or the crops liable to depredation by storms or by wild animals.

In some cases indeed, such tracts of country will be excluded from the regular Revenue Settlement altogether, and placed under some system of fluctuating assessment (p. 191). But apart from such extreme cases, there is always scope for the classification of estates, villages and landholdings as more or less 'secure.'

Care of Boundary marks.—The care of Boundaries and Survey marks is of importance both for the security of rights, for the prevention of disputes, and for obviating the loss of the *data* of survey, a loss which if permitted might result in the necessity for a new survey.

The Revenue Acts will all be found to contain provisions [1] (apart from those relating to demarcation and fixing of boundaries for Survey and Settlement) for the *maintenance* of marks. Every landholder is bound to erect and maintain boundary marks; and the village officers are charged with the duty of reporting any injury to such marks, and any cases in which marks are out of repair [2]. If the order to erect or restore a mark is not obeyed, the Collector has power to do the necessary work and recover the cost (as if it were an arrear of Land Revenue) from the parties concerned. He has also power to apportion the cost between adjacent owners. If there is any dispute about the boundary line, the Collector only recognizes existing possession; and any party objecting, must have recourse to a civil suit to establish his contention.

Penalty for injury.—There is usually a penalty for injury to

[1] In Bengal and Madras where there are no Revenue Codes—see Bengal Act V of 1875; and for Madras, Act XXVIII of 1860.

[2] The Panjáb Act has thought it desirable to specify this as one of the legal duties of village officers: the neglect would consequently entail a criminal liability under the Penal Code. There is a similar law in Burma.

marks, and a provision for a reward to informers in case of injured marks. The Indian Penal Code has also a provision for the punishment of malicious injury to marks. The chief Revenue authority has power to prescribe the form and material of boundary and survey marks.

Boundary marks in raiyatwárí countries.—It will be remembered that in *raiyatwárí* countries, the marks are fixed and unalterable, having been originally adjusted with reference to the separate occupancy rights. In these places, the holdings have to be kept correct, and the boundaries maintained, according to the maps. All sales, &c. proceed with reference to the recognized survey lots, or authorized and recorded subdivisions of them, and this is a matter perfectly well understood. In other districts, some boundaries are, in the nature of things, unalterable; but otherwise there is no rule that the Settlement boundaries must be maintained; fields change and so do the limits of shares, and interests; the maps have accordingly to be kept correct to the facts.

Record of changes in proprietorship. Dákhil-khárij or mutation of names.—Under all systems, great care is taken to record all *changes in proprietary right* (or occupancy right). On this depends the correctness of the records, that is to say, that the work of survey and Settlement is not lost, by gradual and unreported changes which would make the land records cease to correspond with existing facts. Whenever, therefore, a change takes place, by gift, inheritance, sale, or mortgage with possession, there is a process known as *dákhil-khárij* (i. e. putting in and taking out). The former owner's name is removed and the new one put in; this secures the title to the land (p. 198), and also informs the Collector as to who is the right person to answer for the Revenue. When a change is reported, a public notice (for a fixed time) is posted up, and the Collector will only sanction the change being entered on the record when it is found that the transaction is an accomplished fact, that possession has been given, and that there is no dispute.

For it will sometimes happen that on the death of a land-owner, co-sharer, &c., a person will claim to have his name substituted as being the adopted son; and collaterals will come forward and deny the adoption, or the possession of the claimant; or a vendee from *a widow* will ask for record of his purchase, and the family object that the widow has only a life-interest and was not entitled, under the circumstances, to sell: here the Collector may refuse to recognize the transfer, and refer the parties to the Civil Court to settle the matter: the change will only be recorded when a final decision has been obtained.

The whole object of the land record system (I do not apologize for repeating) is to obviate future re-survey and re-record, by seeing that the initial maps and records of Settlement are kept correct and in conformity with facts at the time. Good records mean, the security of titles, the impossibility of encroachment on subordinate rights, and the facility of decision in case a dispute occurs, and especially in all kinds of cases between landlord and tenant. The repeated inspections of land, and the due writing up of the village-papers (p. 29), are the means relied on to secure this object.

3. Partition of joint estates.

Under all systems, there may be joint estates or joint occupancies, and partition may be desirable. All the laws prescribe that this operation is within the sole jurisdiction of the Revenue Officers. The Civil Courts do not act except there is dispute as to the right of a claimant to be a sharer at all, or as to the extent of his share. The actual land to be given to each, and the apportionment of the Revenue responsibility, these are matters which can be effectively adjusted only by persons who have a Revenue Officer's experience.

The Land Revenue Acts contain general provisions. But there are a vast variety of points of detail which can only be dealt with by Rules under the Act, or are enjoined as matters of practice, by the Circular Orders of the Chief Revenue authority.

Perfect and imperfect partition.—As to the law of partition, only two points can here be noticed. In countries where there is a joint estate (whether a village or a larger landlord area), there may be a partition which leaves the Revenue liability of the whole intact, and merely allots the separate holdings for personal enjoyment ('imperfect partition'), or there may be one which completely dissolves the joint liability ('perfect partition'). Some laws do not allow the latter except at Settlement, and for special reasons (p. 174).

In Raiyatwárí countries, the partition has further to respect the fixed survey-numbers or lots, and the partition may not result in lots below a certain minimum size. This will be realized by reading secs. 113 ff. of the Bombay Revenue Code.

In partition, there are always some lands which are left undivided (graveyards, common wells, &c.). The chief difficulty in making a partition is that, in any joint holding, each member usually has had *de facto* possession of certain fields, in the past; each will be eager to keep these; and it is not always easy to effect this, with reference to the value of land and the extent of each share; but in a good partition it will be effected as far as possible.

Partition law.—In Bengal, there is a special Partition Act (Bengal Act VIII of 1876). In Madras, Act I of 1876, and Act II of 1864, secs. 45, 46, make provision for Permanently settled estates. No special law exists for the partition of raiyats' holdings; that is a matter which depends on the rules of survey and the permissible subdivision of survey-numbers.

4. Appointment of Village Officers.

Disputes as to the right to the office.—This is also a matter for the Revenue Officer's decision only. The succession to the office of headman, and sometimes to that of *patwárí*, may be a matter of custom, and it may be hereditary: sometimes the rules allow a certain elective element; but there are very often rival claimants, or objections are raised to a person nominated by the Collector, on the ground of unfitness,—his being much in debt, having no sufficient interest in land in the village, and the like. Such cases are numerous and are generally contested in appeal as far as possible.

There will be usually found provisions in the Land Revenue Act, Rules and Circulars.

Watandár Offices in Bombay, &c.—In Bombay there is provision regarding the village accountant in secs. 16, 17 of the Revenue Code; and as here there may be hereditary Officers remunerated by special holdings of land (*watan*: p. 27), there is a special Act (Bombay Act III of 1874) which may be referred to; also for Sindh, Bombay Act IV of 1881. In Madras, there are several Acts and Regulations relating to the *Karnam* or village accountant in Permanently settled estates and in other villages. Madras Regs. XXIX of 1802, and II of 1806, refer to hereditary officers in estates; Madras Reg. VI of 1831, and Madras Act IV of 1864, refer to such officers in general. In Bengal, Reg. XII of 1817 is still in force, but *patwárís* do not exist except locally; and the whole village system has no vitality under the landlord estate system.

5. Minor Assessments.

Lands to be assessed apart from the general district Settlement.—Alluvial tracts near rivers.—From time to time lands held Revenue-free, or of which the Revenue has been assigned, lapse, and it becomes necessary to assess them and determine who is to be settled with; or waste land is colonized and new villages are established; and there are various other occasions in which lands have to be assessed—apart from the general Settlement of the whole district. One frequent cause in the Panjáb (and other provinces much traversed by rivers flowing through alluvial plains), is the alteration of lands which appears as soon as the floods subside, when the rainy season is over. In some cases, the action of the river is so violent, that an entire area in the vicinity is excluded from the Settlement and put under a system of fluctuating assessment; but where that is not necessary, it is still desirable either to make provision (1) that whenever the *entire area of the village* has been affected to the extent of ten per cent. or more, the whole Revenue is to be re-adjusted (and its apportionment among the co-sharers); or (2) to separate the permanent lands from those liable to river action, and *demarcate a separate 'alluvial chak'* or circle which may require to be re-measured and re-assessed after each rainy season, provided that a certain minimum degree of change has taken place. In these circles of course, as the Revenue will be reduced on account of land washed away or rendered unculturable, so additional Revenue may be assessed on new land formed, or on barren land that has been rendered culturable by a fertilizing deposit. It is the making of these minor Settlements, with the survey work and inspection and reporting that they involve, that afford such excellent opportunities for training the junior officers and qualifying them for larger Revenue powers and duties.

6. Advances to cultivators.

Under the head of the care of estates, might have been included a brief notice of the fact that Government makes advances (to be recovered in certain convenient instalments) to enable agricultural improvements to be made. These advances, in fact, have always been customary in India, under the name of *taqávî* (written *tuccavee*, *takkávî*, &c.; the word is Arabic and literally means 'strengthening' or 'coming to one's aid'). They are governed by Act XIX of 1883. An 'improvement' includes all works of providing wells and other means of irrigation which can be effected by private effort, as well as drainage, reclamation, enclosure, and any other works which may from time to time be declared by the local Government to be works of 'improvement.' The instalments may not extend (as a rule) over more than thirty-five years. The Act makes provision for the form of application for a loan, and for the security (and liability of the land itself to answer) for repayment.

Private works of improvement exempted from assessment.—It also makes the important provision that when an improvement has been made by private effort, and the land comes to be re-assessed under a revision of Settlement, the improvement is not to be taken into consideration; and as in certain classes of work, this exemption cannot go on for ever, the protection is effected by declaring periods of years for which a certificate of the improvement will hold good, so that no increase can be levied during the currency of the period (see p. 190).

Additional powers of making loans.—In the year following the publication of this Act, a further law (Act XII of 1884) was passed, which empowers loans to be made (under rules) to owners and occupiers of land, for the relief of distress, the purchase of seed or cattle, or other purpose not specified in the (above-mentioned) Land Improvement Act, 'but connected with agricultural objects.'

Other branches of public business connected with land. Sources of Information about Revenue duty.—There are other matters of which notice might be taken, but they are only indirectly connected with Land Revenue Administration. Such are the valuation of land in case of its being taken up for a public purpose under the 'Land Acquisition Act, 1870'; and various duties connected with District Boards and (in Bengal) with committees in connexion with drainage works and embankments; and there are various functions of a Collector under the Provincial Canal Acts. In districts where there are still waste lands for disposal, it is the Collector to whom application must be made under the Rules; but these have already been sufficiently noticed (pp. 56 ff.). It only remains to be said that for a complete study of the direct Land Revenue duties of Collectors, it is almost exclusively in Bengal and Madras, that a number of Acts and Regulations have to be referred to; in all the other provinces, there is one Land Revenue Act or Regulation which contains the whole law. In Bombay this Code has indeed to be supplemented by a few Acts dealing with some of the special tenures, but that is all.

In the Bombay Presidency there is no Tenancy Law to be separately studied, nor is there in Burma, Berár or Assam.

'Rules' under the Land Revenue Acts.—In all Provinces, however, it is essential to have the 'Rules' which the Local Government is empowered to make under the Revenue Act. In some cases (e. g. the Panjáb Act) the collected Rules form quite a complete code of detailed instructions; and the rules, when duly sanctioned, have the force of law.

'Circular orders.'—There are also 'Circular Orders' or Standing Orders in all provinces, issued by the Government or by the chief Revenue authority or both, which give detailed instructions on matters of practice, official routine and business details, and in some cases contain valuable explanations of the Act, and call attention to changes in the law. They are to be had in provincial volumes, to which additions are from time to time made as circumstances require.

GENERAL INDEX.

THE END.